3995
80E

INTERNATIONAL SECURITY AND ARMS CONTROL

INTERNATIONAL SECURITY AND ARMS CONTROL

Edited by

Ellen Propper Mickiewicz and Roman Kolkowicz

New York
Westport, Connecticut
London

Library of Congress Cataloging-in-Publication Data

International security and arms control.

    1. Arms control—Congresses. 2. Nuclear
arms control—Congresses. 3. Security,
International—Congresses. I. Mickiewicz,
Ellen Propper. II. Kolkowicz, Roman.
JX1974.1596 1986   327.1′74   86-15073
ISBN 0-275-92186-7 (alk. paper)

Library of Congress Catalog Card Number: 86-15073
ISBN: 0-275-92186-7

First published in 1986

Praeger Publishers, 521 Fifth Avenue, New York, NY 10175
A division of Greenwood Press, Inc.

Printed in the United States of America

∞

The paper used in this book complies with the Permanent
Paper Standard issued by the National Information Standards
Organization (Z39.48-1984).

10 9 8 7 6 5 4 3 2 1

Contents

Contributors

Kenneth Adelman is Director of the Arms Control and Disarmament Agency.

Howard Baker, former U.S. Senator from Tennessee and Senate Majority leader, is now a partner of Vinson & Elkins.

Harold Brown, former Secretary of Defense, is now Chairman of the Foreign Policy Institute at Johns Hopkins University.

Zbigniew Brzezinski, former National Security Advisor, is now Senior Advisor at Georgetown University Center for Strategic and International Studies and Herbert Lehman Professor of Government at Columbia University.

McGeorge Bundy, former Special Assistant to the President for National Security, and later President of the Ford Foundation, is now Professor of History at New York University.

Norman Dicks is a U.S. Representative from Washington.

Anatoly Dobrynin is the Ambassador to the United States of the Union of Soviet Socialist Republics.

Thomas Downey is a U.S. Representative from New York.

Ralph Earle II, former Director of the Arms Control and Disarmament Agency and Chief U.S. Negotiator in SALT II, is now a managing partner of Baker & Daniels.

El Sayed Abdel Raouf El Reedy is the Ambassador of Egypt to the United States.

Richard Garwin is an IBM Fellow at the Thomas J. Watson Research Center. He also holds faculty appointments at Columbia, Cornell, and Harvard universities.

Albert Gore, Jr. is a U.S. Senator from Tennessee.

Gerhard Herder is the Ambassador to the United States of the German Democratic Republic.

John Howe is Director of the Defence Arms Control Unit in the British Ministry of Defence.

William Hyland, Editor of *Foreign Affairs*, was a career State Department analyst of Soviet and East European affairs and a member of the National Security Council staff.

David Jones (Gen., USAF, ret.), is a former chairman of the Joint Chiefs of Staff.

Henry Kissinger, former National Security Advisor and Secretary of State, is now Chairman of Kissinger Associates, Inc.

John Lehman is Secretary of the Navy.

Kinya Niiseki is Chairman of the Board of Directors of the Japan Institute of International Affairs.

Sam Nunn is a U.S. Senator from Georgia.

Joseph Nye is Dillon Professor of International Affairs at Harvard University. Formerly he served as Deputy Undersecretary of State for Security Assistance, Science, and Technology.

Robert O'Neill is Director of the International Institute of Strategic Studies in London.

William Perry, former Undersecretary of Defense for Research and Engineering, is now managing partner of H & Q Technology Partners.

Qian Jia-dong is Ambassador for Disarmament of the People's Republic of China.

Friedrich Ruth is the Federal Government Representative for Questions of Disarmament and Arms Control of the Federal Republic of Germany.

James Schlesinger, former Secretary of Defense and Secretary of the Department of Energy, is now Senior Advisor to the firm of Lehman Brothers Kuhn Loeb, Inc.

Brent Scowcroft (Lt. Gen., USAF, ret.), former Assistant to the President for National Security Affairs and Chairman of the President's Commission on Strategic Forces, is now Vice Chairman of Kissinger Associates, Inc.

Agha Shahi was Foreign Minister of Pakistan.

Helmut Sonnenfeldt, Visiting Scholar at The Brookings Institution, was a Counselor for the Department of State and a Senior Member of the National Security Council.

Ted Stevens is a U.S. Senator from Alaska.

Sergei Tarasenko is Deputy Chief of the United States Department of the Ministry of Foreign Affairs of the Soviet Union.

Cyrus Vance, former Secretary of State, is now a partner of Simpson, Thacher, and Bartlett.

Evgeny Velikhov is Deputy Director of the Kurchatov Institute of Atomic Physics, Vice President of the Soviet Academy of Sciences, and Professor of Physics at Moscow State University.

Preface

In 1983, the Carter Center of Emory University initiated a two-year program to investigate questions of international security and arms control. This complex nexus of issues, set in the context of deteriorating relations between the United States and the Soviet Union and increasing concern with nuclear questions worldwide, was to be considered by a number of political and military leaders, diplomats, scientists, and scholars from around the world. Repeating their earlier collaboration in programs at the Carter Center and the Ford Library, former Presidents Jimmy Carter and Gerald Ford joined forces to press actively for the clarification and analysis of these critical issues and the wide dissemination of the resulting information.

In May 1984, a day-long symposium was held at the Carter Center, chaired by President Carter. Four arms control policymakers and negotiators addressed specific questions relating to the practice and lessons of negotiating with the Soviet Union and the prospects for the future of arms control. Ambassadors Gerard C. Smith and Ralph Earle II, who headed the SALT I and II teams respectively, former Secretary of Defense Harold Brown, and former State Department Counselor Helmut Sonnenfeldt provided an analysis based on the collective experience of three administrations.*

A second symposium, chaired by Presidents Ford and Carter, was held at the Ford Library in November 1984. In the first half of this program, physicists Michael May and Richard Garwin and General Brent Scowcroft examined new developments in weapons technology and their impact on arms racing and security. In the second part, then Assistant Secretary of State for European and Canadian Affairs Richard Burt, former National Security Advisor Zbigniew Brzezinski, and William Hyland, editor of *Foreign Affairs*, commented on Soviet–American relations in the context of changes in the Soviet political system.

Both of these symposia helped to set the agenda for a week-long gathering at the Carter Center in April 1985. At the beginning of the week, three study panels of distinguished experts from several countries, including the Soviet Union, met for several days in private. Their analyses and reports served as a framework for the discussions and recommendations of the public consultation which followed.† The panels considered three clusters of issues:

---

*The edited text of this symposium may be found in *The Soviet Calculus of Nuclear War*, edited by Roman Kolkowicz and Ellen Propper Mickiewicz (Lexington Books, 1985).

†The reader will find the list of participants in the study panels and the text of their reports in the Appendix.

- What kinds of weapons are stabilizing or destabilizing to the strategic and political relations of the superpowers, and how do new technologies affect this relationship?
- How does the proliferation of nuclear weapons affect international stability and national security, and what measures might be taken to minimize that threat? How are international stability in general and the superpower relationship in particular affected by regional conflicts, and what might be done to minimize or assuage these chronic outbreaks?
- How do diplomatic and political factors enhance or inhibit prospects for significant arms reduction? What role do negotiations and treaties play, embedded as they are in the wider political context and subjected though they be to pressures from domestic as well as allied policy interests?

The objectives of the consultation, as defined in President Carter's opening remarks on Soviet–American relations and global security, were: "...to inventory those things that our two countries have in common, and how we might build on those common interests to have a better and more peaceful life for all people. We've assessed some of the differences that divide these two nations and how some of those differences might be assuaged or minimized or even eliminated...and we've assessed...the differences that exist between our two nations that are permanent in nature just because we have a different doctrine and different forms of government."

The reader will see, in the pages that follow, how these and related issues were addressed by the more than 50 participants representing nine countries at the consultation. Certain major themes emerged from the 11 hours of discussion; some of the key issues included:

The mixed record of arms control negotiations in curbing significantly or halting the arms race. Some of the participants were fundamentally pessimistic, such as Henry Kissinger, who asserted that "we are essentially out of ideas on arms control that make any major contribution except in the symbolic field of having made progress." He was joined by Secretary of the Navy John Lehman, who described the history of arms control as "...a sad one, because it has not really increased in any measurable way the security of either country." They were not alone in their assessments of this decades-long process, but others pointed out that whatever the distance between expectations and results, the absence of arms control initiatives and the failure to negotiate are likely to result in a net increase in insecurity.

Most participants emphasized the importance and even the urgency of the need to persist with arms control and to pursue more seriously diplomatic means toward the goal of slowing down and reversing the dangerous direction of the new arms race. And most saw the prospects for success as dependent on the larger scope of the political interactions between the superpowers.

The impact of strategic nuclear weapons and technologies on international stability was discussed at length from several perspectives. There was a general agreement that strategic stability is a fundamental objective of the United States and the Soviet Union; however, there was disagreement as to its specific meaning and the ways of obtaining it. The U.S. approach to the achievement and maintenance of strategic stability was defined as an emphasis on enhancement of the survivability of strategic forces and the minimization of their vulnerability to surprise attacks. This key objective was to be pursued by several means, including: (a) concealment, mobilization, and reduction in the size of forces; (b) enhancement of command and control capabilities; and (c) modification of force balances on each side through arms control agreements.

Soviet participants favored general sharp reductions of strategic forces without specifying the particular levels or numbers.

The complex problem of offense-defense strategies, specifically the implications of the proposed Strategic Defense Initiative ("Star Wars"), provoked lively discussion and disagreement, particularly among U.S. and Soviet participants. Strongest support for SDI came from members of the Reagan administration, who, in the words of Secretary of the Navy Lehman, found it to be a more "morally and intellectually satisfying" strategy than the concept of balance of terror implicit in the Mutual Assured Destruction doctrine, because the former would "protect the populations rather than avenge them." However, other U.S. participants, such as former Secretary of Defense Brown, expressed "serious reservations, to put it mildly, about SDI, on technological, military/strategic, and political grounds," and specifically concerning its feasibility and advisability.

Nonetheless, U.S. participants were in general agreement, with some caveats, that "we can't get the SDI genie back into the bottle." Moreover, given the fact that the Soviets for years have been spending large amounts of money on research, development, and deployment of strategic defenses, American participants felt it made sense for the United States to proceed with its own SDI research programs. Soviet participants strongly rejected SDI, and remained skeptical about notions of Soviet–American cooperation and sharing of these evolving technologies.

The role of alliances and non-aligned countries in the contemporary international political context, and the dangerous flareups of regional conflicts received the attention of numerous participants from many countries. There was a general agreement that while the ability of the major powers to intervene effectively in regional conflicts has diminished, their interest in maintaining their influence and control in the world has not declined correspondingly. As the conflicts in Vietnam and Afghanistan demonstrated, effective external intervention is difficult and costly, suggesting the need for a greater reliance on, and support of, better cooperation among the countries of the relevant regions.

While the proceedings of the consultation were characterized by a generally positive attitude on the part of the participants, by an appreciation for the gravity of the issues under discussion, and even by an urgency to look for constructive solutions to these contentious issues, nevertheless, representatives of the governments in Moscow and Washington tended to assign the burden of responsibility for the current international strategic and political impasse on each other. Ambassador Anatoly Dobrynin maintained that U.S. policies are designed to assure American superiority and that American nuclear forces are tailored to a strategy of prevailing in a nuclear war. On the other hand, several American participants with experience in the current and past administrations pointed out that it was the Soviet Union which was arming at a rapid rate, and which was seeking strategic superiority in their quest for new opportunities for relatively risk-free intervention and aggression in various parts of the world. Dobrynin also described Soviet–American relations as "tense, complicated, and unstable" and warned against American illusions concerning a U.S. ability "to race [the Soviet Union] into some sort of military, economic, and political weakness.".

The consultation concluded on a hopeful and positive note, with several constructive recommendations put forth by the individual panels and summarized by President Carter:

- Continued adherence to the Interim Agreement on Offensive Nuclear Weapons and to the SALT II treaty;
- Retention of the Antiballistic Missile Treaty;
- Achievement of a comprehensive test ban through gradual reduction of permissible levels under the Threshold Treaty;
- Continuation of meetings by top political leaders and the establishment of frequent meetings by military leaders from both sides; and
- Minimization of linkage between arms talks and Soviet–American disagreements and conflicts elsewhere in the world.

The superpower summit in Geneva in November 1985 and the continuing arms control negotiations have, again, confirmed the critical importance of the issues raised at the Carter Center consultation. The proposals and options identified there are still central to a deliberate and prudent improvement in the security of the superpowers and of the other nations of the world.

Session 1
Alliances, Proliferation, and Regional Conflict

President Carter: I'd like to say how delighted we are, at the Carter Center of Emory University in Atlanta, to have such a distinguished group to consider perhaps one of the most important issues that affect our own nation and other countries of the world. When President Ford and I were serving in the Oval Office we both had to be eager students, learning from every possible source, as best we could, the relationship between our country and the Soviet Union, and, of course, arms control is an integral part of that relationship. In the minds of many people—not excluding presidents themselves—it is a kind of a measuring rod of the current, ongoing relationships that irrevocably tie arms control to other issues, for instance, regional conflict. They certainly are closely related.

We have spent the last three days with distinguished panelists from our country and the Soviet Union, China, Japan, Great Britain, France, East Germany, West Germany, and several other nations on Earth, trying to assess the basic ties between our countries and how relationships between the Soviet Union and the United States affect other people on Earth. We've tried to inventory those things that our two countries have in common, and how we might build on those common interests to have a better and more peaceful life for all people. We've assessed some of the differences that divide our two nations and how some of those differences might be assuaged or minimized or even eliminated with better understanding, cultural exchange, diplomatic procedures, and even negotiations and summit conferences. And we've assessed also some of the differences that exist between our two nations that are permanent in nature just because we have a different doctrine and different forms of government, different geographical locations on Earth, different ties to our allies, and so forth, and also how those differences might be endured without departing from peaceful relations. We will analyze, in these next two days, how our own actions affect our allies and those nations closest to us and other countries around the world; how regional conflicts might be assuaged or minimized in their importance or sometimes aggravated by decisions made in Moscow or Washington; what individual weapons systems are stabilizing or destabilizing; how new technologies affect this relationship. We also will assess, as best we can, how the superpowers and others can minimize the inclination of non-nuclear nations to proliferate the nuclear threat—which is dangerous enough in the hands of a nation with a stable government, but much more dangerous in an unstable country or in the hands of terrorists—and of course we'll also discuss in a very frank way the use of public relations—how each country tries to put forward its best foot and appeal to world opinion, sometimes known as propaganda, but I think that is part of the process as well.

The format for these sessions will be that each chairman of one of the three panels will first make a presentation of about 20 minutes, no more, and then we'll have distinguished respondents make presentations following the Soviet statement of interest. I might make it clear at this point that the Soviet delegation has participated in the panel discussions and has joined in, in most cases, with the reports of the panels themselves. Following the chairman's report, President Ford and I reserve the right to ask a follow-up question or make a statement, if we wish, before the panelists respond. I might say, as I told the group last night, that, since all of the presentations are being made by experts who in some cases have devoted their lives to these subjects, we want them to make their presentations in understandable language, because we have a lot of people in this audience. My guidance to them is to speak so that even a peanut farmer or a movie actor can understand what's said. So, with that introduction, let me welcome President Ford here as co-chairman of this session. We hope the sessions will be exciting and interesting to the audience, and productive in the enhancement of better relations between our countries, all nations on Earth, and the furthering of peace. President Ford—we're very delighted to have you with us.

President Ford: Thank you very much, President Carter. It's a high honor and a great privilege for me to participate with President Carter in hosting this gathering of such a wide variety of talent. It would be inexcusable for me to take a great deal of time to welcome all of you when we have so much of substance to discuss in the next two days, but, on the other hand, I would be very remiss if I didn't extend a very warm welcome to all of our foreign guests, from the Soviet Union and other countries, and to extend to Democrats as well as Republicans a warm welcome to participate in these two days' activities; and of course we are delighted to have so many people from the academic world who can have such a significant impact on the educational process of discussing the issues. Last fall President Carter and I had a preliminary gathering for this at the Ford Library on the campus of the University of Michigan, and it was a foundation for this much more in-depth discussion and was helpful in refining some of the issues and laying the basis for the discussions here for the next two days.

It seems to me that our objectives can be several: number one, it is highly important that the American public see representatives from the United States government and the Soviet Union discussing the very important, critical, controversial issues that will be confronting our negotiators in Geneva. At the same time, it will be very beneficial to the American people to see the ramifications on the international front, and of course it's important for the public to get the impression from the United States' point of view that those from both of our major political parties are seeking to sit down and discuss in a proper atmosphere the issues and possible solutions to the problems that have plagued relations between the Soviet Union and the United States over a period of many years. May I say we're delighted to have all of you here, and we solicit your active participation. President Carter and I will do our best to keep things moving, because there's a lot of work to be done. Thank you very much.

President Carter: Our first panel report will deal with three specific issues, and I think you'll notice as the consultation goes on that we've tried to divide the three panels' responsibilities, but there inevitably will be some overlap. In this first report the subjects are alliances, the proliferation of nuclear explosives to other countries, and how to handle regional conflicts. The chairman of this panel is Dr. Robert O'Neill, who is the director of the International Institute of Strategic Studies in London.

Robert O'Neill: Thank you very much, Mr. President. The panel, which is composed of analysts from North America, Asia, Europe, and the Pacific, sees major problems ahead in terms of the security of our vital interests, the management of East-West relations, the limitation of regional conflicts, and the control of the spread of nuclear weapons. Any serious prescriptions for improving international security must rest on an understanding of the major social, economic, and political changes which have occurred in recent years.

Levels of literacy and urbanization have increased dramatically. Mass mobilization in the political process has spread, often in radical forms. The economic gap between the richest and poorest countries has increased. Modern weapons are more widely available. These and other changes during the past 40 years have helped to create a world in which the ability of the major powers to shape events in other countries has steadily declined. At the same time, terrorism, often supported by governments, has increased in scope and scale. The net result is that the world has become less manageable and risks to its safety have multiplied. There are grounds for believing that some of the major challenges to the world's community in the coming years, such as the problems of food production for a rapidly growing population and in social and economic development, can successfully be met; but this success may be uneven, and some countries or regions are likely to face critical problems and serious instabilities. The temptation for more countries to look to nuclear weapons and other mass destruction weapons as a source of security or simply to relieve their frustrations in this situation will remain strong. So will the likelihood that outside powers will be drawn into regional disputes and thus increase the risks of wider conflict.

How then should we deal with these issues? First, let us take the role of allies and alliances—for the United States and its friends. The alliances built up after World War II served to protect against the threat of further Soviet expansion, and they have been outstandingly successful in preserving peace and security. The United States and its European and Pacific allies all wish to maintain and enhance the strength and cohesion of their relationship. But they face difficult problems in doing so. A generation has come into power in all of these countries that had no direct experience of World War II, the realities it taught, and the relationships and attitudes which the experience of major conflict formed. Western European countries also have a need to accelerate the pace of economic and technological change and thereby face difficult problems, both for their internal policies and their relations with the United States. Aspirations for ending the division of Europe created by the Second World War remain strong in Western Europe. But the means of achieving this objective are elusive, giving rise to a growing sense of frustration.

The strategic context of the Atlantic alliance has been changing in recent years, notably as a result of the continuing strengthening of the nuclear and non-nuclear forces of the Warsaw Pact. In the view of some, this change has already brought NATO to a point at which de facto it has a no-first-use policy on nuclear weapons because the threat to use nuclear weapons has been increasingly self-defeating. Moreover, changes of public attitude towards NATO strategy are increasing the desire to move away from the traditional reliance on the threat to use nuclear weapons early, if at all, in the face of Warsaw Pact attack.

Among the Pacific allies of the United States, some similar trends can be seen. In Japan, concern about growing Soviet military activities in the region is real. But there is also anxiety at what many Japanese see as an exaggeration of the Soviet threat by the United States. As a result, confidence in United States military judgment is weakened. In Australia and, even more, in New Zealand, concern about reliance on nuclear weapons as a central element in security policy has grown. The fact that recent disagreements between the United States and New Zealand on the subject of nuclear warship visits have not been contained as in the past has gravely threatened the fabric of the ANZUS [Pacific Security Treaty] alliance, although it remains of great importance to all three partners.

None of these developments has affected the importance that all allied governments, save perhaps New Zealand, in these circumstances, continue to attach to nuclear deterrence as the prime element in their security policies. But there has been a growing desire for a diminished reliance on the threat to use nuclear weapons, especially in the early stages of a war. It has been accompanied by a growth of concern among the Western European allies about the degree of their reliance on U.S. military assistance. There have been some signs, however, that the allies are prepared to increase their capacity for self-reliance both in Europe and in the Pacific. In NATO there is support in principle for the introduction of new non-nuclear forces within the overall context of a strong nuclear deterrence. But non-nuclear weapons are more expensive and are also labor intensive, while the manpower available for European defense is declining, for demographic reasons. The absence of progress towards closer political integration also remains an obstacle to a stronger European pillar in the alliance. At the same time, pressures within the U.S. Congress are once again raising the possibility of a cutback in U.S. support for NATO.

Alliance problems are not confined to the West. The Warsaw Pact remains a powerful and substantially effective military alliance. But it can never hope to be the political community based on free association that the Atlantic alliance represents. We would, however, be foolish to underrate its strategic power, which is being rapidly modernized and extended, and which casts a long shadow even in time of peace.

The development of the U.S. Strategic Defense Initiative [SDI], popularly known as "Star Wars," has further complicated relations between the United States and its allies. Considerable doubt has already been expressed in the scientific community about the technological feasibility of defending populations in the foreseeable future. But if strategic defenses prove feasible, they may undermine the credibility of the strategy of flexible response. If defense of population centers against strategic nuclear attack proves feasible for the United States and the Soviet Union, Western Europe would still be exposed to conventional attack against which there could be no nuclear response or deterrence. Should strategic defenses prove feasible only for key military installations, Western responses to aggression based on first use of nuclear weapons against such targets would become increasingly difficult and unlikely. For these and other reasons, including the future of the ABM [Antiballistic Missile] treaty, opportunity cost, and problems of technology transfer, America's allies see many questions which must be examined before any attempt to deploy strategic defenses is made. At the same time, the allies acknowledge that a program of prudent research should be pursued by the United States because the Soviet Union is already active in this field.

Allied public opinion is puzzled, however, that such high priority should be given to the SDI at this time. The recently resumed arms control negotiations in Geneva have to grapple with formidable problems that were not resolved in the 1981–83 negotiations on strategic and intermediate nuclear systems. This array of issues is made even more difficult to settle by the additional requirements posed by the possibility that strategic defenses might be deployed both on Earth and in space. The Chinese and Japanese members of the panel recalled an old maxim of both nations—there is a sword for every shield and a shield for every sword. Strategic defenses will foster new forms of offense. Military competition will continue. Nuclear weapons cannot be disinvented, nor can their destructive power be wholly negated.

With careful management, these sources of strain need not lead to serious disruption of U.S.-allied relationships. There have been certain signs of strength and continuity in these relationships in recent years. The basic facts that led to the formation of the Atlantic alliance have not changed, notably the division of Europe and dependence upon the U.S. security guarantee. The divisive issue of strengthening the theater nuclear force balance in Europe by the deployment of new U.S. nuclear weapons has, for the most part, been successfully managed. The harmony of views on the need for a strong defense policy in the face of the modernization of Warsaw Pact forces has grown. The peace movement in Western Europe that came to light in the early 1980s is now less active as a political force, although its ideas have left a mark on all major political parties. Even the concerns expressed about the SDI fit into a familiar pattern of European anxieties which may be reduced by careful alliance management. There is, however, no ground for complacency. The current controversies on the SDI and new concepts of conventional defense using advanced technologies, such as highly accurate battlefield missiles, could slow progress toward the needed enhancement of allied military capabilities and also offer opportunities to the Soviet Union to exploit internal alliance disputes.

Second, let us consider the problems of regional conflict. The most important regional conflicts, notably those in the Middle East, Central America, the Indian subcontinent, and Southeast Asia, all derive from persistent, long-lived causes within the social, economic, and political structures of the regions. Such conflicts are likely to endure, and, in view of the explosive potential of the combination of social tensions, ethnic differences, and economic strains, to grow in number and intensify. The growth of terrorism as a normal tool of both governments and subnational groups, for example in Lebanon and Central America, and the increasing use of force in violation of the U.N. Charter, as in Afghanistan, are symptoms of this increasing disorder. The challenge to the international community is to find ways of either resolving these conflicts or living with them without their causing a further breakdown of regional order and wider and more dangerous confrontation at the global level.

There is general agreement that the ability of the major powers to intervene effectively in regional conflicts has diminished. But their interest in maintaining their influence and control in the world has not declined correspondingly. As the conflicts in Vietnam and Afghanistan have shown, effective external intervention is difficult and costly. In addition, domestic politics in the United States in the aftermath of Vietnam make it hard for the U.S. government to use military force except where quick and easy success is likely. Some people draw the conclusion from this situation that the superpowers should define the range of their security interests more narrowly and reduce their involvement in regional conflicts, thereby minimizing the prospect for multiplication of incidents that could, if mishandled, lead to a superpower confrontation. Since in the nuclear age any one such incident could be fatal, there is a need to establish more firebreaks to inhibit the spread of local conflagrations. Other people are skeptical as to whether such superpower restraint is achievable in the foreseeable future, given the expectation of continuing U.S.-Soviet competition. Such people argue that the superpowers have more influence over the course of regional conflicts than the first view admits. Even if the direct control of the major powers is diminished, they still have means of indirect control, such as through the supply of armaments, and they will use them.

The panel accepted that Western countries should think in terms of a broad definition of security: comprehensive security, as the Japanese call it, which embraces economic, social, and political, as well as military, aspects. In this connection, the promising signs of increasing regional cooperation in solving regional problems that have emerged in recent years should be strongly encouraged. The Association of Southeast Asian Nations [ASEAN], the Gulf Cooperation Council, and recent diplomatic moves between Brazil and Argentina are all examples of this trend. The Organization of African Unity, although hitherto less successful, should also be encouraged to take a greater responsibility for resolving regional disputes in Africa. The Contadora process in Central America is another form of regional initiative that deserves encouragement. For these purposes, and also as the basis for some of the more radical solutions that may be appropriate to some regional conflicts, such as the resettlement of populations, Western countries will need to devote greater attention and resources than in recent years to economic assistance through both bilateral and multilateral arrangements. This policy will not be popular in countries whose national budgets are already strained. But the short-term domestic advantage of failing to support such policies will be dwarfed in the long term by the dangers that will result.

Third, how should we approach the problem of the spread of nuclear weapons? The acquisition of nuclear arms by additional nations continues to pose a grave risk to world peace. None of the panel accepted the view, sometimes expressed, that further proliferation could be seen as contributing to regional or global stability. All agreed that the effort to halt and reverse proliferation should receive higher priority at the national level. The successful coordination of U.S. and allied nonproliferation efforts has been important in increasing the effectiveness of the international nonproliferation regime. This coordination should be continued and, if possible, extended. The international nonproliferation regime, which includes the International Atomic Energy Agency, bilateral and multilateral nuclear trade agreements, and the Non-Proliferation Treaty, has done much to retard the spread of nuclear weapons and deserves continued active support.

There are a number of states whose nuclear activities have raised proliferation concerns over the past decade, including Argentina, Brazil, India, Iraq, Israel, Libya, Pakistan, and South Africa. Attempts by some of these nations to build or expand nuclear weapons capabilities are posing greater dangers and necessitate increased nonproliferation efforts by the international community. During the 1970s, a number of these nations appeared to be pursuing the acquisition of nuclear weapons through commercial purchases of sensitive, nuclear plants as part of their civil energy programs. The nuclear supplier countries successfully curtailed sales of these installations, especially enrichment and reprocessing plants capable of producing nuclear weapons material. However, the emerging nuclear weapons states have turned increasingly to developing such installations—in effect dedicated military installations—themselves, both by indigenous efforts and by illegal acquisition of nuclear technology from more highly industrialized states.

Nuclear technology controls remain important to counteract these trends, and efforts should be made to bring new nuclear suppliers to cooperate with a supplier restraint regime. But emphasis must be placed on a broader array of tools for stemming proliferation, including diplomatic pressure, sanctions, and incentives to increase the costs to would-be proliferators of developing nuclear arms. Regional measures for addressing specific non-proliferation challenges deserve further support. If, as recent reports suggest, Argentina and Brazil have agreed to open their nuclear installations to mutual inspection, this would represent a confidence-building measure of considerable importance. A no-nuclear-explosion pledge by India and Pakistan might similarly serve to reduce nuclear tensions in that region.

Finally, the proliferation of chemical weapons, which are also weapons of mass destruction, may pose even greater near-term dangers than the spread of nuclear arms, and may be more difficult to control. Moreover, the acquisition of chemical weapons by one regional power may encourage the acquisition of nuclear weapons by a regional rival. Iraq's recent use of chemical weapons in violation of the Geneva Protocol suggests the need for greater international attention to this difficult problem.

Let me now leave you with the panel's recommendations. The most important consideration arising from the panel's discussion is that we must pay greater attention to the speed with which the world is changing and the directions that these changes are taking. The affairs of the world are becoming more complex to manage, and this complexity challenges us to find better ways of preserving security. Information technology can help, but can only supplement what we ourselves, both in government and as private citizens, know and understand about our security problems and interests. We draw attention to the following conclusions:

(1) The United States, as the leader of the West, must not only maintain its strength but also pay greater attention to the views and interests of its allies, in order to preserve cohesion and effectiveness in the Atlantic and Pacific alliances. Continued divergences in the way in which the United States and its allies perceive threats and responses raise new challenges for alliance management. The debate on the utility of strategic defenses can be expected to intensify in coming years.

(2) The Western alliances have a strong record of achievement in terms of maintaining peace and security, but all the allies face greater responsibilities for improving the management of global affairs. Their active involvement will continue to be

needed in all major dimensions of the East–West relationship—political, military, economic, and social. Allied participation in these areas has often been important in the past, but even greater efforts will be called for in the future, if East–West relations are not to be permitted to drift into areas of danger.

(3) Military capabilities of the Soviet Union and the Warsaw Pact can be expected to continue to develop, and pose an increasingly serious challenge to Western security. This challenge is presented not only in the form of military confrontation, but also in terms of attempts to divide the alliance and neutralize it politically. Hence, special attention must continue to be devoted to meeting both sides of this politico-military threat.

(4) The West should develop and allocate the resources necessary to implement longer-term strategies for preventing or limiting regional conflicts. Leadership must, in most cases, come from the United States, but in some situations, as has been the case in the past, individual allies must be prepared to play a leading role. Most urgent action is required in respect to the Middle East, but problems elsewhere, such as in Central America, Southern Africa, Afghanistan, Kampuchea, and the Korean peninsula, have potential for escalation and must be addressed. Failure to act and to accept greater responsibility for initiatives is likely to lead to increased risks, both for Western security interests and for global stability.

(5) The development of regional initiatives to enhance security both nationally and collectively should be encouraged. Organizations such as ASEAN and the Gulf Cooperation Council have shown what can be done. They are worthy of continuing Western support and cooperation, and offer lessons for nations in other troubled regions.

(6) The threat of terrorism is becoming more serious as more potent means of violence are acquired by people in desperation in both developed and developing societies. Short- and long-term remedies must be sought.

(7) Nuclear proliferation remains a potent threat to world order. New technology and increased concern by potential nuclear powers about regional threats require renewed vigor in our dealing with this problem. Firm controls on the transfer of nuclear technology must be maintained, and new ways of thwarting the clandestine diffusion of this technology must be devised. The cause of nonproliferation must be kept high on the international agenda. Incentives for proliferation must be dealt with as part of a wider policy for strengthening security both regionally and globally. None of these problems can be solved in a context dominated by unremitting East–West hostility or the perspectives of any single nation-state. The recommendations of this panel must stand together with those of the two panels on Soviet-American relations. Thank you, Mr. Chairman.

President Carter: I think you all noticed that this committee has covered a very wide range of subjects in a very succinct way. During the coming discussion we will have a chance to explore some of these matters in more specific terms. One of the most gratifying elements of our consultation here has been the very distinguished delegation sent by General Secretary Gorbachev and the Soviet government. The delegation, which represents the Soviet military and the foreign ministry in Moscow, as well as the academic and scientific community, has participated in the panel discussions. We are particularly honored to have Ambassador Dobrynin, who has now been in our country a number of years; he's the senior diplomat in Washington among the ambassadorial corps. I think he's been here 20...how many years? [*Dobrynin:* 20 plus something.] 20 plus something; he doesn't know exactly. And we'll be very eager in each case to have the Soviet delegation make a statement on these same issues, recognizing that they have been involved in the panel discussions and have been part of the presentations in general. We'd like to call on him now to comment as he sees fit.

Anatoly Dobrynin: Thank you, President Carter. Well, I shall not exactly be directly involved, because this panel went on without our participation. I have just arrived, and my colleagues concentrated mostly on military questions and, I should say, arms control. Probably I will have something to say in the course of the discussion today, but we would prefer to deal with the important issues of disarmament, arms control, and our relations with the United States in our major address. Thank you very much.

President Carter: Ambassador Dobrynin will make a comprehensive Soviet statement this afternoon following the second presentation.

One of the most intriguing aspects of this panel's discussions was the interrelationship between regional disputes, which sometimes assume enormous importance in the consciousness of the world public, on the one hand, and the continuation of arms control on the other hand. I'd like to call now on the former Secretary of State, Henry Kissinger, a distinguished leader of our country, to make the first response among the panelists.

Henry Kissinger: President Carter and President Ford, first of all let me thank both of you for inviting me to come here. I believe that this conference is important in its own right, but it's also extremely important as a demonstration of the need for bipartisanship in the conduct of our foreign policy. We cannot continue to reassess our foreign policy every four to eight years without becoming a factor of instability in the world, both to friends and adversaries. Cy Vance and I have talked about this, and I believe that both presidents are making a great contribution in assembling such a forum. Frankly, Mr. President, I think we're making great progress when the Soviet ambassador is present on the panel discussing the strengthening of NATO—a subject to which I know he is dedicated. [*Dobrynin:* All my life.] I look forward to the contribution he will make as our discussion develops, especially with respect to what might be the most effective strategy for containing the Soviet Union. For the benefit of southern senators, from North Carolina particularly, I hope there is no symbolic significance to the fact that Anatoly has been placed to the right of me. [*Dobrynin:* But looking from the audience, I'm to the left of you.] Before I answer your question, Mr. President, I'd like to make one or two comments about the presentation that we have just heard, keeping in mind all the adjectives you used yesterday that we should keep in mind in formulating our comments; they are not easy to meet for somebody whose native language was German.

Let me just make a few comments where I did not agree with the statements that have been made because I don't want to let them go unchallenged. I cannot accept the proposition that the de facto policy of NATO is no first use of nuclear weapons, and I do not think any such statement should be permitted to pass unchallenged. I believe that this would be a very dangerous course that creates the impression that we would prefer to be defeated with conventional weapons than resort to nuclear weapons. It is also totally inconsistent with later statements that have been made in the paper about the reliance on nuclear weapons. I fully agree that it is highly desirable that nuclear use be avoided and that one should not resort to it lightly, but I hope the de facto no first use is not something that remains in the final paper. I believe also that a balanced discussion of allied relationships should not only concentrate on the alleged loss of confidence by our allies in our judgment, but also on some doubts that may have arisen about American confidence in allied judgments. It is statistically improbable that the United States is always wrong, and therefore I think a rational discussion should concern the issue of the merit of the arguments and not just the criticisms that are made, sometimes for domestic consumption. Third, with respect to the Soviet threat—whether the American perception of it is excessive—I think one ought to analyze, if Anatoly will permit it, what it is before we can judge. Finally, with respect to the theory of the Strategic Defense Initiative (on which you have a panel that will discuss technical feasibility, on which I'm not competent to make a judgment) I cannot accept that these weapons are always attacked on two grounds: that they are unfeasible and that they are destabilizing. They can only be one or the other. Now, I will address only the argument that if it were possible to have a defense, leaving aside the question whether it is, that that would be against allied unity and would weaken the American willingness to defend Europe. I would say a much more plausible case could be made for exactly the opposite proposition. I do not believe that the total vulnerability of populations is an assurance of the willingness to undertake defense, and indeed I believe that there is a political, strategic, and moral obligation to move away from a concept of attacks on population centers. I do not think that democracies, and maybe even nondemocracies, can indefinitely sustain the proposition that only the threat of mass extermination can preserve the peace; I believe that we owe it to ourselves to discuss the SDI idea in such a context, and I leave aside the question of its feasibility.

There is one other point I have to make with respect to the paper. There are many areas of the world in which we should be afraid of the potentiality of escalation and in which we should, perhaps, make sure other nations get involved. I would not include Korea among those. The only potential for escalation in Korea is aggression from the North, and I think we should make absolutely clear that without military aggression from the North, there is absolutely no possibility of escalation in Korea; and to turn that into a global issue involving NATO and other countries and to say that there's a crisis in Korea, other than a direct military attack along a clearly demarcated line, I think, is creating a needless source of friction.

To address your question, however, I have believed—and I had the privilege of working with Anatoly on the subject under President Ford's and President Nixon's direction—that the easing of relations between the Soviet Union and the United States is an important element, a crucial element, of world peace. I do not believe it can be achieved exclusively in the arms control field, especially since (until the panel can meet this afternoon) I believe we are essentially out of ideas on arms control that make any major contribution except in the symbolic field of having made progress. In the period in which, I think, significant progress was made, in the 1970s, there were always political discussions going on side by side with the military discussions. Anatoly will remember the Berlin discussions, the European security conference discussions,* and a host of political discussions that accompanied the arms control negotiations. And we have seen with SALT II that if there is an explosion in some part of the world, if the political conflict gets too great between the United States and the Soviet Union, then the arms control process will not be possible to sustain, or be sustained, or will simply become a means of ratifying what exists anyway.

Arms control is extremely important. We must accompany it by political discussions. I believe that a lot of fun has been made of the principles of international conduct that were established—negotiated—in 1972;** certainly, principles of restraint are not self-implemented. If we had not had the national tragedy of a loss of executive authority which created the oddest coalition between liberals and conservatives—liberals who disliked President Nixon, and conservatives who disliked the Russians—so that we lost the political basis for further negotiations, we would surely have gone on to concrete political discussions on mutual restraint which might or might not have succeeded. But I would simply emphasize that they must be part of an agenda that is given great importance, though I hope not as much drama and publicity as the arms control negotiations are getting, because they are not really very conducive to that sort of dramatic business. I would urge that the arms control negotiations be accompanied by some quiet political dialogue in which we ask ourselves where we want the world to be ten years from now, and not simply repeat by rote all the slogans of the last period, and move toward a solution in that manner. Excuse me for going on a little too long.

President Carter: Our next commentator on the panel is Joseph Nye. Mr. Nye is Dillon Professor of International Affairs at Harvard University and has served as Deputy to the Undersecretary of State for Security Assistance, Science,

---

*The Conference on Security and Cooperation in Europe, which opened in mid-1973 and culminated in a summit in Helsinki for the signing, on August 1, 1975, of the final act of the conference.

**The Agreement on Basic Principles of U.S.–Soviet Relations, signed in Moscow, May 29, 1972, after the signing of the SALT I treaties.

and Technology. We are delighted to have Joseph Nye comment at this time.

Joseph Nye: Thank you, Mr. President. Rather than comment on the whole report, let me mention the context within which I want to focus on the particular issue of the nonproliferation of nuclear weapons. In the last two years, the Kennedy School at Harvard has had a program we call "Avoiding Nuclear War." Rather than starting with arms control, we started with the question: Are there things you can do to reduce the probabilities of nuclear war in a significant way? And as we've gone over the different ways in which nuclear war might start, we have found that while there are five significant paths, the most dangerous path is likely to be escalation from a regional crisis—basically the subject matter of this panel. And that within that path of escalation from a regional crisis, the greatest dangers will be things which lead to loss of control, to complications, to thwarting the rational strategies we otherwise would follow. In that context we found that the issue of the nonproliferation of nuclear weapons is extremely important. The spread of nuclear weapons to third countries would greatly complicate the problems of managing regional crises, into which we might be drawn whether we liked it or not, as well as allow prospects for terrorists to use to disrupt regional balances as well as the societies of the great powers. So in that sense, I very strongly concur with the report's suggestion that the issue of the nonproliferation of nuclear weapons is not merely an issue which has seen its day and passed, but one that presents a major security problem for the future. Let me begin by asking three questions: To what extent does proliferation really matter? Is the situation hopeless? and, What can be done?

To what extent does it matter? Well, there is a view that if stable deterrence has been achieved in the U.S.–Soviet relationship through nuclear weapons, why wouldn't this stabilize regional relationships, such as the Middle East or Southern Africa or Latin America, and so forth? And when we hold nuclear weapons while going to conferences in Geneva and telling other countries that they should not acquire them, is this not hypocritical on our part? It seems to me that the answer to that question is that if the conditions were the same in those other relationships, it might be hypocritical, and it might be cultural arrogance. But the conditions are not the same. If you look at the technologies for the control of nuclear weapons (the special electronic combination locks, the special procedures for communication) which are present in the U.S.–Soviet relationship, and realize they would not be present for the new countries who would acquire nuclear weapons, you very quickly see that you can't assume that what's stabilizing in one relationship would be stabilizing in another. Similarly, if you look at statistics of where governments fall apart—where military coups occur, where civil wars occur—many of these include countries which would be in the list of countries trying to acquire nuclear weapons. Not only that, but when a country first acquires nuclear weapons the weapons are likely to be quite vulnerable and quite easy to be preempted or struck first by a regional neighbor whose fears are stimulated by it. In that sense, I think the conclusions from our "Avoiding Nuclear

War'' book, *Hawks, Doves, and Owls*, are correct: that the prospects for the use of nuclear weapons are much higher among the new proliferators than they are in the U.S.–Soviet relationship. In that sense, I believe that the argument that trying to stop proliferation is cultural arrogance is wrong. On the contrary, it is a common security interest and one which deserves to be placed much higher on our agenda.

If so, however—let me address my second question—is the situation hopeless? Very often we are told that the horse is out of the barn and that I might be right on question one but there is not much to be done on question two. I think that's a mistaken metaphor. To reformulate the metaphor, it matters how many horses are out of the barn and how fast they're escaping. Remember that, in 1963, President Kennedy expected that there would be something like 25 countries with nuclear weapons by this time. In fact there are less than a third that number, and I would argue that that difference is of profound significance in terms of security and the ability to manage the destabilizing effects of the spread of nuclear weaponry. In other words, it has proven quite possible to manage and to slow the rate of spread of nuclear weaponry. We've done it, and it's extremely important then that we continue to do it and not be misled by metaphors such as "the horse is out of the barn."

So let me take you to my third question: What can be done? I will list seven things—some of which are mentioned in our report, some of which are additional—and I'll elaborate briefly on these seven points. The first thing to notice, before discussing the seven points, is that sometimes people will say, "Well, proliferation is a technical problem, or a political problem," as though one were opposed to the other. It's both. A nonproliferation policy has to walk on two legs—a technical and a political leg. And people who say: "Well, it's a 40-year-old technology; it's bound to spread; there's nothing you can do about it," should think carefully about the circumstances and the experience of Libya. Libya's had lots of money and for fifteen years has tried to get a nuclear weapon and has not been able to do so. Technological restraints do matter. They're not the only thing that matters, however, because over the very long run, unless you pursue political restraints in addition to technical restraints, you're not going to have a firmly based policy. So the seven points that I'm going to mention stress both political and technical points.

The first, and perhaps the most important, is giving diplomatic priority to the issue of nonproliferation. There has sometimes been slippage in this dimension, and the diplomatic priority comes both in bilateral relations with particular countries—sometimes it pains us in other parts of our relationship to take a strong stand about proliferation—and it also comes in terms of maintaining the alliances which have been a central feature of this report. If one looks at the alliance structure, we see that not only have the alliances maintained the overall balance of power in the world since 1945, but they've had a lot to do with the fact that there are probably some thirty countries that could have nuclear weapons today but less than a third of that number have done so. So maintaining the alliances and at the same time maintaining the diplomatic priority of the issue is probably the most important question.

The second point is—as the report stresses—the maintenance of the regime, the instruments of the Non-Proliferation Treaty, and the International Atomic Energy Agency in Vienna, which sends out its inspectors. I think that's extremely important, in the sense that it places the burden of proof on the would-be proliferator. In a world in which sovereign nation-states have the right of self-defense, the fact that 120 countries have said that they do not presume that that includes the right to have nuclear weapons, is a point of no small significance. If we didn't have it, we would certainly miss it. And maintaining those instruments, while not sufficient for a policy, is absolutely necessary. In that sense one has to welcome, as the report does, China's admission and participation in the International Atomic Energy Agency as a significant strengthening factor.

A third point is the maintenance of the Nuclear Suppliers Group and the guidelines that it has created for being restrictive in the supply of certain technologies which are directly related to the production of nuclear weaponry or can be used in that fashion. And here again, as the report notes, it's important to bring in new suppliers—countries like India, Argentina, and others—to see that it's in their self-interest to maintain the same set of standards. That again strikes me as a feasible proposition.

A fourth issue is the development of sanctions to be applied if a country does indeed violate these norms and does develop a nuclear weapon. Now you might say: "Well, sanctions are widely discredited in international politics—they just don't work." Not quite true. You have to be careful about how you think of sanctions. If you think of sanctions as saying: "I don't like what you did and I'll never play with you again," obviously, that's not the way the game of international politics is played. The game will always go on. But if you think of sanctions more as a severe penalty in a hockey game, in which you know the game will go on, but it is very expensive if you incur that penalty, then sanctions do make a difference. It may not reverse the action that has just occurred, but it sure can make the next player an awful lot more careful in the calculations he makes about the actions he's going to take. So, thinking ahead to the next case of violation of these International Atomic Energy Agency safeguards or the next case of a nuclear explosion, and thinking ahead to developing sanctions that are analogous to a good ten-minute penalty in a hockey game, will have a powerful effect on the rate of future proliferation, even though it doesn't stop the case in which it is directly applied.

The fifth point on my list is the issue of zones. We can try to reinforce non-nuclear zones such as the one in Latin America and to think of new devices, such as reciprocal visits in South Asia between India and Pakistan. One might envisage an agreement for no further explosions, or some such arrangement.

A sixth point on my list would be the relationship of U.S.–Soviet arms control to the maintenance of the Non-Proliferation Treaty. There is a review conference which will come up in Geneva late this summer or early autumn, and in the Non-Proliferation Treaty there is an article which says the superpowers will take steps to reduce their own armaments. Sometimes people say: "Well, that doesn't matter all that much; it's there largely for window dressing. The treaty really rests on the point that it's good for regional security and that you wouldn't stop certain countries from carrying out their policies whether you did or did not take steps in the U.S.–Soviet relationship." There's some truth in that. There are many specific cases of proliferation that can be affected only by direct bilateral diplomacy, and what happens in U.S.–Soviet disarmament is irrelevant. But notice something else. In ten years the whole treaty comes up for review. It has to be renewed in 1995. I would submit to you that if there is no progress in U.S.–Soviet arms control negotiations by that time, it is going to be extremely difficult to get renewal of that treaty. And in that sense, I don't think it's quite feasible to imagine that over the very long run the United States and the Soviet Union will continue to pile up more armaments without at the same time being caught in an argument on this Non-Proliferation Treaty, which will lead to its erosion, and, I think, to a loss of our own security over the longer term.

The seventh and final point on my list is the importance of enhancing U.S.–Soviet cooperation on nonproliferation. This is an area where, despite the bad relations that we have had in the past, we have managed to maintain a modicum of cooperation. However, it's a cooperation that could be greatly strengthened on both sides, both on the American and the Soviet side. I would submit that with those seven points there are things that we can do. They may not totally stem the spread of nuclear weaponry, but they certainly can continue to slow it down so that we're better able to manage its destabilizing effects and less likely to find that proliferation will contribute to that most likely scenario which we identified as leading to the onset of a nuclear war: escalation growing out of a regional crisis in which there's loss of control because of third actors who basically are outside of the strategic calculation. So in that sense I think the report is exactly right on proliferation. I would only wish to underline it, which is what I've just done.

President Carter: Last May, when my wife and I went to Hiroshima as part of our trip to Japan, I decided, as the first major American official to visit there since the Second World War, to make a statement on the interrelationship between the use of atomic weapons as they existed back in those rudimentary days, as formidable as they were, and the need to maintain world peace. There were several thousand people assembled there, at what is known as "Ground Zero." And it was a vivid reminder to us of the devastating consequences of the potential use of nuclear weapons. In preparation for this consultation, in private and in the previous efforts of our own Carter Center here, the Japanese—both in the government and in the business community—have been extremely interested in what we might do in the enhancement of peace, the lessening of the nuclear threat, the promotion of human rights, and so forth. And I'm very pleased that Prime Minister Nakasone has designated a strong delegation of Japanese representatives here today. Now we'll hear from Mr. Kinya Niiseki, who has come to represent the government of Japan. He's Chairman of the Board of Directors of the Japan Institute of International Affairs. Ambassador Niiseki, we're glad to hear from you.

Kinya Niiseki: Thank you, Mr. President. I feel very privileged to take part in this very important meeting. On this occasion, I would like to make a brief comment on the importance of disarmament efforts in the context of nonproliferation. As pointed out in the report of the study panel, nuclear proliferation would aggravate political tensions and contribute to greater instability in the world. However, as long as the sense of insecurity exists, the threat of sanctions may not always discourage countries with technical capabilities to make nuclear weapons from trying to do so. In view of the review conference of the Non-Proliferation Treaty scheduled later this year, which Professor Nye has mentioned, it's necessary to try to eliminate the sense of distrust of the non-nuclear weapons states toward the Non-Proliferation Treaty regime. Non–nuclear weapons states always emphasize that the nuclear weapons states are discriminatory against them. Therefore, it is very important for the superpowers to pursue the current arms control negotiations in Geneva in good faith for the purpose of reducing their arsenals of nuclear weapons. Japan, as an ally of the United States, is pretty aware of the difficulties with which the United States is faced with negotiations with the Soviet Union. However, unless something is done, in time the discontent prevailing among developing countries may reach a dangerous point.

As an important measure for nuclear disarmament, the Limited Test-Ban Treaty came into force more than twenty years ago, but underground testing of nuclear weapons is still permitted, and actually a number of underground test explosions are being carried out by the nuclear weapons states. I remember when President Eisenhower, who was the founding father of the "Atoms for Peace" program, cited the failure to achieve a comprehensive test ban as the greatest regret of his presidency. And President Carter, also, made clear at the outset of his administration that a comprehensive test ban treaty is what we needed. In this regard, I must say, it is very unfortunate that negotiations on a comprehensive test ban treaty came to a standstill. I believe now is the time when nuclear weapons states, in particular the superpowers, should exert their efforts to find a way toward a more practical solution of the problem. If a comprehensive test ban can't be achieved at one stroke, we should try to invent a second-best measure. Mr. Shinkaro Abe, Foreign Minister of Japan, proposed in the Conference on Disarmament in Geneva last summer a so-called step-by-step formula. According to his proposal, underground test explosions of a yield now considered technically verifiable will be taken as a threshold, and an agreement will be reached on banning test explosions overstepping this threshold. Then the threshold will be gradually lowered by improving the verification capabilities, hopefully to zero in the not very distant future. And Japan is prepared to make available its advanced technology of seismic detection (as you know, we have many earthquakes in Japan) to increase the verification capabilities. I think under the present circumstances this step-by-step formula is the most realistic option left to us, and this will open up a way for an early realization of a comprehensive test ban treaty.

Finally, I would like to mention in this regard that the Chinese delegate to the general disarmament conference, Ambassador Qian Jia-dong, who is sitting on this stage as one of the panelists, said recently in the conference that his country, China, which had not signed the Limited Test-Ban Treaty, would reconsider its position and join a working group on the treaty to ban nuclear test explosions. I think it was a very important and encouraging suggestion. Thank you very much.

President Carter: That's an extremely encouraging and enlightening statement. The so-called step-by-step approach to constantly lowering the level of nuclear tests permitted is a practical way to resolve some almost insurmountable obstacles we've faced in the past. I recall in Vienna, when we were negotiating the final stages of SALT II, that we and the Soviet Union and the British were trying to conclude a comprehensive test ban agreement. We had gotten down to the point of fairly good understanding about how possible tests might be detected, how the reports might be made, and so forth, but there was a difference about how many sensing devices would be located within Great Britain, as contrasted with ten on both sides—ten for our large country and ten for the Soviets' large area as well. This particular proposal put forward by Mr. Abe in Japan might certainly be worthy of exploration.

Our next panelist to comment will be John Howe from Great Britain, who is the Director of the Defence Arms Control Unit in the British Ministry of Defence, and we are grateful that Prime Minister Margaret Thatcher has sent him to represent Great Britain.

John Howe: Mr. Chairman, I feel very privileged to be here under your chairmanship and in such very distinguished company. The advantage of speaking fourth or so in the batting order is that several of the points one had wanted to make have been made already far more eloquently than one might have achieved oneself. I shall, therefore, try to be brief.

The paper and the presentation seem to me to be admirably comprehensive and cover a very great deal of ground and at least three very large themes. I think that one underlying motif, though, which is common to almost all the analyses we've heard, is the significance of the superpower relationship for other countries and in relation to regional problems. That relationship is indeed of the greatest importance to everyone, wherever they are on this planet. And I just wanted to touch, in that context, on the importance of arms control agreements.

I certainly agree with Dr. Kissinger that arms control agreements cannot be simply a surrogate for dialogue at the political level. But agreements do have a particular value, partly symbolical, partly real, in helping to stabilize and regulate that all-important superpower relationship. And so the connection, I think, of this theme with the process that is now starting or restarting at Geneva is perfectly obvious.

If I can turn next to that part of the presentation which deals with regional conflicts, my perspective on this is naturally a European one and is rooted firmly in the NATO alliance. There has been, in fact, a rather interesting evolution of thinking within NATO over the last few years in relation to what we from within NATO call the out-of-area problem. About three years ago or so, NATO went through rather a bad patch in relation to that problem. It was thought by some of the Europeans—some of the more conservative Europeans on these questions—that the American administration at that time was trying to propel the alliance toward acknowledging some kind of collective responsibility in relation to the preservation of security outside the NATO area, and clearly this proposition would have aroused considerable sensitivity and considerable difficulty. As a result of discussion in the alliance, it became clear that really no such proposition was ever on the table. What the alliance does now recognize, though, is, first, that the United States and indeed other members of NATO may well, in the defense of good and strong interests, either individual or collective, need to deploy outside the NATO area, and that the defense-planning mechanism of the alliance has to address that problem and decide how, on a contingency basis, it would best make good any shortfall in its capabilities. So there is a defense-planning implication. The second principle was fairly clearly established, that responsibilities for the preservation of security outside the NATO area rest on individual governments, not on the alliance machine as a whole. It is interesting in this connection that the paper and the presentation stressed the responsibility of individual governments, rather than any collective responsibility. I was left wondering whether the panelists had reached any conclusions about the role of military strength as distinct from political and economic influences in contributing to stability outside the NATO area. One has to look at problems of stability in terms of all the instruments at one's disposal, and not just military instruments.

Let us turn next to one of the main themes of the paper, which is a theme that occurs at almost every conference at which defense and security issues are discussed, and that is the Strategic Defense Initiative—certainly a dominant theme in any gathering such as this. The paper touches, as again Dr. Kissinger noted, on the decoupling argument: the argument that a complete defensive screen protecting the United States could leave the Europeans and others outside the screen vulnerable, and that this might have implications for the American strategic relationship and the strategic guarantee to her allies. I agree with Dr. Kissinger that the argument can be argued both ways. One can argue that a strong and safe

America would in fact be even more likely to fulfill its obligations to allies than an America which is vulnerable. But there are other questions, very lively and important questions, to which the SDI gives rise, and these are very much under debate at the moment. I think the paper perhaps may slightly exaggerate the extent to which the SDI is, as it were, a divisive issue at the moment within the alliance. I mean there is complete unanimity among all those European leaders who have spoken on the legitimacy and the need for a research program, and that is what the SDI is at the moment. What might follow from that, the implications that it might have, are, of course, much more open questions, and our own attitude in the United Kingdom, I think, is fairly well known: our own attitude would be colored very much by the implications for the ABM regime, which we see as an extremely important part of the arms control achievements of the last decade or two, and by the implications for deterrence strategy. One of the main questions in many European minds, in fact, is whether the more fundamental prospectus of the SDI of producing a leakproof defense is achievable, and whether its pursuit is likely to enhance or weaken public support for NATO and alliance policies.

The paper touches on the question of reduced reliance on nuclear weapons as an objective of the SDI. I think one has to be rather careful not to take it as too self-evident that reduced reliance on nuclear weapons is a valid objective. I think there's an open question there. Would a world in which almost total reliance was placed upon conventional strength be in fact safer? It would certainly be a very different one. And I think it would be wrong to think of European opinion, at least, on the question of the nuclear threshold and reliance on nuclear weapons as monolithic. There is a debate on the issue.

Finally, if I could just touch on the section in the analysis on nonproliferation: I agree very much with what the paper has to say on this. It is an extremely important area. It is also significantly an area in which, I think, there is very important common ground between the Soviet Union and the West, and that is itself an important and significant fact. Also, it is an area which we are right to take extremely seriously and to be concerned about, but it is actually an area in which we do have success to record—as Joseph Nye has noted. Twenty years ago the thought that in 1985 there would still only be five nuclear weapons states would have at that time seemed incredible, and that is a success for the regime. I certainly do not want to imply any kind of complacency, but the point I want to make is that it is a regime which is in the interests of everyone—not just of the nuclear weapons states, but of everyone. The question of a comprehensive test ban treaty has been raised by our Japanese colleague in this connection. It is a very important issue, but there are indeed formidable difficulties, largely in terms of verification, as indeed has been acknowledged, in the achievement of any such treaty, and I think it would be a great pity if the strength and continuation of the nonproliferation regime were in some way held hostage to success in achieving a comprehensive test ban treaty. That probably concludes the points I wanted to make. Thank you.

President Carter: Throughout the latter months of my own administration after we were able to normalize relations with China, we had a constant input of advice and counsel and comment from Beijing through the ambassador in Washington, and also directly from Vice Premier Deng Xiao-ping, who came to visit our country, quite interested, obviously, in the relationship between our nation and the Soviet Union; very careful not to form any semblance of an alliance with one of the superpowers versus the other one; and also interested, of course, in the question of how nuclear weaponry should be handled. Yesterday, I received a personal message from Vice Premier Deng Xiao-ping, giving his best wishes to the consultation with hopes that the results would be relayed to China and recommending very highly Mr. Qian Jia-dong, who will represent China and who will now make a comment concerning issues that we've addressed. So, representing the People's Republic of China, Mr. Qian Jia-dong.

Qian Jia-dong: Thank you very much, Mr. President. Thank you also for inviting China to send representatives to this important event. I'm very happy to be here.

As it happens that I come from a country, China, which is not a member of any of the military alliances, it may be of interest if I add a few words to the report to explain more fully the independent policy pursued by my country.

As is known to all, China is right now embarking on an arduous task of modernization. We need a peaceful international environment. To oppose war, to safeguard peace, and to strive for disarmament are the main objectives of China's foreign policy. To this end we wish not only to establish friendly relations with all the countries of the world on the basis of the Five Principles of Peaceful Coexistence, but also to see the amelioration of the strained relations between the two military alliances, between the East and the West in general, and between the two major powers in particular. It is recognized throughout the world that the United States and the Soviet Union have a special responsibility toward maintaining international peace and security and achieving disarmament. The reason is very simple, for it is they who possess over 95 percent of the world's total nuclear weaponry, and it is they who are actually engaged in the ever-accelerating arms race. We are glad that negotiations between the two superpowers have now been finally resumed or restarted. We hope that this time they will demonstrate genuine political will, truly undertake their responsibilities, negotiate in good faith, and come up with results in the interests of all and detrimental to none, or in other words, really conducive to world peace. Such results could be, for example, a reversal of their arms race, whether in the nuclear field, in the conventional field, or in the field of outer space, and a sharp reduction of their existing nuclear and other arsenals. In order to create an atmosphere and conditions favorable to their negotiations it would be of significance, we think, for them to begin with a pledge to the non–first use of nuclear weapons; to stop deploying new intermediate nuclear forces, and to refrain from developing, testing, and deploying outer space weapons. Such steps are not excessive and should be attainable.

Of course international security and disarmament are not just matters for the two major powers. They are the concern of all countries. China, for one, knows of its responsibilities very well. We don't shirk them. We wish to see the complete elimination of all nuclear weapons. As early as 1964, we unconditionally pledged not to be the first to use nuclear weapons, and we also unconditionally guaranteed never to use nuclear weapons against non–nuclear weapon states. But it goes without saying that unless the two major powers take the lead in cutting back their armaments, any talk of disarmament would be of little significance, if not entirely meaningless. Once they have done so, things will be very easy for the other nuclear states. All countries of the world, be they members or nonmembers of any military alliance, are independent and equal in status in international affairs, and can have their roles to play in all matters related to international security and disarmament. They can voice their own views and put forward their own proposals. In so doing, they are in fact helping the two major powers in their negotiations. Such views of their allies, as well as of other countries, should be seriously taken into consideration by the two major powers. I happen to come from Geneva, where I represent China in the Conference on Disarmament, the sole multilateral negotiating forum for disarmament. The conference has been very unsuccessful in the past years; we hope it can fare better this year. The CD and the bilateral talks are not mutually precluding, but complementary to each other. If we can achieve something in the CD, it will only be beneficial to the bilateral talks.

On the question of regional conflicts, while causes for such conflicts might be many, the root cause, in my view, lies in the sharp rivalry between, and the policies of power politics pursued by, the two major powers. We often hear them saying that they have interests in this part of the world or in that part of the world. If we look around the world, there is practically not a single "hot spot" where we don't see the fingers of the two powers put in. They either infringe on the sovereignty or interfere in the internal affairs of countries concerned, and in some cases even resort to direct military aggression or intervention. Needless to say, instead of alleviating such conflicts, this will only aggravate them. Some regional conflicts might be "purely" indigenous in the beginning, but because of the meddling by the two major powers the nature of such conflicts changes, and their solutions become even more difficult to find, and—I might add, as some of my colleagues have mentioned—this entails also the grave risk that the regional sparks might flare into a global conflagration.

What is the way out, then? I think of the following points:

(1) It is imperative for all countries, particularly the superpowers, to abide strictly by the United Nations Charter, or in more concrete terms, the Five Principles

of Peaceful Coexistence. There are over 150 countries in the world with widely varying conditions. Peace and security can be preserved only by observing these principles. The recent settlement between China and Britain on the question of Hong Kong is yet another example of the vitality of these principles.

(2) All foreign interference must be stopped and occupation troops withdrawn immediately.

(3) The countries concerned should be left to themselves to settle their own problems in a peaceful way.

(4) In this process a role in the form of good offices, peacekeeping, etc., by the United Nations or appropriate regional organizations should be encouraged.

(5) For the major powers, if they really want to play a constructive role, efforts to cut down their military expenses and to increase their contribution to the economic development of the developing countries would be a commendable option.

Now, on the question of proliferation: it is indeed a question of legitimate concern to all countries. China is not a party to the Non-Proliferation Treaty, but this does not mean that China stands for proliferation. On the contrary, China is against proliferation. It does not encourage, nor is it engaged in, any proliferation activities. China did not join the NPT because we consider the treaty a discriminatory one. We are critical of it. Why? In the first place, the treaty, while prohibiting specifically and strictly the non–nuclear weapon states from acquiring nuclear weapons, provides only in very vague terms obligations for the nuclear weapon states to reduce or eliminate their nuclear weapons. Second, in spite of the fact that the non–nuclear weapon states party to the NPT have relinquished voluntarily the nuclear option, this is not compensated by any guarantee from the nuclear weapon states party to the NPT not to use nuclear weapons against them. Third, in the field of peaceful uses of nuclear energy, although certain rights are promised to the non-nuclear states, they are in fact prevented from enjoying these rights owing to increasingly strict measures taken by the major nuclear suppliers under the pretext of preventing proliferation. So from the above one can hardly believe the treaty has really served its purposes and this is borne out by the actual state of affairs: while there has been no horizontal proliferation all these years, vertical proliferation by the major weapon states has been going on all the time.

We recognize the importance of nonproliferation. The point is how to achieve this objective. A number of measures have been suggested in the report and in the comments of Mr. Nye, but in my view the best approach would be for the two major nuclear powers to stop their nuclear arms race and agree to disarm as early as possible. Once they have begun to reduce their nuclear weapons, there would no longer be any convincing rationale for non-nuclear states to go nuclear. Thank you.

President Carter: As I expected, the Chinese comment has been very sharp and to the point, and also quite critical of the United States and the Soviet Union. I think all of you are looking forward to this afternoon for a much more direct discussion with Soviet participation, but perhaps later on this morning they would like to respond to some of the points made. This is, as President Ford has pointed out, the third session in the process of our understanding more about U.S.–Soviet relations, with emphasis on arms control. The first one was about a year ago, in May of 1984, when we reviewed, here at Emory University at the Carter Center, the history of negotiations; the status of existing agreements, very few of which have any legal status at this point; the difference in perspective as to how negotiations are conducted and the purposes that are to be achieved by the United States and the Soviet Union; and the reasons why agreements were concluded as finally formulated. And last fall we had a discussion at President Ford's library at the University of Michigan campus, concerning, primarily, new technology, new kinds of weapons systems that were being evolved or in prospect, and how they might impact on nuclear arms control and the relationship between the United States and the Soviet Union. One of the most stimulating and effective spokesmen there, in my opinion, was our next speaker, Helmut Sonnenfeldt. He is a former member of the National Security Council staff and now a visiting scholar at the Brookings Institution. We're very delighted to have Helmut Sonnenfeldt here this morning.

Helmut Sonnenfeldt: Thank you, President Carter and President Ford. I'm very pleased to be back here. You've put me, at least from the vantage point of the audience, on the extreme right of this panel, which may say something about the selection process that you engaged in. I want to compliment the organizers of the conference for putting this topic up front. I do believe that issues of war and peace in the present era hinge crucially, first, on the effectiveness of our alliances; second, on the prevention of exploitation for geopolitical manipulation and gain, and of the inevitable regional animosities and instabilities from which this world suffers and will suffer; and third, curbing the problem of nuclear proliferation, one of those issues that could prove to be extremely damaging to the peace of the world. Of course, the discussions that will take place later with respect to direct conflicts with the Soviet Union and arms control issues are of great importance, and certainly of intrinsic interest as well.

I think it is worth recalling that all the major crises of the last 40 years—crises which perhaps came close to bringing us to the verge of conflict—did not occur over some abstract or theoretical issue related to the arms race, but rather occurred in very specific areas of the world where interests and ambitions clashed and where third and fourth parties, in many instances, were involved. Thus, disturbing as questions of military policy and programs are, and desirable—and indeed essential—as it is to try to achieve agreed arrangements in the arms control area, the question of managing ambition, interests, and global instabilities is at the very core of the problem of war and peace in the world, including war and peace between the two superpowers.

As regards the alliance—and again some of these matters will be discussed later—I want to underline what Dr. Kissinger said earlier. Defense and deterrence in the Western alliance continue to depend on credible nuclear deterrence. Many problems have arisen about that long-standing strategy, and it is indeed the case that the NATO allies have been looking for ways—to some degree successfully—to reduce the reliance of NATO on early recourse to nuclear weapons should deterrence fail. I think that effort should continue, as should the effort, in consequence, to increase and improve the conventional capabilities of the alliance. At the same time, it is of considerable interest—and Mr. Howe reinforced it just a moment ago—that in the discussion over SDI the Europeans seem, in a sense, to have rediscovered the importance of nuclear deterrence. I think that for the period before any successful research in the area of SDI may lead us to a substantial reduction in reliance on nuclear weapons we do indeed have to maintain the nuclear component of deterrence. Indeed, I would hope that this apparent rediscovery in Europe of the importance of nuclear deterrence will improve the possibilities for NATO to solve some of the long-deadlocked problems concerning nuclear strategy and the role of nuclear weapons in the defense of Europe over which we have labored so long and so hard in every administration with which I have been associated and in those since then as well.

As regards the problems of Third World—if I may use that misleading term—Third World conflicts, the report lists the areas of past and present instability and danger. It has struck me that for whatever reason—and one can argue about them at length—during the last five years, despite the very bad tone and atmosphere in American–Soviet relations and the deadlock or even disruption of arms control negotiations, the incidence of real crises and confrontations in these Third World areas has gone down dramatically compared to all previous periods—name any five-year period since 1945 and compare it to the last five years. I do not know exactly why that is or whether there is a permanent trend. I would hope that perhaps there is—that perhaps a certain caution has entered into the calculations of those who make decisions in these matters that wasn't always present in the past. Without reciting them all, just remember the Cubas, Congos, Angolas, and Afghanistans, and the three wars in the Middle East, the Vietnam war, and the Korean war—all of which spilled into superpower confrontations, if not indeed almost direct conflict. We should not minimize it when there are no crises of this sort every six months or every year.

Whether this can be attributed to the farsighted nature of the agreement on Principles of Conduct that was negotiated before the summit meeting of 1972,* to which Dr. Kissinger referred, I don't know. I rather doubt it. I think it probably has more to do with very careful calculations of what the risks and the benefits are of various forms of conduct. And I tend to be rather skeptical about the feasibility of putting in a formal code of conduct the sort of thing we have been experiencing in practice over the last five years. We may be more in a phase

---

*Basic Principles of Relations Between the United States of America and the Union of Soviet Socialist Republics, signed May 29, 1972.

of careful conduct than of grand structure in our relations with the Soviet Union. I would like to see that extended, perhaps through the kinds of consultations this administration has offered and engaged in, and the Soviets seem to have agreed to undertake, on various of these problems, perhaps by other ways. But, at any rate, I would like to observe this phenomenon and to note that at least in that respect—and it is important, considering the history of the last 40 years—these five years have not been all bad—on the contrary.

I would like to make one further comment, which relates to nonproliferation. The means for dealing with that problem have been recited in the paper, and there has been discussion of it around the table. If one examines the list of potential proliferators, it is evident that some, at least, maintain the nuclear weapons option because of severe fears concerning their own security and survival—a severe sense of threat stemming from neighbors which in several cases are supported by a nuclear power. Pakistan is one of the prime candidates for such fears. I don't believe that a nonproliferation regime per se can cope with the security concerns that lead countries and their leaders rightly or wrongly to want to preserve the nuclear option. Ultimately, therefore, proliferation is intimately connected with the security situation that prevails with respect to the particular countries which may be on the threshold of acquiring nuclear weapons. This factor would not necessarily apply to Khadafi, and the situation regarding Argentina and Brazil may have different components. But it almost certainly applies to Pakistan, Israel, and South Africa, and it has applied at various times to South Korea, and others. This aspect of the problem should be borne very much in mind.

One of the ironies of the Non-Proliferation Treaty and the nonproliferation regime is that while it has been signed by 150 countries, those who haven't signed it—the ones we are concerned about—are precisely the ones that may see themselves as having a valid security motivation for preserving the option.

One final comment—and it is not intended to be facetious. We just heard two of our colleagues raise the issue of vertical proliferation, as it is called— that is to say, the reluctance or the refusal of the existing nuclear powers, particularly the two superpowers, to do something about their own nuclear stockpiles and reliance on nuclear weapons. As a source of motivation for potential proliferators, the argument is mentioned in the report as well: because the superpowers refuse to accept effective limits on nuclear weapons, other countries are entitled at least to have the same option. Well, apart from the fact that the United States has in fact, for a variety of reasons, greatly reduced the size and explosive power of its nuclear weapons stockpile, one should at least take account of the fact that the Strategic Defense Initiative seeks to deal with problems of strategic defense by non-nuclear means, as distinct from the antiballistic missile systems of the 1960s and 70s. Therefore, those around the world who are particularly concerned about what the superpowers are doing about nuclear weaponry, when they are concerned about proliferation, should at least give some weight to the potential impact on proliferation of increasing American interests in non-nuclear defenses. Thank you.

President Ford: Thank you very much, Helmut. The Soviet delegation has requested that they make their observations and comments this afternoon, so if I might, let me make a comment or two.

Mr. O'Neill gave us a full menu of issues and challenges. I would like to comment on one or two aspects of this very broad coverage of problems around the world. Beginning in the late 1960s and running for the next eight to twelve years, there was a policy, as I understood it, of the United States and the Soviet Union seeking to move forward on nuclear negotiations, but simultaneously there was an equal effort, not as dramatic, not as visible, to solve some of the so-called political problems that would appear from time to time. The progress on nuclear negotiations is best reflected in SALT I and the ABM treaty, and the negotiations that my administration undertook in Vladivostok, which, in my judgment at least, gave us a good framework for further negotiations.

One of the deepest regrets of my administration was that we were never able to finalize the progress that was made at Vladivostok. President Carter's SALT II negotiations were a further extension of this policy of nuclear negotiations with considerable success between the Soviet Union and the United States, and it would be my observation that even though those negotiations never achieved the maximum that was hoped for by many, the observation can be made, and fairly so, that the two superpowers managed the problem of a nuclear confrontation. From my personal friendship and experience with other individuals who have served in our White House, I know of no American president who would want to get our country involved in a nuclear war with the Soviet Union, and from my one personal experience with a Soviet leader, I do not believe that he, representing that country, would want to undertake such a confrontation. So if you isolate the nuclear negotiations, it's my judgment that we have managed the problem extremely well.

Now, I also concur with the observation made by Henry Kissinger, Mr. Howe, and Helmut Sonnenfeldt to the effect that as we proceed in this one direction on nuclear negotiations, it's equally mandatory that we proceed down the road of trying to solve political problems—although the scorecard from the late 1960s, up until 1980, was not perfect—some of those problems were very complicated and very controversial, but I think there is a scorecard of reasonable success. And the fact that those problems were dealt with was a sign of common sense and maturity. Now, unfortunately, there were some—who had no responsibilities—who were somewhat critical of this approach. Regrettably, the process—or the program—was given a label, and I am not sure that some of the critics understood the label, and I am not sure some of the critics understood what was accomplished or what was sought. But nevertheless the pressure from that group, I think, to a degree at least, hampered and hindered the process of trying to work not only on nuclear problems but also on political problems, and the consequence was that some of those problems that might have been solved, unfortunately, were not.

Now, the menu of problems in Mr. O'Neill's paper is so large and so significant, it seems to me that we should not only urge the two superpowers to work on nuclear negotiations, but we ought to be equally concerned with and take action on this other shopping list of issues that not only are serious in a regional way or other ways, but also have the potential and the possibility of developing into a much more significant and controversial problem between the superpowers themselves. I look forward to the opportunity of hearing the subsequent discussions this afternoon on military and other matters. I would like to raise a question with my friend, Hal Sonnenfeldt: You weren't, by any chance, ignoring the problems in Kampuchea or the problems in Central America, which, it seems to me, are serious challenges where both of the superpowers, for one reason or another or in one way or another, do have an interest and are in one way or another participants. It seems to me—at least—I have seen little or no evidence of any effort in that area, or in either one of those areas, for some political action, as far as the two superpowers are concerned.

Helmut Sonnenfeldt: No, I certainly was not ignoring them. I was commenting on, if you will, the next stage, which is the stage of confrontation. I do view with great concern the introduction of extraregional superpower involvement in the Western Hemisphere. That does indeed, I believe, have potential for the sort of confrontation that I was hoping we might have put behind us. I think it needs to be handled with extreme caution and perhaps should even be the subject of some straight talk in consultations. I also view with concern the events in Kampuchea. Perhaps I might say to our Chinese colleague that the role of the regional great power there is quite crucial, and to expect some resolution of that situation, which is already extremely tragic in terms of the human suffering, and which could become potentially very dangerous in terms of what it means to Thailand and the region as a whole, is serious, and one cannot ignore the fact that the Soviets are now present militarily in Cam Ranh Bay and elsewhere in Vietnam. But here again one would have to explore the reasons in detail. We have not, the United States and the Soviet Union, come to a direct, toe-to-toe or head-to-head confrontation. We could cite other cases—the Middle East; the Soviets and Cubans are still in Angola; they certainly still are in Afghanistan, and I do worry very much about the threats that are made against Pakistan from time to time in various ways—so we are far from being out of the woods. My comment related to the peculiar circumstance that, with all of these problems that continue to be there and do continue to have a potential for crisis, we somehow have navigated over the last few years in such a way as not to be alerting any forces and having the kinds of problems that we faced in various places that I mentioned in my comments.

President Carter: One of the most interesting questions that has arisen is how the world might deal with a nuclear threat in a region where one nation might have a nuclear capability, the capability of producing nuclear weapons, and a next-door neighbor doesn't have the ability. One of the prime responsibilities, I felt, was to implement the Treaty of Tlatelolco,* which would make the south of this hemisphere free of nuclear weaponry. And now almost all the nations there have confirmed and ratified this treaty. And I think there has been a lessening of tension, for instance between Brazil and Argentina; as has been mentioned previously, Brazil has ratified the Tlatelolco Treaty and in a recent visit that I made to Argentina, following the replacement of the military junta by a democratic regime under President Alfonsin, they're completely dedicated to peaceful prospects for Argentina in the nuclear field. As many of you remember, in 1974 there was a so-called peaceful nuclear explosion in India. This created a wave of concern throughout the world, but I think the concern was certainly highest in Pakistan. Pakistan has been mentioned several times this morning in connection with the question of whether proliferation might proceed in that region of southern Asia. The Ambassador of Pakistan to the United Nations, Mr. Agha Shahi, will make a brief statement now about Pakistan's position on the question of proliferation, in view of the fact that India has demonstrated an ability to produce explosives which they have not followed up. Ambassador Agha Shahi.

Agha Shahi: President Carter, President Ford, ladies and gentlemen: Silence is golden, but when reference is being made to Pakistan in the context of proliferation of nuclear weapons—and many among you think that in this field Pakistan has played some kind of villainous role—it would only lead to a gross misunderstanding about Pakistan's nuclear activity if I were to remain silent. However, before coming to the question of nonproliferation in the context of NPT, the Non-Proliferation Treaty, I would like to make a comment or two in regard to what was said by members of the panel on the subject of regional conflicts.

It may be a matter of satisfaction from the perspective of the superpowers that they have not allowed themselves to be drawn into confrontation over regional conflicts—such as those mentioned by Mr. Sonnenfeldt. While we welcome this restraint, it must also be stressed that the views and interests of the regional states need to be taken into consideration by the superpowers in their regional competition. For instance, in regard to the situation arising from the Soviet military intervention in Afghanistan, Pakistan wanted it to be dealt with as a question between the regional states and a superpower. But it has now become an East–West issue, and is implicit with the threat of further escalation because of recent developments in the policies of the United States as well as the Soviet Union. I wish the panel had also addressed the question of finding a solution to the problem of Afghanistan, especially in view of the threat of an escalation of conflict in that tragic country. If the scale of violence were to increase, Pakistan would be faced with an inundation of many million more refugees. I

---

*The Treaty of Tlatelolco (1947) bans nuclear weapons in Latin America. The United States has not ratified the treaty but has agreed to observe its major articles.

should think that in a forum of this kind thought might have been given to addressing the concerns of the regional states as well as the Soviet Union in order to find a solution to the problem. For example, one comes across the apprehension voiced in Soviet news media that if the Soviet Union were to withdraw its forces from Afghanistan the retreat would lead to a bloodbath of pro-Soviet elements in that country, considering the bitterness with which this tragic conflict is being waged. I think that such concerns also need to be addressed, and I ask myself whether, in the context of restoring regional peace, the role of the United Nations in peacekeeping operations could not be explored, through the provision of peacekeeping contingents from socialist countries to replace the occupation forces. A peacekeeping force, operating under a U.N. mandate, and governed by U.N. principles of peacekeeping, would be altogether different from an occupying force. Such a peacekeeping force should be able to reassure all sides about their safety and security of life and property, and promote a climate conducive to political reconciliation and a solution of the problem in accordance with the principles of international law.

Coming now to nonproliferation, I do not think that many countries of Africa and Asia can take consolation from the fact that there has been no horizontal proliferation since the conclusion of the NPT. That may be so de jure in terms of the provisions of the NPT, which gives formal recognition to the nuclear weapon status of the five permanent members of the United Nations Security Council. But for all practical purposes, many countries must take into account the fact that by now there may be as many as seven or eight nuclear weapon powers—two or three more than the de jure five recognized by the NPT. The problem of horizontal proliferation has therefore become further exacerbated.

Mr. Nye made some valid comments about the dangers of a further spread of nuclear weapons, but Mr. Niiseki and Mr. Sonnenfeldt have rightly pointed out that the inducement to proliferation arises from the acute sense of insecurity felt by certain non–nuclear weapons states. The policies of penalties and sanctions now being resorted to may find a place in the diplomatic armory of the superpowers. But it seems to me that they would have to look beyond punitive measures if further proliferation is to be halted. Since the Soviet Union and the United States are in complete agreement about the dangers of horizontal proliferation and have decided to cooperate closely to curb this threat, why should they not also give thought to extending their cooperation to the provision of effective security assurances to non–nuclear weapons states?

At the time the NPT was being debated in the United Nations, the three nuclear weapon powers, the United States, the Soviet Union, and Britain, came forward and said they would extend security assurances in the nature of positive guarantees to take action under the charter of the United Nations if a non-nuclear weapons state was threatened with aggression accompanied by the use of nuclear weapons. But it soon became apparent that the security assurances extended by the three nuclear weapon powers added nothing to the general provisions of the charter of the United Nations against aggression, thereby leaving the situation in regard to the security of non–nuclear weapons states exactly where it was— in other words, as insecure as before these assurances were extended.

The non–nuclear weapons states also clamored in the United Nations for negative guarantees—that they would not be threatened with nuclear weapons by the nuclear weapon powers. I well remember, President Carter, your address to the U.N. General Assembly Special Session on Disarmament in 1978, in which you put forward—you did, on this question, take a big step forward—your formulation on the nonuse of nuclear weapons against non–nuclear weapons states which were not in alliance with the nuclear weapons powers. What the non– nuclear weapons states have been trying to do in U.N. forums is to find a formula by which the non–nuclear weapons states outside the security systems of the two major nuclear weapon powers could be extended some positive guarantees—of protection against nuclear aggression or blackmail. I do not wish to go deeply into this complicated question. But I would suggest that, in the consideration of the dangers of nuclear proliferation, the insecurity of non–nuclear weapons states should be addressed as the central issue, and thought should be given to the question of extending to these states effective guarantees, both negative and positive. There have, of course, been separate unilateral statements on negative guarantees by the nuclear weapon powers, but these assurances remain inadequate because there is as yet no agreed common formulation in regard to their substance, much less their incorporation in a treaty so as to generate confidence in their credibility.

Insofar as Pakistan is concerned, it put forward the idea of reciprocal or bilateral inspection of the nuclear facilities of India and Pakistan. It's a matter of profound regret that this offer has not been seized upon in South Asia. Argentina and Brazil deserve to be congratulated for having entered into a mutual inspection agreement, according to what has been stated here. I should think mutual inspection would be a great confidence-building measure in South Asia. Those countries of this region which do not wish to become parties to the NPT on grounds of principle or do not want to make a declaration jointly to renounce nuclear weapons or are opposed to the establishment of nuclear weapon–free zones, would still be able to ensure nonproliferation through bilateral inspection arrangements.

Finally, I would like to make a point or two in regard to the NPT. Apart from the reasons given by Mr. Nye why the nuclear weapon powers should bring about nuclear disarmament—for the reason that the NPT is due for renewal in another ten years, and there will be a great problem about its renewal unless the nuclear weapon powers give evidence of their good faith by carrying out some nuclear disarmament—apart from that, I think it is most important that credible security assurances should be extended to non–nuclear weapons states. What the non-nuclear weapons states also find very difficult to understand is the reluctance of the nuclear weapon powers to conclude a treaty banning underground nuclear weapon tests. How can you simultaneously promote nuclear disarmament or reduction of nuclear armaments, while the nuclear weapon tests permit you to make qualitative improvements in nuclear weapons, improvements that tend to destabilize the nuclear deterrent about which we have heard so much? If only the nuclear weapon powers could make a beginning and pick up the suggestion made by Mr. Niiseki about progressive reduction of the threshold of nuclear explosions, confidence among the non–nuclear weapons states about the good faith of the nuclear weapon powers in engaging in disarmament negotiation would be restored. I should also say that during that 1978 U.N. conference session on disarmament, and even before then, Pakistan had expressed the hope that the two superpowers would give evidence of their good faith in disarmament negotiations by reaching some agreement in the Vienna talks about the balanced reduction of conventional weapons* so that a way would be opened toward agreement between the Soviet Union and the United States on no first use of nuclear weapons. It is difficult to understand why even ten years of negotiations have not led to any progress whatsoever toward a mutual and balanced reduction of conventional armaments of the NATO and Warsaw military blocs.

Finally, in regard to what Mr. Sonnenfeldt said—that the non–nuclear weapon powers should take into account the fact that the SDI is an attempt to move away from nuclear armament—I think this is much too complicated a subject. I myself am particularly confused, because I have come across opinions of other experts who maintain that SDI is going to lead to a vast increase in both offensive and defensive nuclear armaments. Thank you.

President Carter: Mr. Ambassador, can I ask you one question? Did you state that Pakistan has proposed to India mutual inspection of the nuclear installations of both countries to assure no more production of explosives?

Agha Shahi: Yes, Mr. President, when I was Ambassador to the United Nations and subsequently a foreign minister, we proposed to India a nuclear weapons–free zone; we proposed bilateral inspection on a reciprocal basis; we proposed a joint declaration to renounce nuclear weapons, and other nonproliferation measures. I think several of the suggestions that have been made are worthy of being pursued.

President Carter: And all those proposals still are viable?

Agha Shahi: Certainly; they were also put forward formally in the forum of the United Nations General Assembly.

Helmut Sonnenfeldt: Just a quick comment on your first point, regarding Afghanistan. Of course, it should be resolved, but it is obviously extraordinarily difficult. I think that the goal of everyone concerned with regional peace and avoiding escalation of the conflict should be the restoration of a neutral and non-aligned Afghanistan. The question, of course, is whether the Soviet Union can see its way clear to accepting a government in Afghanistan that would command

*The Mutual and Balanced Force Reductions negotiations, commenced in Vienna in 1973.

the support of the people and permit the refugees to return—indeed, would have the confidence of the refugees so that they would return. In my view, because of what has happened in the last five years, any such government in Afghanistan is likely to be anti-Soviet. On the other hand, any government that is pro-Soviet is likely to have to be supported by Soviet bayonets in order to survive, and is never going to be of the kind that will enable the refugees to return from Pakistan. Perhaps people more able to work with the dialectic than I am can resolve this dilemma, but it seems to me that is the essence of the problem, and I wish it could be resolved along the lines of the first proposition that I put forward.

I won't comment further on the nuclear matter except to say, in regard to the comprehensive test ban, that we did take a step in that direction in the period of the Nixon and Ford administrations with the threshold test ban, but regrettably it was not submitted to the Senate for ratification. It has now become controversial on grounds of verification, but I believe that precious time was lost when that treaty was not submitted after it was completed at the end of the Ford administration.

Henry Kissinger: On the issue of Afghanistan: I think it is absolutely insoluble if it is discussed in terms of pro- or anti-Soviet governments in Afghanistan. I think one ought to separate the issue of the convictions of the government from the security problem. If the Soviet Union has a military concern in Afghanistan— that it could be used by any country for any military purpose—I believe that a constructive discussion would be possible and that Soviet concerns about Afghanistan as a military base, directly, indirectly, or in any other form, should be met. What form of government then exists in Afghanistan, how it votes in the United Nations—I hope the superpowers have become mature enough so that the individual views of the government need not necessarily be decisive if the security problem can be resolved. I think if the issue of Afghanistan is ever to be satisfactorily resolved, one should separate the security problem from the composition of the government. The United States has no particular interest, as far as I can tell, in any particular type of government—certainly not in an anti-Soviet government in Kabul. What we have an interest in, and what other countries have an interest in, is the absence of a military occupation of a neighboring country. And I think if we could separate the security issue from the issue of the self-determination of the Afghan people, and if that were agreed upon as an agenda, all the other countries could go very far toward meeting Soviet concerns. That seems to me to be the way of approaching it.

Helmut Sonnenfeldt: My point, President Carter, is that in order for the refugees to return, there has to be a government in Afghanistan that has credibility, or they won't return and there is no solution. But such a government in Afghanistan seems to have been unacceptable to the Soviet Union, and that's where security and the nature of the government link up with each other.

Anatoly Dobrynin: Well, I do not want to sound as pessimistic as Mr. Sonnenfeldt. In his variations there is practically nothing, no solution. We do not believe in this. And as far as the government of Afghanistan, too, now, we have a process through the United Nations. The Secretary General of the United Nations is actively involved and, as far as I understand, all the parties immediately involved in the situation are supportive and, I hope, the government of Pakistan is too. This is my impression, at least. They are meeting from time to time, unfortunately on a rather rare basis, usually because the Pakistan government doesn't want to recognize the government of Afghanistan. This makes it rather difficult because, in the opinon of Afghanistan, the main problem is the continued intervention from the territory of Pakistan. Once this is solved, then the whole issue will be solved, because we will not keep troops there, I can assure you. With concurrence of the Afghanistan government, our troops will go home. We don't seek any bases; if we did we could have already created one, some air base near the Far East—we have not done it. So this shows our strategic intentions— whether we really wanted to use this conflict for strategic purposes, or rather, because we are very interested in the security of our southern borders. This is as far as we'll go on this Afghanistan business. We wish that there would be more vigorous discussion through the United Nations, through the Secretary General. I think we are going to meet within one or two weeks or months. And let's really use this in particular—the neutral United Nations—to facilitate this decision. I think it's possible to, and for the time being, it's really the only thing we could do.

My second remark is about the security of nonproliferation of non-nuclear states. Well, I'll put it this way: Dr. O'Neill talked about confidence, and so on. We made a declaration—a unilateral declaration—that the Soviet Union is not going to aim nuclear weapons at any state which is non-nuclear or doesn't have nuclear weaponry on its territory. This is an obligation we undertook unilaterally. We are quite prepared to sit down with the United States or other nuclear powers and to sign a treaty. There is not really a problem for us to deal with with this particular question. We do understand the concern of the non-nuclear states, and we are prepared to meet this concern of the non-nuclear states. A reluctance (I am just following what Ambassador Shahi just said) of nuclear powers to conclude a test ban: yes, we have already signed two treaties, in '74 and '76—I mean Soviet-American treaties on test bans. Unfortunately, up till now, these treaties are not ratified by the United States Senate. We are prepared to ratify and sign, I would say within several months, maybe two months, after you do, if you give a guarantee from your side that you would. We've inquired with your government. They refuse to do it up till now. So this is the situation. They want to have some additional guarantees. In our minds, really, if the treaty was good enough in 1974, even in 1974 we had enough—both sides had the technical means—to detect the tests. Why don't we have it now? And then the second point: in this particular treaty we have a protocol which says: once this treaty is ratified, a special mechanism will be set up in order to find improvement in the detection. So we feel it is quite possible to ratify and to have at least these two treaties of 1974 and 1976 ratified.

The last point is about the comprehensive test ban treaty. I think it was President Carter who mentioned that we were very close, really. There was a discussion between the three nuclear powers at that time: the Soviet Union, the United Kingdom, and the United States. And he mentioned how we were very close; our differences at that time were over how many boxes—at that time they were called black boxes—should be put on British soil—not on American, not Soviet. We agreed. I don't want to say that the British were troublemakers, but in this case they did not agree. But we agreed with the United States and they agreed with us about those black boxes, about how many we would have. We repeatedly—I emphasize, repeatedly—in the last two or three years, including this year, addressed the United States government: "Let's resume those negotiations, with the United States, with the United Kingdom, and the Soviet Union. We are prepared to sit down, even tomorrow." The answer was: "No, no, no." I am not in a position and have no theory to explain why. But this is the situation that exists. I understand the worries over non-nuclear powers, but we don't like it either. It could be and should be. We are convinced that we have enough technical means now to detect nuclear tests. So it is high time to have a comprehensive test ban treaty. And as for the nonuse of nuclear forces, I welcome the statement by the representative of Pakistan, because we are trying to convince our dear colleagues from United States to do the same. Thank you.

President Carter: There have been several comments made from both the non-nuclear powers and also from Ambassador Dobrynin concerning non–first use and nonuse of outer space and the comprehensive test ban. I'd like to presume on Secretary Kissinger, if he would, to present. . .I'm glad he came back to life. [*Kissinger:* I was just telling Anatoly Dobrynin that he has refined the art of making Americans feel guilty.] Secretary Kissinger was involved along with—obviously—Presidents Nixon and Ford, in some of these agreements, and I would like for Secretary Kissinger, if he will, to explain the American position on the comprehensive test ban and its restraints on us; on the demand for non-first use of nuclear weapons and also the prohibition against the use of space for offensive or defensive weapons. We'll discuss this in more definitive terms after lunch, but since Secretary Kissinger will not be on the stage then, I wonder if he would respond now.

Henry Kissinger: Let me deal with the no-first-use issue first. A number of individuals that I have very great regard for, one of whom is here,* wrote an article on that subject. I agreed with the objective in the sense that we should be in a position where we would not be obliged to use nuclear weapons at an early stage or maybe at any stage. In other words, that we should be able to resist conventional attacks by conventional means. I have opposed making that an official doctrine—that we would never use nuclear weapons first—because the implication is that we would prefer to be defeated with conventional weapons,

---

*McGeorge Bundy, co-author with Gerard Smith, Robert McNamara, and George Kennan, of "Nuclear Weapons and the Atlantic Alliance," in *Foreign Affairs,* Spring 1982.

that we would accept a defeat with conventional weapons, rather than use nuclear weapons. That leads to the absurdity that we will resist a defeat with nuclear weapons only if nuclear weapons are used against us. This I cannot accept. I think we have to maintain the principle that an attack on NATO will be resisted with nuclear weapons if necessary. Hopefully, NATO will put itself into a position where it may not have to make that choice. I oppose enshrining it in a doctrine, and I do not want the Soviet Union to get the misapprehension that a war in Europe could be won with conventional weapons without a nuclear response— without seeking to imply that the Soviet Union has any intention to launch an attack. But alliances have to be based on a military strategy. This is my first objection to the no-first-use doctrine, and the second is that we continue to have a defense policy that de facto relies on nuclear weapons and then stigmatizes these weapons, which creates a gap in our perception.

The second problem has to do with the various test bans. The threshold test ban was negotiated in the Nixon and Ford periods; it spanned both administrations. And I was involved in its negotiation under the direction of two presidents. Therefore I strongly supported it and support it today. We thought, at the time, that the detection system was adequate. Actually the threshold test ban was then not submitted for ratification in the two succeeding administrations for two entirely opposite reasons: in one administration because they thought it didn't go far enough, and that one should really aim for a comprehensive test ban; and in the current administration because it went too far and because they found flaws in the inspection system. Now this raises the fundamental question about verification. No verification system is going to be foolproof. The analysis that has to be made with respect to verification is whether the scale of violations is or can be of sufficient magnitude to threaten the purposes of the treaty. Our judgment at the time was that, with respect to the threshold test ban, while some violations might be conceivable they could not be of a scale and of a consistency to achieve a significant advantage, and, in fact, there were some collateral benefits, such as on-site inspection, for civilian users, that we thought were of importance. I believe one of the lessons to be learned from the experience of the threshold test ban is that without some bipartisanship in our considerations we will be on a constant roller coaster in these negotiations.

On the comprehensive test ban, frankly, I am not a good witness because I have never studied it in sufficient detail to have a strong view one way or another. I have an instinctive reaction on the ground of its constantly adding to the stigmatization of weapons on which our security depends. On the other hand, I have never taken a heroic position. In our administration it was not thought feasible to go that far. We went as far as we went, which was to the threshold test ban, because we felt that the scale of violations was such that we could protect ourselves within the limit.

On outer space: I have been very sympathetic to an attempt to keep nuclear weapons from being placed into outer space, and consider that a desirable objective. I must say I have also gradually been converted—not by the administration, whose various explanations of strategic defense are so manifold that it is difficult to know which one they're pushing at any particular moment—but I have been gradually convinced that the question of strategic defense requires really prayerful consideration from the point of view of third countries, from the point of view of governments relying, for the indefinite future, on total vulnerability as an element of security. But I would far prefer that weapons that are in space be non-nuclear, and so I have reluctance to place nuclear weapons into outer space.

President Carter: There are a lot of people who are reluctant to place any kind of weapons in space, and I happen to be one of them. I think that the essence of the question on the comprehensive test ban was addressed when we completed the SALT II negotiations in Vienna in 1979. There has been opposition in our own country from those responsible for the maintenance and reliability of nuclear arsenals, to be sure that we could indeed assure ourselves that the triggering device on nuclear weapons was reliable. This would require a very low threshold, and I think that the essence of it has been expressed very well by Mr. Niiseki, that the limited test ban could be constantly lowered approaching a comprehensive test ban, but never below what we were certain could be verified by detection mechanisms that were available at the time. And so as science lets us be more and more sure that we can detect any violation, we would lower those thresholds. At this point, we could lower far below the present limits of the test bans, indeed. [*Kissinger:* Mr. President, I would support that statement totally.] There's a large area for possible negotiation and successful negotiation on this question. I made a proposal to President Brezhnev in 1979 that we omit Great Britain from the discussions because the major obstacle to concluding the comprehensive test ban was how many black boxes would be placed in Great Britain. The British were quite reluctant to have ten black boxes in their country; they claimed they were too expensive. We talked about who would even pay for them, and the question was should there be one, two, or three, and it's unfortunate that we weren't successful then. But the option is still open.

We are going to adjourn in about six minutes, and it would be only fair to let Bob O'Neill, the chairman of this panel, respond to some of the comments that have been made, and I'll ask him in the interest of time to limit his comments to those points that have been disputed in his presentation.

Anatoly Dobrynin: Excuse me, Mr. President. I just would like to make one remark about the discussion here—the lovely discussion about how it's not a good thing to put atomic weapons in outer space. I just would like to remind that we have a treaty prohibiting the placing of nuclear weapons and other weapons of mass destruction in outer space; so our discussion was very useful but it's not specifically relevant.

Robert O'Neill: My remarks will be brief. Dr. Kissinger, unfortunately, did not have a chance to study the paper this morning, and I think his opening comment may have been based on a misunderstanding. When I referred to the view of some people that NATO's strategy had already come to a point of de facto non–first use, I was referring, of course, to one strand of public opinion, but I did mention in the paper that none of those developments had affected the importance that all allied governments continue to attach to nuclear deterrence as the prime element of their security policies and, their desire to retain a doctrine of first use in certain circumstances, although moving away from early first use.

With regard to the SDI, I was simply pointing up questions that need to be resolved in the next few years. We are at the start of a lengthy debate on the future of the strategic postures of both sides and the desirability of moving in the direction of acquiring strategic defenses. We should not become heated at this point, but we must recognize that there are major questions in front of us. When they are addressed in the context of other alliance problems, which may become aggravated by different causes in the next two or three years, there exists clearly a continuing problem of maintaining cohesion among partners. On John Howe's comment, which was also reflecting one of Henry Kissinger's: of course America's allies want America to remain strong. The question about the desirability of the acquisition of comprehensive strategic defenses relates, in the minds of allies, not so much to the United States by itself but to the Soviet Union. If both sides are protected against any nuclear retaliation, then the allies fear that their own security interests will be jeopardized in the process. Flexible response becomes less credible, and stability may be degraded.

President Carter: This afternoon at two o'clock we'll reconvene. The discussion, will, I think, be a much sharper one as we present the points of view of the Soviet Union and the United States on the subject of weapons, strategy, and doctrine. We'll hear this afternoon from Brent Scowcroft, who's the chairman of that panel.

Session 2
Weapons, Strategy, and Doctrine

President Carter: We have a new audience this afternoon, and I'd like to explain very briefly what we've done. We spent the last three days with three separate panels addressing important issues that will be discussed now in public. This morning we explored the ideas of alliances—of the two superpowers primarily, the problem with nuclear proliferation, and regional conflict. And this afternoon we have a major discussion that will more deeply involve the Soviet representatives here, entitled, "Weapons, Strategy, and Doctrine." In just a few minutes I'll introduce our first speaker, Brent Scowcroft, who will present a very brief summary of what his panel has proposed for consideration. Following that, we'll have the Soviet presentation that will include this morning's subjects, as they see fit, and also these this afternoon, and then, following that, we'll have comments from the distinguished panelists on the stage with me, and, as I said earlier, President Ford and I will comment or propose questions whenever we see fit. At this time, it's a great pleasure for me to introduce Brent Scowcroft. He's been deeply involved at the top level of government, not only in previous administrations but also in exploring some of the possibilities for the present administration's policies. He's headed the Scowcroft Commission; he's a former lieutenant general in the U.S. Air Force; he was an assistant to the president for national security affairs; he was chairman of the President's Commission on Strategic Forces in 1982, and now he's Vice Chairman of Kissinger Associates, a consulting firm. It's a great pleasure for me to introduce General Brent Scowcroft.

Brent Scowcroft: Thank you very much, Mr. President, President Ford. The membership of the panel to discuss the role of strategic weapons strategy and doctrine in the U.S.–Soviet relationship was bilateral in the sense that it was comprised of American representatives over a fairly wide spectrum of attitudes on these issues, and also Soviet representatives; it did not have members from other countries. The subject this afternoon is of, I might say, neuralgic concern, not only to the countries involved, but to individuals, and it is difficult to keep an objective and anodyne approach to the issues involved. Nevertheless, we tried. I plan to touch on only some of the highlights of our discussion, divided into three major categories: first, the factors that have influenced strategic weapon development on each side; the centrality of the notion of strategic stability (which I will define a bit later); and some issues and options for the future.

We first turn to an analysis of the factors which have influenced the procurement of the strategic forces which both sides have today: this within a fairly technical framework, that is, outside of the overall political relationship, of course, of which the weapons themselves are only a manifestation. So what we say has to be put in this kind of a larger framework. We really focused on the evolution of U.S. concepts of deterrence in the sense of strategic ideas from the early days of the existence of nuclear weapons and the U.S. decision to substitute nuclear weapons for conventional strength in the defense of Europe, which subsequently became known as extended deterrence. We reviewed the modifications in strategic doctrine, with different periods reflecting different technologies and different political administrations, emphasizing various aspects of retaliation, up until the present time where we're witnessing the reintroduction of the notion of strategic defenses into the issues involved in the strategic balance.

In addition to the influence of strategic concepts on the character of strategic forces, of course, there have been a number of other factors at work on one or both sides, such as: the military traditions of the two sides, which have emphasized, naturally, those kinds of weapons and concepts with which the military services on each side are more comfortable; the momentum of technology itself and the creation of new military opportunities which seem to be apparent within the technology; the influence of domestic politics and the political weight of organizations involved in weapon development, that is, both inside military establishments and within military-industrial areas; the perception of geopolitical needs of each side and the differing problems, as perceived by the two sides, that they face; and, importantly, the sort of action-reaction impulses which have stemmed basically from the antagonistic nature of the U.S.–Soviet relationship. On this point—that is, the action-reaction phenomenon—the Soviet representatives claimed (and I would like to point out that when I speak here of the United States and the Soviet Union, I'm talking about the views of individuals—you can ascribe them, to whatever extent you wish, to those of governments, but in each case, the panel members were speaking in their individual capacities) that the United States had in each case initiated new weapons, new technological developments, and that the Soviets simply responded to U.S. developments. The U.S. participants sharply dissented from that notion and suggested a number of counter-examples—which again is an illustration of the complexity of sorting out the influences on strategic weapons developments. One other factor—in a sense stemming from this—has been the fact that the two sides have been somewhat out of cycle with each other in terms of deployments of major weapons systems and forces. The United States has tended to go in spurts of significant development and then remain in a static state, whereas the Soviet Union has pursued more of a steady, constant development. The result is that as these curves change, you have this perception on each side of being ahead or behind. This, in addition, has exacerbated the tensions resulting from action-reaction, tendencies that have added to the difficulties of the arms control process. Now, in this whole aspect, the Soviet participants, while not describing doctrine and strategy as it relates to the construction of Soviet forces, indicated their belief that the United States had sought in the past and still is seeking strategic superiority and a first-strike nuclear capability.

Notwithstanding the competitive tendencies which have been created by these weapons policies over the years, the panelists did note several factors tending toward convergence. And these factors stem from one central point, and that is the realization that we are on a single planet, and therefore we must seek to preserve it. This has several consequences: one, which was discussed at some length this morning, is the shared interest in preventing the spread of nuclear weapons to additional states. In addition, the certain knowledge on each side of the disaster that a nuclear war would represent has resulted in a consequent caution in approaching situations which could lead to such conflicts. It is easy to overemphasize the influence of that, but I think it is true that perhaps one of the remarkable things is that—given the tension between the two sides since 1945—I think one can adduce that concern over the possibility of nuclear war has played a role in increasing the caution with which the two sides have engaged in confrontations which, in a different age, might have resulted in war. These general convergent forces have tended to produce some stability in the overall political relationship and have tended to set some bounds to this basic antagonism. This overall kind of stability, fragile though it is, is strongly influenced by the stability of strategic forces themselves; that is, by the degree to which these forces encourage or are immune to attack, which is basically the definition that we use for strategic stability. There was a consensus among all the panelists on the centrality and importance of strategic stability and of the value of enhancing strategic stability in increasing the overall stability of the relationship between the two sides. However, after agreeing on the basics, the criteria of strategic stability and the means of improving it, the U.S. and Soviet participants differed sharply, and, within the U.S. side, there were also a number of differences.

The U.S. side noted several steps in the weapons field which could improve strategic stability, for example: adding to the survivability of strategic forces and reducing the chance that they could be destroyed by a side which would choose to attack first; vulnerable forces, that is, forces which could be destroyed, could add dangerously to the military incentive to strike in case of a crisis. Also, reducing the value of individual military targets would likewise reduce the military incentive based on a differential advantage in the force used compared to the force destroyed, to destroy those targets in a first strike. The Americans also thought that it was important to insure the adequacy and invulnerability of command and control systems before and during any nuclear conflict, to remove the notion that the opposing leadership could be destroyed or denied the ability to use its military forces. And lastly, they considered it important to reduce the possibility of surprise or of misperception. Such measures could reduce the tension in any crisis and relieve the sort of hair-trigger nature of anticipation which could otherwise result.

The Soviet participants, by and large, rejected these notions of improving strategic stability by modernization or modification of existing forces. They felt that new weapons were destabilizing or at least changed the environment in ways that are difficult to predict in advance and are usually sharply negative. They felt that renouncing new weapons, the arms race, first use of nuclear weapons, and force, was in general the right way to improve strategic stability.

The U.S. participants pointed out that there are a number of cases where new weapons could greatly enhance strategic stability, such as, for example, the replacement of large missiles with a number of warheads in fixed sites by single warheads and smaller missiles, hopefully mobile or otherwise less vulnerable. In terms of acting on measures to reduce force vulnerability, one U.S. participant suggested that there were three broad alternative courses of action: First, to modify the character of offensive forces through concealment, mobility, change in size; second, to modify the balance on each side through arms control measures; and third, to defend those offensive forces. The American participants generally recognized that there could be tensions between these different alternatives. For example, concealment or mobility which adds to survivability complicates verification of arms control. I believe there was consensus on the U.S. side, however, that strategic stability or increases in strategic stability should not be subordinated to absolute arms control verification. For example, if both sides went in the direction of the small single-warhead mobile missile, the stability of the relationship would be such that absolute verification would not be so necessary because the risk of developing a strategic imbalance would be less. On the third option, that is, the defense of strategic forces, there seems to be a U.S. consensus that strategic defense had to be explored as an option to reduce strategic force vulnerability. That exploration had to include the costs, feasibility, the political implications, as compared with other options, to improve survivability. There was concern expressed by the Americans about the potential problems with strategic defense, such as the difficulty of distinguishing between the defense of missiles and of populations and thereby the possibility of triggering countermeasures that might have unfortunate implications. At this point, the Soviet participants observed that a strategic defense such as envisioned by the Reagan administration's Strategic Defense Initiative would not enhance stability or invulnerability; it would stimulate a response in offensive forces, and would, therefore, make arms control reductions in offensive forces impossible and would inevitably destroy the ABM treaty and other arms control agreements.

In addition to the questions relating to stability, American participants identified two issues which would have to be faced as we looked to the future. The first was strategic defense in any of its manifestations, including SDI (whatever its current definition by the administration may be), and the second, allied but separate: the uses of space. On the issue of strategic defense, several participants observed that the issue could not simply be put aside, that technologies are emerging which would facilitate the identification, tracking, destruction of weapons. These technologies themselves raise many questions, including: Can these new technologies—which perhaps promise results in defense that were not heretofore available—work when other technologies will be available to counter such defensive systems? Should the focus be only on ground-based defense or include space-based weapons? Could the technology be banned, in fact, or should there be a U.S.–Soviet collaborative approach to this whole issue? The Soviet participants were skeptical about the prospects for a collaborative approach and favored an outright ban on strategic defense.

On the uses of space otherwise, several questions were raised. Should there be a treaty on ASAT [Antisatellite] weapons? Should the ban on weapons of mass destruction* in space be extended to all weapons? Is there a basis on which to develop even a tacit U.S.–Soviet understanding on the uses of space? One American participant observed that the guiding principle on the uses of space should be the protection of valuable assets which each side presently and prospectively has in space. The Soviet participants at this point stressed the critical importance of banning all space weapons.

In conclusion, a number of specific recommendations were made for enhancing strategic stability. One was to reduce offensive forces on each side to a level of 1,000 warheads. Another notion was that of "de-MIRVing," that is, removing multiple warheads from all missiles as an alternative to deploying strategic defense to defend offensive forces. The Soviets, on these two points, favored sharp reductions in offensive forces without being specific about their levels or character. Another idea was related to stability in Europe and to one of the concerns about the initiation of nuclear war there. That idea was to eliminate very short-range nuclear systems in Europe, to avoid the danger of their being overrun in the event of attack and thus reduce the pressure for their early use. Another participant commented that this suggestion could erode confidence within Europe and thus turn out to be a counterproductive development. Another notion was that the importance of satellites to both sides warranted a ban on ASAT tests and on weapons in space, and the Soviet participants favored this notion. And lastly there was a proposal to agree to discuss in advance contemplated deployments

---

*A provision of the Outer Space Treaty of 1967.

of new systems with the other side, in order to reduce fears, surprise, and perhaps avoid some developments. These suggestions were certainly not all-inclusive, nor was there time to analyze each one as to feasibility, acceptability, or other desiderata. Their common element, however, is an attempt to go back to our central concern, which was to enhance strategic stability as the major objective of improvements in the military relationship between the two superpowers. Thank you.

President Carter: Before we call on other participants to respond to this specific report, I would like to say again how proud and delighted we are to have Ambassador Anatoly Dobrynin here to represent the Soviet Union, along with Dr. Velikhov, who's been designated by General Secretary Gorbachev to represent the Soviet Union. Dr. Velikhov is well known for his research and for the high position he holds within the Soviet academic and scientific community. At this time, Ambassador Dobrynin will respond, not just specifically to the subjects here but more generally, if he prefers, and then following that we'll have the other panelists on the stage give their points of view. Ambassador Dobrynin, we are delighted to have you here and look forward to hearing your comments.

Anatoly Dobrynin: Thank you. I want to thank President Carter and President Ford for the invitation of Soviet representatives to come here: Academician Velikhov, my good friend, General Mikhailov, and Ambassador Tarasenko; they are sitting over there. They came directly from Moscow.

I should say that unfortunately I did not participate in the panel discussions, so for me it is rather difficult immediately to reply to my good friend, General Scowcroft, but I am sure Academician Velikhov, who participated very actively yesterday, will have something to say about this report.

First, I am glad to see yesterday and today many familiar faces—Secretaries Rusk, Kissinger, Vance, Brown, Lehman, Generals Jones, Scowcroft, among others—the people who one way or another have taken part in the shaping of the United States foreign and military policies. As a longtime Soviet ambassador in Washington, I was and am privileged to work closely with some of you to improve relations between the United States and the Soviet Union. Excuse me— my statement probably will be rather lengthy, but please be patient with me because we consider the subject of our relationship with the United States rather important.

There is hardly a need to dwell at length on the importance of Soviet-American relations in today's world. Not only are our two countries by far the most powerful on this earth, but they also symbolize in many respects two opposing, opposite economic, social, and political systems. Their relationship, to a large extent, determines the entire course of international development. At the same time, we are far from looking at the road only through the prism of our relationship with the United States. One should not ignore other members of the international community, including dozens of new states with their own history, own traditions, and their own interests. This, however, doesn't diminish, but increases the special responsibility of the Soviet Union and the United States for the future of human civilization. Now, probably as never before, the world finds itself at an important, maybe even critical junction; it depends primarily on our two countries which road mankind will take—toward genuine reduction in nuclear and conventional arsenals and banning all weapons in space, or toward a further arms race, making even the heavens an arena of competition of weaponry in military posture, thus, inevitably, increasing the risk of an all-out nuclear war.

As of today, Soviet–American relations, quite frankly, remain tense. Are there now any changes for the better in these relations? There is no simple answer to this question. Something gives reason for hope—but there is still a lot that causes alarm. The history of our relations has known its ups and downs. Together we have been through good times and bad times. Presently, as I said, these relations are tense, complicated, and unstable, to say the least. There are some in the United States who regard such a state of affairs as normal, and view confrontation as almost a natural state. We do not think so. Confrontation is not an inborn defect of our relations. There is a good page in the historic record, of course: the close alliance between us, together with other members of the anti-Hitler coalition, in the Second World War. We in the Soviet Union maintain very good memories of the joint struggle against Nazism, more so on the eve of the fortieth anniversary of the great victory. And it is only regrettable and unfortunate that in this country, it seems, some would rather forget the lessons of the war and the common sacrifice for the sake of the victory.

Another example of mutual cooperation was the period of the seventies, usually defined as years of detente—or should I avoid that particular term in deference to President Ford's linguistic preferences? I will not use "detente" anymore. Anyway, in our Russian language, we do not use this word "detente," as you understand it, but we simply say "relaxation of tensions"—nothing more dangerous. What is important, however, is the substance of that policy, based on a mutual recognition of the imperative necessity for the Soviet Union and the United States to coexist peacefully and to build their relationship on the basis of equality, equal security, and respect for the legitimate interests of each other. We don't say that the 1970s were some kind of golden age in our relationship. The period had its own share of tense moments and complications; however, a significant example was set during the presidencies of Nixon, Ford, and Carter for how the Soviet Union and the United States, East and West, must interact to reduce the danger of nuclear war and curb the arms race. Today some people in this country doubt the validity of the agreements concluded to that effect ten or fifteen years ago. But let us ask ourselves: what would have happened if those steps had not been taken? The answer is clear, at least to us: the situation now would have been even much more dangerous.

Unfortunately, the first half of this current decade saw a serious downturn in Soviet–American relations and in the international situation as a whole. Let us look at the facts—the so-called rearmament of America, which, as at least we see it in my country, is nothing but a bid to acquire strategic superiority for the United States. Yet, the strategic buildup on this side of the Atlantic and the deployment of new American medium-range missiles in Western Europe did not add an iota of security, either for the United States itself, or for its NATO allies. It has only made it necessary for the Soviet Union to match all this with countermeasures of our own. But neither did this add much to the security of my own country. Lately of special concern was the American decision to go ahead with the "Star Wars" plan, the concept of creating this full-scale antiballistic missile system, based in space as well as on the ground. In brief, in our opinion, the world is now faced with the prospect of the militarization of outer space, with the serious consequence of such a menace. Some people are even joking in my country that it is ironic how political and military leaders of a country with a strong religious following like the United States would want to spread the arms race to the heavens while the Soviet atheists have a problem with this very unfortunate and extremely dangerous idea.

No less disturbing is the accompanying change in the philosophy here as far as the Soviet–American relations are concerned. Back in 1974 President Ford said, and I quote, "As nations with great power we share a common responsibility, not only to our own people, but to mankind as a whole. Of course, we must avoid war and the destruction that it would mean. Let us get on with the business of controlling arms. Let us contribute through our cooperation to the resolution of the very great problem facing mankind as a whole." I could quote along the same lines from a very thoughtful, very interesting speech made by President Carter in Vienna in 1979. But the Cold War mentality, unfortunately, has left a very strong imprint on human minds. The basis of our relationship is often portrayed more as a struggle between good and evil, with the Americans, naturally, as the good guys. The pyramids of Egypt may or may not make some sense, but the pyramids of weapons, well, maybe there is a moral side to this, by the way, to justify the gross misuse of human efforts. Animosity sometimes is cultivated toward other countries. Of course, Cold War thinking is very simple. There is a crystal-clear goal: to bring the enemy down. The more damage you inflict on the other party, the better off you are. You can appeal to jingoism, suspicion, and hostility toward those who live and look differently. We live then in a two-dimensional world of black and white, and you can describe your political problem in one minute on television prime time. By contrast the philosophy of detente—excuse me that I use it—or peaceful or constructive coexistence, is much more difficult to master. One has to be broad-minded and tolerant enough to realize that the relations between the United States and the Soviet Union are not a zero-sum game in which one side wins exactly as much as the other loses, but that, despite all differences and difficulties, both sides have some overriding mutual interests. And one has to realize that the restraint, moderation, and readiness to compromise, even though they require not only more wisdom but greater political courage as well, are preferable to self-righteousness, arrogance, and the inclination to play tough. And the Cold War has left behind not only a lot of preconceptions, but also some built-in mechanisms—I mean the mechanisms of the arms race, the existing military and political alliances, as well as other parts of the huge infrastructure created in the service of the Cold War, such as the bureaucracies and organizations for psychological warfare, and similar activities. All these mechanisms seek to ensure their own survival. This means that they have to generate international tensions, spur on military rivalry, and sow distrust.

In the last five years we have seen just how stubborn the legacy of the Cold War really is. We have seen, as I mentioned, the recommitment to the achievement of military superiority, which has led to a steep rise in international tension and increased threat of war. We have seen that anti-Soviet rhetoric and a tough style have a very negative effect on the substance of Soviet–American relations. Although we do not take every diatribe literally, we cannot ignore them as merely rhetorical exercise, for such words shed light upon the real feelings and intentions of their authors. True, we do compete in many ways in the international arena. It's also true that this competition stems from certain fundamental differences of our social, economic, and political systems; however, in our view, that is no reason for starting to fight. We are in favor of a competition where each system will have to prove—in the conditions of peace, of course—who is able in the long run to ensure economic and social prosperity, a better quality of life, the satisfaction of the cultural and spiritual needs of individuals along with their material well-being. Who will persist in this is to be proved by strength of example and not by strength of arms.

We would like to remind you, ladies and gentlemen, that you have a history of more than 200 years, but we exist three times less. When we will celebrate 200 years, we will see what kind of achievements we might have. And then despite all the differences, we have one overriding interest—the overwhelming mutual interest in survival in a nuclear age. It would be proper, in this context, to recall what John Kennedy said more than 20 years ago in his American University speech: "In the final analysis our basic common link is the fact that we all inhabit this planet, all breathe the same air, we all cherish our children's future and we all are mortal."

Let me emphasize again that the differences in our political and social systems should not, we believe, be a reason for starting a fight or a nuclear war. We do not seek military superiority over the United States. At the same time, we simply couldn't afford to permit the other side to gain superiority over the United States. At the same time, we simply couldn't afford to permit the other side to gain superiority over us. This is not in any way a threat—it's simply a fact of modern life. That is the essence, in a nutshell, of our approach to the entire complex relationship with the United States. Recently the new general secretary of our party, Mikhail Gorbachev, again restated the Soviet Union's readiness, provided the United States is also ready, to actually work to improve Soviet–American relations. Our new leader said in his maiden speech: "We will firmly follow the course of peace and peaceful existence. To goodwill the Soviet Union will always respond with goodwill, as it will respond to trust with trust." The Soviet Union's choice is clear: stopping the arms race on Earth and preventing it in space.

Is it possible for the Soviet Union and the United States to come to a sensible agreement to clear the present-day logjams on the way to a safer world? We do believe it is possible, moreover imperative, that we come to such an agreement. Despite doom, gloom, and despair by some, we in the Soviet Union are convinced the solution can be found, provided the political will is there. Again, the experience of the 1970s demonstrates that when there is a political will, the chief results are within reach. After all, three previous American presidents were able to negotiate important arms control agreements with my country. For that, however, it is extremely important to recognize the reality of the world and to give up the illusion that it would be possible to deal with the Soviet Union and the socialist community of nations from a position of strength. It is an illusion, first of all, to hope to race us into some sort of military, economic, and political weakness vis-à-vis the United States and the West. Of course the arms race has put a heavy burden on us. But it may be interesting for you to know that we are still trying to keep the prices of essentials for our population on the same level. I should say, for instance, that we practically haven't changed the prices in the last 30 or 40 years on food, apartments, public utilities, and public transportation. Health care and education, of course, continue to be free. But of course continued escalation of the arms race will force some additional drain on our economy, and, we have to admit, some necessary austerity. What is going on meanwhile in your own country you know better than I do. The Soviet Union has everything it needs to build its own future for centuries ahead—vast natural resources, big territory and population, great industrial, technological, and scientific potential. And of course you shouldn't doubt the resolve of the Soviet people to defend our own way of life. The Second World War proved it rather decisively.

Coming back to the central question of our relationship—I cannot but point to the all-too-familiar attempts to justify the continuous build-up of United States military arsenals by invoking the so-called Soviet threat or imbalance of forces in favor of the Soviet Union. Such allegations are, in our opinion, misleading. Strangely enough, this worked on so many occasions in the past, and it continues to work even now. Take for example the so-called "bomber gap" or the "missile gap" in the 1960s. This simply did not exist, but it served its aim to realize support for high military appropriations. Or in the early 1980s we heard similar complaints about the "window of vulnerability." While immediately before— a few months before—during the Vienna summit, the United States president, the secretary of defense, and the chairman of the joint chiefs of staff (and they are all present here) acknowledged the existence of rough strategic parity with the Soviet Union. At the same time it may be revealing that at no time, now or in the past, have the American generals ever said they would exchange their so-called weakness for the Soviets' so-called strength. Who should you believe? Of course it was not only a one-sided exercise. We have our share in all this arms race. But I could tell you quite frankly that in developing the most important new types of arms we really were following the Americans. Unfortunately, it seems that some American politicians have not been able to get over the fact that they cannot use force against the Soviet Union without inviting a retaliatory blow.

Last, there has emerged a very misguided and, as you say, extremely dangerous trend, a search for new ways to use force—such ways that supposedly would not endanger the United States itself. This trend is multifaceted. One process that deserves a special note is the search for new weapons systems, new doctrines and methods of targeting military forces—all designed to make nuclear war winnable. There is the counterforce doctrine, the idea of selective and surgical strikes, and limited nuclear war. There are attempts to introduce certain rules of the game in nuclear and military conflicts so as to make them more thinkable. Surely, a peace based on deterrence is far from the ideal, and in the long run, neither too stable or even durable. Deterrence, the principle of mutual fear, generates stress by itself. We have here an example of that monstrously perverse logic which is imposed by the balance of terror, as it is now. One has to remind others constantly of one's ability for mass murder in order to assure one's own security. The dilemma cannot be solved within this framework. On the one hand, it has to be admitted that war has become meaningless. On the other hand, you have to prepare for war around the globe and emphasize your readiness to start it. No matter what the regional intentions are, this logic, if you cling to it permanently, inevitably leads to brinkmanship. It is no surprise, therefore, that many people now are looking for some alternatives to Mutual Assured Destruction. But the concept of MAD is cherished not by only those who detest war and insist on drastic reduction of weaponry, but by those who are still in favor of the arms race. Now we are confronted with a very strong effort to tip the balance of terror in favor of the United States. The American nuclear forces are being tailored to the strategy of prevailing in a nuclear war. The Trident II submarine, the MX missile, the B-1, the Stealth bombers, the cruise missiles, and the Pershing II are the toys of this deadly game. We have our own, of course. But it really does not make life easy.

All this is said not in anger or purely for the sake of criticism. President Carter invited us yesterday to share our mutual concern and fear, and that is exactly what we are doing today before the American audience. Our perception is that the development of United States' doctrines and weapons systems was designed to assure superiority. This is our interpretation; if we are wrong, please prove otherwise. And this remains the direction of the current U.S. strategic policy, including the Strategic Defense Initiative. Recently the Soviet Union and the United States entered into new negotiations on nuclear and outer space arms in Geneva, which is, undoubtedly, a positive step. The successful outcome of these talks will depend upon how faithfully both of us adhere to the agreement reached by our foreign minister, Andrei Gromyko, and your secretary of state, George Shultz, as to the subject and objectives of the negotiations; namely, that the issues of space weapons and nuclear arms, both strategic and medium-range, are to be considered and resolved in their interrelationship—I repeat—in their interrelationship. In other words, the aims of the talks are defined as follows: not to start an arms race in space, but to stop it on Earth, and to start a radical reduction of nuclear arms—their total liquidation being the ultimate goal. That is a very simple definition of the talks. They will affect the course of Soviet-American relations and world developments as a whole. Some people, including some people here, say the Soviet Union's purpose is to divide NATO over this particular issue. Well, I don't know—maybe that is a good idea, but the mere fact that such a concern exists in the United States shows there is something wrong with the whole doctrine. Otherwise, why worry about it? So what is happening now in the United States? I quote my new general secretary, Mr. Gorbachev. In his words, "It is basically the same banking on superior strength and not even considering this. Diplomacy and negotiations themselves are very often still subordinated to missiles and bombers. The people who are supposed to conduct talks in Geneva on behalf of the United States are hastily summoned from the negotiation table to Washington to help push new strategic arms programs through the United States Congress."

There is intense propaganda in favor of "Star Wars" in this country. It is even contended that these plans make strategic weapons more negotiable, and that, by creating space weapons, it is possible to arrive at the elimination of nuclear arms. To be direct, it's a rather strange method. Just as the advent of nuclear arms did not eliminate conventional types of arms, but only generated an accelerated race in the manufacture of both nuclear and conventional arms, the creation of space weapons will have only one result: the arms race will become more intense and encompass new spheres. This is our conviction.

Now, American politicans rather loudly worry about some Soviet ICBM a thousand miles away. But what would the American people say if, as a result of the "Star Wars" doctrine, they had over their own heads some new, very destructive arms or weaponry? The Soviet people, I can assure you, don't like this perspective for themselves. That's why we are against this doctrine. Having lived for some time in Washington, I am aware of the intense rivalries between the Redskins and the Cowboys. I am sure that neither the head coach of the Redskins nor their offense would believe it if somebody started to sell them the idea that the Cowboys drafted a new defense line for humanitarian reasons and not to beat the Redskins in the next season. I would even venture to predict the Redskins' reaction: they would definitely recruit bigger, quicker, and stronger guys for their offensive line.

Well, I will probably not be revealing a big secret about the negotiations which are going on now in Geneva by saying that the general impression we have so far is that the United States is not willing to discuss with us anything specific about space until they have completed the research stage of their program. It will take several years, as it was announced. But, by the way, with whom would they negotiate after this—there will be a new administration, I guess. But the fact is that the United States entered into the negotiations with us under the agreement—which was signed, I gather, by the other two foreign ministers, Gromyko and Shultz, and this agreement stated that we should consider and resolve the three sets of issues—space, strategic and medium-range weapons—in their interrelationship. We still hope that this particular agreement, which was signed by the two ministers on behalf of their governments, would be fulfilled. Should both sides take this path of reason, it would truly mean a decisive turn in a positive direction, not only for Soviet-American relations, but for the entire world situation. This planet is our common house, and we should proceed from our common interest in preserving it. An important example is our shared interest in nonproliferation—prevention of the spread of nuclear weapons to additional states. We have cooperated quite well, even during these last years. This is a good example that we could really cooperate. If one has to sit at the negotiating table—and now specifically to achieve the reduction of arms—then, according to common sense, one should at least refrain from increasing these armaments further. That is why we propose that the United States and the Soviet Union introduce, for the entire duration of the talks, a moratorium on the development, testing, and deployment of space arms and freeze their strategic offensive arms. At the same time, the deployment of American medium-range missiles in Europe should be terminated and, correspondingly, the buildup of the Soviet countermeasures. At the same time, Mikhail Gorbachev, our general secretary, has declared a moratorium on the development of medium-range missiles until November. The United States hastily rejected our proposal. We regret that, but I promise you we will study very carefully any proposal which, we hope, will be forthcoming. What else could be done, meanwhile, during this first stage of negotiations? We have had only four weeks of working there. We think there are certain things we could do. We could make, for instance, a mutual pledge of no first use of nuclear weapons, or nonuse of force between the blocs, or resumption of talks on a complete and comprehensive ban on nuclear weapons tests between the United States, the United Kingdom, and the Soviet Union, which were interrupted by the U.S. administration. We are prepared to resume these negotiations any time. Or for instance, why not proceed to ratify the well-known test ban agreements of 1974 or 1976?* It could be done now, and during these negotiations—it could be a good stimulus to all the negotiations in Geneva. We are in favor of it in any case.

The Soviet Union is prepared to apply the same kind of positive attitude to

---

*The Treaty on Limitation of Underground Nuclear Weapons Tests (July, 1974) and the Peaceful Nuclear Explosions Treaty (1976) prohibit any nuclear explosion with a yield greater than 150 kilotons or a group of explosions exceeding 1,500 kilotons, collectively known as the "Threshold Test Ban Treaty."

other areas of our relationship with the United States, not only on the cardinal problems of arms control and prevention of war. We are prepared to work together with other countries in searching for ways to facilitate the settlement of conflict situations in different parts of the world. We are ready, as we mentioned recently once again to the United States government, to seek together a solution to regional problems, be it the Middle East, Central America, Southern Africa, Cyprus, or other hot spots, including the situation in Afghanistan.

Moscow and Washington have begun, through diplomatic channels—quietly so to speak now—to discuss some of these issues—at least to exchange views, as was the case in our recent consultation on the Middle Eastern problem. Although we haven't advanced very much so far, the fact that such a dialogue is at all possible is in itself encouraging and we welcome it. Of course, much can be done—and to our mutual benefit—in normalizing and developing bilateral ties and exchanges between the Soviet Union and the United States. There were some shifts in this area of our relations for the better: a restoration of some of the contacts which had been interrupted or suspended, certain activities in a number of heretofore largely moribund bilateral cooperation agreements. But still it's more or less a departmental diplomacy. Practical results are few and not very significant. Nevertheless, again, there are good signs, and on our side we are ready to move further ahead. Our impression was that the American side was willing to do so too; we welcome this. All these questions could be among the topics for discussion alongside the key issues of Soviet–American relations. As is well known, a positive attitude for a summit meeting was expressed by President Reagan and General Secretary Gorbachev. The time and place will be the subject of subsequent arrangements. We are convinced that a serious impulse should be given to Soviet–American relations at the high political level. Meanwhile, both governments—we agree on this—should conduct these relations in such a way that it would be obvious to everyone, to our people, to other countries, that the political processes of the United States and the Soviet Union are oriented not toward hostility and confrontation but toward the search for mutual understanding and peaceful development, to arms control and important, quiet political dialogue. As you know, both governments have agreed that Foreign Minister Andrei Gromyko and Secretary of State George Shultz will meet on May 14 to discuss the whole range of questions of Soviet–American relations. We wish them success. Let me say in conclusion that we regard the improvement of Soviet–American relations not only as an extremely necessary, but also a possible, realistic matter. Possibilities for improving these relations do exist, as well as for improving the overall world situation. This possibility should not be missed now. Thank you very much.

President Carter: I think Ambassador Dobrynin gave a very good reason for the length of his speech—it's a very important relationship, and we have to remember, too, that they are making two responses since they skipped over this morning's opportunity. I thought he had some very stimulating and interesting comments to make about the present, past, and future, and now we'll hear some responses both to what Ambassador Dobrynin had to say and also to the original presentation by Brent Scowcroft. The next speaker formerly worked in the National Security Council; he was then employed at a high position in the Department of Defense, and now he occupies what to me, a few years ago, was the most important single position in the United States government, and that was secretary of the navy. When I was in the submarine force, I thought the secretary of the navy was tops, and maybe the president was somewhere below that position. We're delighted to have Secretary of the Navy, John Lehman.

John Lehman: Thank you, Mr. President. While certainly it's not tops, Mr. President, it's only second to the presidency, still. I was dismayed to hear Brent's summary of the panel, and I must say I disagree with what seems to be the consensus of the assumptions describing how we got to the state of deterrence that we are in today. Through it seems to run, as Brent described it, an action-reaction syndrome theory, that somehow we are all poor cogs in a large universe that is predetermined by the material aspects of the weapons and the forces that are beyond men to guide. The military structure that we have today—the nuclear weapons we have—are not some result of a mindless determinism of our environment and the materiel we deal with; they are the result of conscious, informed decisions by human beings. This is a hobbyhorse of mine, because it's the very same heresy that afflicts our procurement and other aspects of our defense establishment today: the idea that somehow organization charts and bureaucracies are what determine decisions and outcomes. I disagree with that completely. The weapons systems we have were decided upon to meet military missions—military missions perceived by intelligent human beings over the last thirty years. The history of arms control is a sad one, because it has not really increased in any measurable way the security of either country. And one of the reasons is that it was this kind of Manicheanism that underlaid the approach that we took to negotiating arms control. I believe that we have made a fundamental change in that assumption in the way that we go about arms control negotiations today.

We see an opportunity, at this point, to find that common ground where intelligent, pragmatic decision-makers on both sides can agree to get on with major reductions in the nuclear weapons we have, not because they got there by some mindless process, but because the balance and the opportunities that those deployments presented at various times are no longer there. I believe the history of the sixties and the seventies is a history of Soviet building of weapons and their seeing, as pragmatists, benefits derived from those expensive deployments. As Secretary Harold Brown had said, very aptly, the history of that period was that we built in the early part of that period, and then the Soviets built, and we stopped building, and the Soviets built. In the hopes that the arms control process itself would stop what was assumed to be an action-reaction cycle, we allowed very destabilizing disparities to develop in the continuum of deterrence. As a result, arms control became impossible to achieve in a meaningful way, because why should the Soviets stop deploying an average of two hundred new ICMs [Increased Capability Missiles] a year while we were deploying none? Because they could see, they could read in our press, they could read in the world discussion of the issues a very marked shifting in the perceptions of how the strategic balance was seen; they could see a perception in the world that they were gaining a large measure of superiority in the strategic equation, which in turn opened up new opportunities of relatively risk-free intervention and activism elsewhere in the world. So, this false assumption that we brought to arms control conditioned the Soviets to continue building because it yielded real benefit. I think that cycle has been broken. The rearming that Ambassador Dobrynin spoke of, begun in the last administration and in the latter part of the seventies and continued vigorously the last four years, has re-established the basis to begin to pursue real reductions on the basis of common sense. We have programs underway in the MX, the new bomber programs, the Trident program, and the D-5 missile and other modernization programs, particularly in the most important of all President Reagan's strategic initiatives and the least reported upon: the development of the vertical dimension of deterrents through greatly increased investment in redundant command and control communications. Heretofore, we have looked at arms control only in the horizontal dimension, measuring the things that verification means could see and count, numbers of silos, numbers of submarines, numbers of missiles. President Reagan has concentrated a major part of his approach on the vertical dimension of survivability over time: the stabilization of the deterrent, the building of a robustness in command and control and of survivability that makes the advantages of any potential first strike, or the advantages of any major investment by the Soviets in civil defense, disappear over time. We have re-established now an unprecedented opportunity. We have many more missiles and weapons on both sides than are needed for an ideal, stable nuclear deterrence, and now we are approaching it with a realism and a pragmatism that will yield results. This common ground is made up of several obvious elements.

First, it's very expensive for our military establishments and our economies to support the level of strategic weapons we have today. We have real, legitimate military tasks in the military that are not being met because of the burden of expenditures in the nuclear field, and so we have an obvious common interest in reducing the numbers and expense of maintaining this apparatus, which will exactly coincide with the perception of their degree of uselessness. In the seventies the Soviet military had no incentive to reduce, because they had clear benefits from maintaining their edge. Today they are going to lose that edge, and maintaining those high numbers of expensive submarine-based missiles, expensive land-based silos and bombers, is, therefore, simply not there. The margin of return is not what it was in the seventies, and that holds great promise. Also, there is a more realistic approach to verification. Obviously, the lower we go in numbers, the more destabilizing any imbalance will become, and the more important absolute numbers, as opposed to relative numbers, become. Therefore, verification becomes more, not less, important the lower we go in the numbers of systems. In my judgment we have exhausted the opportunities that nonintrusive verification has provided for arms control. It will still remain a fundamentally important part of any arms control verification system. But to really achieve the promise that I believe is there, we now have to move on to much more extensive verification methods. Now there is a trendy wisdom in Washington that the Soviets will never accept on-site inspection and intrusive inspection. I would be interested in hearing the ambassador and some of the Soviet participants' discussion of on-site inspection issues. I think they are getting a "bum rap." They did accept intrusive on-site inspection for the PNE [Peaceful Nuclear Explosions] treaty that was negotiated, and I think they should be willing to carry verification along this path in the future. We in the U.S. military see nothing particularly abhorrent about it. We have testified repeatedly in the Navy Department that we can certainly accept on-site inspection of naval ships if that is what is negotiated in an arms control agreement on a reciprocal basis. I would be interested in hearing General Mikhailov's views as to what the Soviet military's position on intrusive on-site inspection might be. Lastly, the Strategic Defense Initiative is, contrary to the Soviets' current position, very much in our mutual interest, and I think they will come to see why. I can very well understand why it is that they oppose it today, because it is a system—an approach—that certainly capitalizes on the great advantage in the technological innovation the United States enjoys. But conceptually, spending our resources in maintaining deterrence through protecting our populations rather than avenging them is a morally and intellectually satisfying concept, far more satisfying than the balance of terror that has been an assumption of much of our deterrence policy over the last thirty years. And I believe that reorienting our expenditures in strategic deterrence to defense can only be stabilizing, and not destabilizing. I reject the suggestion by some of the Soviet commentators that they will simply react by attempting to build more, bigger, and better offensive weapons. They will not do that because it simply does not make common sense, and I think whatever one might criticize about Soviet strategic policy over the last thirty years, it makes a great deal of common sense, consistently, from their point of view. So I believe that SDI is going to lead us toward a much more stabilizing future. I believe that it does not have to be one hundred percent in order to achieve that stabilization. A little bit goes a long way. Every little bit that is effective further dilutes the confidence that would tempt any offensive strike. So I see much common interest.

In the treatment of the theater nuclear balance in the study panel's paper, although it wasn't extensively treated, I don't find any interesting suggestions. Perhaps it might be pursued further on. Clearly, the policy advocated by some that we should attempt to move our posture in NATO toward a one-to-one matching of land divisions in the balance doesn't make any sense for a coalition of democracies. The Soviets have about 178 active divisions today. We are hoping to get to eighteen by the end of the decade. Clearly, an attempt to convince the world that we are prepared to fight a war of attrition against a totalitarian regime with that many land divisions and that large a land force is not believable, and of course it is strategically foolish, because it simply does not recognize the great advantages in technological innovation and in flexibility that the free-world alliances have. It is that that we must continue to use in order to deter the overwhelming land force strength that the Soviets and their allies have maintained permanently in an active posture in the Eurasian landmass. So, unfortunately, theater nuclear weapons have been part of that balance of imbalances and they are not going to go away by attempting to convince the Europeans that the battle of the Somme was a more acceptable form of warfare than a deterrent based on theater nuclear weapons. Other than that, Brent, it is a great report. Thank you.

President Carter: I don't think I have ever heard a clearer or more forceful presentation of the radical departure of the Reagan administration's policy toward nuclear arms agreements—both those reached in the past and those that might be reached in the future. That is a very important thing for this audience, throughout the nation and the world, to understand. My own inclination is to wait till later to respond to Secretary Lehman's open and implied criticism of what our own administration and those of Presidents Ford, Nixon, Johnson, and Kennedy tried to do in reaching what we considered to be agreements negotiated in good faith on both sides, basically stabilizing and beneficial in their ultimate effect, and also, in general, complied with on both sides. There have been some deviations by the Soviets and by the United States from the interpretations of the agreements. Those complaints have been submitted to the Standing Consultative Commission as agreed, and in most cases, have been resolved satisfactorily. But I think we've seen here a clear departure in American policy on this crucial issue of arms control, explained in a very forceful and clear way.

President Ford: If I heard you correctly, John, you said that many of these new weapons were initiated under this administration or the preceding one. You're either uninformed or didn't tell the true story. As you know, the research and development of the MX started in 1975 and continued in 1976 under my administration. The B-1 bomber was initiated in our administration. I won't comment on what happened after that, but as you well know, because you were in the Defense Department, it was started in our administration. The cruise missiles: the ALCM, the SLCM, and the GLCM, all were begun in my administration. So I hope you were just inadvertently inaccurate. [*Lehman:* I accept your criticism.]

President Carter: The next presentation will be very significant because we will be hearing from a man, Secretary Harold Brown, who has the far-reaching ability to analyze very complicated scientific issues. He's the former president of Cal Tech, as you know—a notable scientist in his own right. He is a former secretary of the Air Force. I asked him to be secretary of defense after I was elected president. He brought to our administration, and to the analysis of nuclear arms concepts and the present situation, an insight that has always been very valuable to me and to all those who have listened to him. And now, I would like to call on Secretary Harold Brown to give the next presentation.

Harold Brown: Thank you very much President Carter, President Ford. It is a great pleasure to be here—even more of a pleasure than I had anticipated, because in the past hour my mind has been subjected to a psychedelic stretching in both directions. I find much that I agree with in what each of the previous speakers has had to say (hard as that may be to believe in view of their apparent lack of overlap). I would observe that slogans on both sides of an issue are sometimes politically effective for a time, but they are usually not useful in the long run, whether we use those slogans to try to substitute what we would like to be for what we really are or whether we would like to substitute what we would like to be true for what is true. Ambassador Dobrynin has said about some U.S. programs what is often argued against them in the United States, sometimes by me. But he has tended to lump all of them together. He lumped together stabilizing, submarine-launched ballistic missiles with potentially vulnerable intercontinental ballistic missiles. He has lumped together Stealth bombers with the Strategic Defense Initiative. And he has mentioned that some of these same objections or concerns apply to Soviet programs, but he has done so only in passing, without mentioning any systems. He has neither claimed nor denied, for example, that SS-18s are stabilizing, as stabilizing as the Soviet SSN-20s (their submarine-launched ballistic missiles). He has said nothing about whether the intermediate-range missiles, the SS-20s, should reassure Europeans or frighten them by being targeted on their cities. [*Dobrynin:* Is it not clear?] Yes, to me, but not from what you said. He hasn't mentioned Soviet contributions to the arms competition in the form of the first ICBMs or the first heavy ICBMs or the first significant antiballistic missile deployments or robust air defense. His more reasonable statements (and they are reasonable) about the limitations of military capabilities, the dangers of the arms competition, and so forth, including the Soviet contributions to those activities, are echoed in the United States. But on my not very recent and rather brief visits to the Soviet Union I never heard much on television about these problems or the contributions of the Soviet Union to these problems.

Now, my Russian is not that good, and things may have changed, so that it may be that one hears the same sort of criticism in the Soviet Union about Soviet military programs that one hears of U.S. programs in the United States from Americans and from the Soviets, but I doubt it. Indeed, this lack of discussion in the Soviet Union about need to compromise, about the wastefulness of one's own military efforts, about the conclusion that there are no real differences, necessarily, in the search for peace—the lack of that in the Soviet Union really reflects one of the differences between our two systems. There is a fundamental competition, but it is more than in social or economic systems; it is also for political influence. It is true that the United States has been an uncomfortable neighbor to some of its neighbors sometimes—that's true of any great power and especially true of a superpower, and it's also true of the Soviet Union. Being a neighbor to a superpower is uncomfortable, but I think I know which one is less comfortable to be a neighbor to. Still, we do inhabit the same world together, and whatever our differences, we have a mutual interest in survival as a general proposition, and a mutual interest in some specific things: preventing nuclear proliferation, for example. As to the claims that stopping weapons development solves our security problems, that needs to be seen in a broader political context of a kind that was mentioned already by General Scowcroft. Certainly the effects of technical and military developments would be very different in a world in which the United States and the Soviet Union were not adversaries. Such a context is not a realistic alternative in the foreseeable future, but if we are going to get to the unforeseeable future, we have to survive in the meantime. And that ought to be our mutual concern.

Let me talk a little bit about doctrine. Deterrence by the threat of retaliation remains the U.S. and allied strategy, not really out of choice but because it is a fact of life—technical life, military life, and political life. We think that such a fact of life deters nuclear attack and perhaps even deters to some degree the threat of conventional attack, by a concern—a mutual concern—about the possibility of escalation to strategic nuclear war if there is a conventional attack. And part of that actually is the possibility of first use of nuclear weapons in the face of an overwhelming conventional attack, which is why the alliance has rejected the proposal for explicitly forgoing the possibility of such a response. It is not clear to me that the Soviet doctrine is the same. It is not clear to me what the Soviet doctrine is about whether nuclear war is survivable, about whether it is winnable. By and large, the Soviet political leadership has expressed doctrines similar to ours. Soviet military writings have not always done so, and it would be useful to have that discussed more explicitly at some point.

Let me turn to the discussion of the goals of nuclear planning and of nuclear arms control in the paper of the study panel. It seems to me that they are to reduce the chance of nuclear war and to limit the damage of nuclear war if it occurs. Unfortunately, sometimes these two goals conflict, and one has to make a judgment about which is more important. Given the likely enormously destructive nature of nuclear war, it seems to me that so far, the clear choice is to reduce the chance of nuclear war. Reducing the chance of nuclear war is the more important goal since (I will come back to the SDI, which apparently is the "King Charles' head" of all these discussions and can never be left out) as to the attempts to moderate its effects—although they are necessary and laudable as, for example, was the idea of limited nuclear options, and the idea of a countervailing strategy—the idea of graduated response and so forth—we need to push them, but we should not have too much confidence in them. And I have the concern that too much attention to abolishing nuclear weapons—laudable as that is—is a dream which can cause us to take our eye off the ball—the ball being avoiding nuclear war by a combination of managing a deterrent strategy and managing the political competition with the Soviet Union. If we miss out on either of those two goals, then the world becomes much more dangerous.

I would note, also, the sacramental purpose of nuclear arms control. For the benefit of our Soviet friends, a sacrament is the outward sign of an inward grace. Nuclear arms control has served in the West—and I think also in the Soviet Union—as a way for political leaders, by the outward sign of engaging in arms control negotiations and thinking that they are important and showing that they consider them important, to show their populations that they do worry about nuclear war (which populations do very much) and that they are trying to do something about it. As with much other symbolism, it can be overdone and it can backfire if it is oversold. But I think it is an important function of arms control negotiations. I would add also that the effect of arms control and of unilateral weapons choices on political relations can be significant and count heavily, because managing competitive adversarial relations to avoid crisis is a very important activity, even while the United States and the Soviet Union are pursuing their respective political goals. My own judgment is that failure in arms control negotiations hurts more than success helps. Unlike some, however, I deny that it is therefore better to have no attempt for arms control or to delay until one's own side is negotiating from a predominant or superior position. Because if you do not negotiate at all then the failure to limit is automatic.

Since there is not much time, let me speak also to the question of conventional forces. I believe that raising the nuclear threshold by lengthening the time that a conventional war might be fought by the NATO alliance along a stable line—lengthening it to, say, 30 days or 50 days—would actually enhance nuclear deterrence. Because if there is no conventional capability, you are thrown entirely on the nuclear deterrent, on early nuclear escalation, and that, perhaps, becomes unbelievable. And if it is unbelievable, then I think my friend McGeorge Bundy and his three colleagues in the "Gang of Four" are right that it becomes dysfunctional. It has to be somewhat believable, and it is more believable, in my judgment, if there is a higher nuclear threshold. I would support Secretary Lehman's judgment that high-technology conventional capability may improve the balance for the West vis-à-vis the Soviet Union and ought to be pursued. I know that our European friends are concerned about the potential damage of a conventional war, even one that lasted only 30 to 60 days, but if they think there is no difference between that and what nuclear war would do, they ought to think again. Thirty years saw miraculous recovery from a great conventional war. Thirty generations would not see a recovery from a nuclear war. I would note that it is important for the United States and its allies to have a substantial land-based conventional capability. It would little profit us, if the Soviet Union were to overrun its contiguous regions—Southwest Asia, Europe—for us to be able to take it out on the fishes in response to the Soviet victory.

Let me turn finally to the Strategic Defense Initiative. There are two ways of looking at its effect on stability, and this is a very telescoped summary. One is: suppose it is perfect or near perfect. One could argue that it would then be bilaterally stabilizing between the United States and the Soviet Union, assuming that both sides have it. (And I assume that if one side has it, both sides will have it, not as a result of a charitable gift but as a result of competition.) On the other hand, it could encourage a non-nuclear war. Given the adversarial nature of the U.S.–Soviet relation, had there been no nuclear weapons, the chances that there would have been a non-nuclear war between our two countries would have been very substantially higher during the past 35 years. One can argue: "That may be true, but if a nuclear war happens, it would be so much worse that it would have been better to risk the non-nuclear war"—and that's an argument you can get into. For the moment, I only argue the stabilizing effect of nuclear weapons, however dreadful a failure of deterrence would be. Even if there were a perfect or near-perfect defense, there could still be a destabilizing effect in terms of relations with others, and certainly the Europeans see this very clearly and are very concerned about it.

Let's now look at imperfect defense. If you are hardly able to defend populations, if by defense you can reduce the number of warheads that fall on cities by a factor of two (which would be similar to the effect of reducing the number of warheads by a factor of two with an arms control agreement) the establishment of such an imperfect defense could again be destabilizing, depending upon the effect of what would happen if one side were able to preemptively attack the defenses of the other, or what one side might gain in a preemptive attack on offensive forces, or both. That is a matter of difficult, detailed analysis, but some has been done, and it appears that it may well be destabilizing. The situation could be even more destabilizing during the establishment of defenses, because the mutual phasing of deployments would be a very, very delicate matter. As you can see—from what I have said here and from what I have said more extensively elsewhere—I have serious reservations, to put it mildly, about the Strategic Defense Initiative: technical, military, strategic, and political reservations about its feasibility and about its advisability. But active strategic defense in its various aspects—air defense, conventional ballistic missile defense with radars and ground-launched interceptors, research on space-based ballistic missile defense— is a fact of life as an issue and as a program, at least as much in the Soviet Union as in the United States. And we ought to confront it as a fact of life and ask ourselves and our allies to explore the criteria for stability and deployment and explore what should be the guidelines for permissible research and development. These are things that Paul Nitze has already raised, for example. We should do them bilaterally with the Soviet Union. And of course we have to make unilateral decisions as to what our programs ought to be; that is not a matter for bilateral discussion. As is the case for other weapons systems and other arms control issues, all this needs to be done within an overall military, technical, strategic, and, above all, political context. Thank you very much.

President Carter: I would like to introduce Dr. Richard Garwin next. He has been a very fine spokesman during this project in analyzing previous arms negotiations and also the impact of technology on future negotiations. He is deeply dedicated to bettering our understanding of nuclear weaponry and arms control. He is an IBM Fellow at the Thomas J. Watson Research Center, and he also holds faculty appointments at Columbia, Cornell, and Harvard universities. That is enough in itself to make him an admirable teacher, and we are very delighted to have Dick Garwin make his presentation at this point.

Richard Garwin: Thank you, Mr. President. I speak from a thirty-four-year involvement with the technology and policy of hydrogen bombs, military satellites, arms control and other aspects of security. I want to begin with a vision of where we could be in 1995 if we focus on our own security and own benefit. This is not a utopia, but is clearly more secure than where we are now. It is a very conservative prescription, because it leaves in place the importance of deterrence, not only of nuclear war but of conventional war; leaves in place the possibility of battlefield explosions and of first use of nuclear weapons; it does not require any technological marvels; and it does not demand that the lion lie down with the lamb.

As Secretary Brown indicated, the key is to maintain a commitment to the deterrence of war by the guarantee that the one who starts the war is going to lose by so doing, and as long as there are rational people in charge—and there are rational people over here—we can maintain that "countervailing strategy," as it has been dubbed in the past. We have now about 25,000 nuclear weapons; the Soviets have a similar number. Of these about 10,000 are strategic nuclear weapons, and a similar number for them—a few less. There is no reason, maintaining this conservative prescription of deterrence, why we should not be satisfied with 1,000 nuclear weapons on either side—1,000 warheads. Of course this could not be achieved if the other three significant nuclear powers in the world— China, France, and the United Kingdom—carried out their plans and built to a level of 1,000 also. So one would hope that they would see it in their interest to have the United States and the Soviet Union reduce by a factor of twenty-five the number of nuclear weapons in their stockpiles, and these other three nations might stop or return to a level of about 300 each.

Such a circumstance—1,000 nuclear warheads—can be managed so as to reduce the vulnerability of the retaliatory force, because there would be a lesser threat on the other side. We would choose a basing system in which we do not mass many warheads together so they can be destroyed by a single one from the other side—as with ten warheads on the MX in a Minuteman silo. (Our total 1,000 would be exhausted if we built 100 MXs, which could be destroyed by one-tenth of the force that the Soviet Union would be allowed.) I would choose to base about 400 single-warhead Minuteman missiles in the existing silos (ten years from now we could modify our system and have a small missile with one warhead, based so as to require the most weapons to destroy it); about 400 warheads on submarines—on 40 existing submarines, only ten warheads per submarine (very inefficient but it would cost less than what we have now on the same submarines) and about 200 air-launched cruise missiles on 100 bombers of whatever vintage we have at that time. So our vulnerability would be reduced from what it is now. We would maintain adequate flexibility to respond to one, a few, or hundreds of nuclear weapons—not by throwing away our nuclear weapons on unimportant targets, not by being unwilling to respond, but by choosing the most valuable targets to destroy with the nuclear weapons that we would use in response. Thereby we would deter not only our own destruction, but we would hope to deter the use of even one or a few nuclear weapons. If necessary, we would provide nuclear weapons against massed troops on the battlefield, in order to maintain the advantage of the threat of nuclear weapons: to keep conventional forces from massing into formations that are more effective conventionally and which are prevented by the threat of use of nuclear weapons. But we would not need nuclear weapons deployed on the battlefield in order to call forth explosions on the battlefield. In fact we have not needed that for fifteen years. We can react more quickly with nuclear weapons from a great distance than we can in calling up nuclear weapons from twenty kilometers away.

There are some implications of such a strong reduction in number of nuclear weapons. It is important for us because it would reduce the Soviet stockpile; we would have to pay for that in reducing our own stockpile; we would both benefit. Most important, though, is not reductions but, as Secretary Brown has said, reducing the likelihood of nuclear war, and now I want to explore how the likelihood of war would be reduced by an appropriate reduction of such magnitude. First, we will never be able to achieve such reductions in this period of ten or fifteen years unless there is a strict limitation on defense, so that deterrence will be possible with this rather smaller number of nuclear weapons than we have now. We have 10,000 strategic weapons; I propose 1,000. At present, we might even be heading toward 15,000 or 20,000 on the existing forces. But if there is no significant defense; if there is strict compliance with the ABM treaty on both sides (and a thorough discussion so that that treaty will cover not only the technology existing in 1972 but the technology which is coming into being and which doesn't quite fit the definition of components which was formulated in 1972) then 1,000 nuclear weapons is more than enough for deterrence.

In fact, in an article in the April 1985 issue of *Arms Control Today* the president's science advisor, Dr. Keyworth, says that ten or twenty nuclear warheads are all that any nation needs for deterrence. I will let him say that, but I think 1,000 are plenty in the absence of significant defense. That "absence of significant defense" really means that we must have a ban on antisatellite weapon tests and on space weapons, because we or the Soviet Union, in the guise of perfecting antisatellite weapons, could develop defenses against ballistic missiles. They would not work very well; I think I could defeat them with penetration aids and with attacks on the system; but I assure you that if the Soviet Union were developing those space weapons and continued ASAT tests we would be unable to achieve these reductions that I talk about. It would be politically impossible; it would be strategically unwise.

The purpose of this ban on ASAT tests and space weapons is not to prevent, eventually, some wonderful defense, if anybody thinks of how to do that 20 or 30 years from now. If the common security would be improved by deploying space weapons, that would be time enough to revise these treaties. But it is to prevent the emergence, in the intermediate time, of new systems which would imperil deterrence and prevent these reductions. In the phase of this low and stable number of retaliatory nuclear weapons, I think we should have a ban—a comprehensive ban on nuclear tests—perhaps achieved, as was indicated earlier, by this declining threshold as the technological means and the human means—the voluntary exchange of information—became a more stringent limitation on the threshold. The main purpose of this nuclear test ban would be to inspire and strengthen collaborative efforts to prevent the spread of nuclear weapons to other countries, which would be a danger not only to us and to the Soviet Union, but to all the countries in the world. As time goes on we ought to explore strengthening the nonproliferation regime by sanctions and guarantees against attack.

Now, what about the Strategic Defense Initiative? Well, what is the Strategic Defense Initiative? It is very difficult to say what it is because, according to Secretary Weinberger and Fred Ikle, strategic defense is the centerpiece of our security, now and henceforth. But according to Paul Nitze, speaking for the secretary of state and the president, strategic defense will be deployed only when it is survivable and cost-effective at the margin—not for decades. And the Strategic Defense Initiative right now is defined by those people who want money to pursue it as a research program—the first five years of which will cost $26 billion. (They don't tell you the next five years is still also a research program—probably about $50 billion—and after that a decision will be made as to whether it will do us any good to develop and deploy.) Earlier today, some things were said about the Strategic Defense Initiative: that it seeks to provide strategic defense by non-nuclear means, for instance. But the Strategic Defense Initiative includes a Department of Energy component with x-ray lasers pumped by a nuclear explosion. Those are not non-nuclear means. It also includes all of the Army's ballistic missile defense program office's activities, including the usual ballistic missile defenses: interceptors armed with nuclear warheads. The problem is not with these nuclear warheads. That is the only way we know now, if we had to, to deploy a ballistic missile defense of limited capability. The problem is with the definition of this Strategic Defense Initiative animal which is a different beast for different audiences.

Is it true that a strategic defense cannot be both ineffective and destabilizing, as Secretary Kissinger maintained? Let me give you an example of a weapon that is both ineffective and destabilizing. If you go to the dime store and buy for one dollar (or whatever you spend at the dime store these days) a plastic handgun, and you go up to an armed guard and point it at the armed guard, obviously this is an ineffective weapon, but it is extremely destabilizing and you are likely to end up dead. Similarly, there are strategic defenses which are both ineffective and destabilizing, and I think we have found one of them in a commitment to a Strategic Defense Initiative program. The problem is not that it will succeed; it will not succeed. It will not succeed, not because our technology is inadequate, but because the defense can be defeated by countermeasures more readily than it can be built. It will not be survivable; it will not be cost effective at the margin. It contains the seeds of its own destruction. For instance, the x-ray laser, which cannot be based in space according to the treaties and which, according to Edward Teller, would be too vulnerable if placed in space like any other defense, would be popped up from submarines or basing facilities on land. But if the other side, the first-striker (whoever that is) has x-ray lasers itself, they would launch them first on little rockets to be above their ICBMs at the moment of launch, and our x-ray lasers struggling to get into view of their ICBMs in boost phase would be zapped by their x-ray lasers. So technological success does not imply strategic benefits.

According to some, we absolutely need strategic defense. I think Secretary Kissinger mentioned "rogue nations," and others talk about countering "accidental launch" of one or a few ICBMs. According to the schedule, even a successful strategic defense initiative program—"Star Wars"—would not give you a worthwhile system for at least ten or fifteen years. What about all those accidental launches during the next decade—are we to do nothing about them? If you are worried, you ought to put a command-destruct link on our submarine-launched ballistic missiles and our ICBMs: the device we use in every test of a missile, so that if it flies out of a test range it is destroyed by a radio command. And ask the Soviets to do the same. The command would be coded, and if the Soviet Union (which is very careful about restraining their missiles) accidentally launched one of those missiles toward the United States, they could destroy it by radio command, and they could immediately phone us up and tell us the code for destroying that particular missile. This would be far more effective, ready sooner, and cheaper than a strategic defense.

Suppose Libya, trying for all these years to obtain a nuclear weapon, bought an ICBM, fitted it with a stolen nuclear warhead, and held New York hostage. If there was ever a reason for covert action, that is one. On the other hand, we could have a backup: our nuclear-armed Minuteman II missiles, capable of striking a silo half a world away within a very short time window and a very small distance error, could easily make an intercept in space and destroy at a distance of 1,000 miles or more from our shores this single warhead launched by a rogue nation. So if we worry about that, that's what we ought to do, not something called the Strategic Defense Initiative program, which is going to drive the Soviet Union to expand its offensive force, to test ASAT systems; and I do not think they would be able to refrain from making a similar system, not because it will work any better for them, but because they have people who love technology as well.

What has kept us from such reductions? The desire to expand—not for expansion's sake, but because we worry recurrently about the survivability of our missiles—their destruction before launch—and so we need more, or different, basing systems. Worse than that is the search, not for superiority—we have never actively sought superiority—but we insist on parity. The problem with parity is that it is precisely equivalent to superiority, because people on the two sides look at the existing balance with different eyes. They envy what the other side has, and they want to build more of that character, so you never hear about our superiority in bombers and air-launched cruise missiles and number of warheads at sea; you hear about the superiority in Soviet throw-weight; in time-urgent hard-target kill capability. When it comes to remedying that deficiency, we rarely do. We do something else. We prize these deficiencies, because if we didn't have them, it would be very difficult to persuade the American public to do what we think needs to be done.

I think we can achieve a reduction, if not to 1,000, then, 2,000—we will live with that for ten, or twenty, or thirty years and see what we can do in further reductions, either in warhead numbers or in tensions. But we must not, in my opinion, go forward with a strategic defense initiative program; we can go forward with some of the research, especially on observation, verification, survivability, but I think we have to abandon a commitment to a defense. A defense which will replace offensive weapons is not feasible; the defenses that are feasible are not desirable because of their side effects. Thank you.

President Carter: Our next speaker will be David Jones, a scholar and an intellectual, a strategist, a distinguished military leader, and former chairman of the Joint Chiefs of Staff. It's a great pleasure to have you here.

David Jones: Thank you, Mr. President, President Ford.

As maybe the only person here that served in a fairly senior position under each of the last four presidents, I would like to make a couple of observations, and I believe they will recognize the problem I'm talking about. This morning when you called for a break, Mr. President, you instructed the group to stand in place and not leave the room, and immediately two thirds left the room, and it just confirms that presidential decisions and instructions are still not always carried out.

Sitting here and listening to all these comments confirms where I believe the U.S. military and—in my private conversations with them—where the Soviet military tend to stand, and that is someplace between the super-hawks and the super-doves. The Joint Chiefs of Staff unanimously have supported all of the arms control agreements we've made—with some reservations in some areas—but through the years they have been supportive of the actions, although not pleased with every detail. They have had many of the concerns that have been expressed by others as to the relationship with the Soviet Union. And there is a greater tendency in all the arguments to be too technical and too simple at the same time. We tend to oversimplify things. My friend John Lehman, talking about NATO, and saying that there is some sort of plan, that we would build to 178 ground force divisions, while he said we have had only 18 divisions on our side. Here in Georgia you would be surprised to know that one of your divisions is not counted by John Lehman, or a lot of other forces in the States are not counted— our great reserve forces, many of which are better than many in the Soviets' 178. He does not count all of our NATO divisions; he does not take into account that the Soviets have one-fourth of their divisions facing China.

Sam Nunn has been the architect of increasing and improving our conventional capability in Europe, but not to fight a World War III, not a long war of attrition in the sense of repeating what happened in the 1940s; more effort is needed to raise the nuclear threshold; it is more complicated than just trying to match the Soviets division for division. With regard to the strategic nuclear forces, I first got involved as a young aide to General Curtis LeMay when he was commander-in-chief of the Strategic Air Command back in the 1950s when we had the "Open Sky" proposals and so forth, and ever since I have been concerned about the oversimplification of talking about strategic parity and who's ahead? and do we have a window of vulnerability? Five years ago all the talk in this country was about the tremendous window of vulnerability. President Ford eloquently talked about the programs that really were started by him or—some of them—even earlier and were continued by President Carter. I disagreed with President Carter on cancellation of the B-1, but if you look at our strategic force today, it's about what was laid out many, many years ago. We are planning to have 100 B-1s. Where we earlier had a consensus in the Congress and strong support for 200 MXs, and some of those MXs would be in the ground today— we are probably going to get 40. My friends in the Congress say 40 to 50 MXs, based in a very vulnerable mode. So with all these puts and takes, it is not much different now than it was five years ago and not much different, from a force standpoint, than it was planned to be by this time. There is more emphasis on command and control—a subject that we pushed very hard. But overall with the strategic offensive forces there has been a change in perception that somehow this window that was open now has been closed. And Ambassador Dobrynin has made a comment that even some Americans have used: that because we have said we would not swap forces, it meant there was at least an overall balance. We are much more of a maritime nation than the Soviets; they are much more of a continental-type nation. We have different force requirements, and that's really what we're talking about when we say we would not swap forces—not "Are they mirror-imaged?" or "Are they totally equal in every regard?" And there are great asymmetries. In my home state of North Dakota there was an old saying that you can drown in a stream with an average depth of three feet. The Soviets have advantages in certain areas and we have advantages in other areas, so it is pretty hard to say whether they are ahead or we are ahead; they are ahead in some areas and we are ahead in other areas, and what we are worried about is that the confrontation may happen in an area in which they have an advantage.

With regard to first-strike capability: that is a term used by a lot of people very glibly, used by Soviets and by Americans and not by most knowledgeable military people on both sides. In my discussions with them I found that the Soviets really don't believe that either side can get a first-strike capability in the sense that one side could take actions to disarm the other side so much by offense or defense that they would not have some retaliatory capability left. Of the 10,000 strategic weapons that Dick Garwin talks about, about five percent of those would kill 100 million Americans if aimed at our cities or close to that number if aimed at Soviet cities—five percent of the largest types of weapons. More Americans would be killed, because our population is more vulnerable and because the Soviets have more megatonnage. But in any case we are talking about hundreds of millions of people. By saying this I do not mean that I believe we have overkill (again a great simplification), that just because we can kill 100 million Soviets with a small part of the force everything else is unneeded. An overall balance is important. It is important to have more than a small force aimed only at cities. That is not a good strategy. We have not had that as a strategy at any time. Our strategic forces are primarily directed against Soviet military targets and only secondarily against what we call their urban-industrial areas. In my discussions with the Soviet military I found that they do not believe any more than we do that either side can win a nuclear war in any meaningful sense of winning a war. In arms control we have found, very frankly, that people at both ends of the political spectrum expect too much from arms control: that somehow it is going to be so successful that all problems will go away and that only different tactics are needed to achieve this tremendous outcome in arms control. It is a slow, tedious process, and the process, in my judgment, is almost as important as the results. You could have both sides scrap 5,000 nuclear weapons today, and we wouldn't be any more stable if the tensions between the countries—the political, and all the other problems—were not in the process of getting solved, and if some degree of confidence by one side in the other side was not established. So the process is very important. But we are very, very suspicious of each other in the arms control negotiations.

I said in jest to one of my Soviet colleagues that we ought to swap positions today rather than wait ten years. What I was alluding to was that, if you go back about twelve or fifteen years, we were for MIRV—multiple independently targetable re-entry vehicles—with large numbers of warheads on one intercontinental ballistic missile—but the Soviets were against it. Now we would like to get the ICBMs "de-MIRVed" to a single warhead, to the Midgetman missile, and the Soviets do not want to go in this direction. We were the ones who advocated ballistic missile defense first, and for eight years we worked with the Soviets on trying to secure ballistic missile defense agreement, and they were reluctant to have it. Now, we are the ones who want to modify the ABM treaty, and they do not want to modify it. The problem is on both sides, and there is great suspicion. The Soviets think we are paranoid. We know they are. The basic suspicions build up. There needs to be a way to somehow break through these tremendous suspicions, and one thing that I have advocated is a good dialogue among military leaders.

I accompanied President Carter to Vienna in 1979 and met with Marshal Ogarkov, and Harold Brown and I met with Marshal Ustinov. My meeting with Marshal Ogarkov was the first time that the senior military people of our two countries had met since General Marshall and Marshal Zhukov met right after World War II. And I found that meeting very useful, not so much in the plenary sessions but in the one-on-one with Marshal Ogarkov. In discussing the issues there were clear misperceptions, clear suspicions on both sides, and I thought: what a tragedy it was that all these years we did not have a dialogue at the senior military level. I know that in the navy it has been fruitful that after incidents at sea the senior military people meet and are able to work out small problems—not the major problems between our countries, but they work out some. I think there is one area where a meeting of top military officers could be very helpful, in quiet, not negotiating, not trying to take over the jobs of the secretaries of state or the negotiators: that is on verification. Both sides express concerns about verification. The Soviets expressed some concerns about our side, and we said we are meeting every treaty obligation, and we say to them, we are convinced that you are not abiding by certain agreements. The Standing Consultative Commission is not working very well now, and one reason is we are trying to verify treaties that have not been ratified, and that makes it much more difficult. If we could sit down and try to examine some of these suspicions and misperceptions of each side, such as those relating to verification, there could be better understanding. Secretary Kissinger said this morning that in coming to any agreement we recognize you cannot verify it one hundred percent, but any deviations from it would destroy the value of the agreement in the first place. The problem is that when there are anomalies or variations or violations, it may not impact upon the balance but it certainly impacts upon subsequent negotiations and creates increasing suspicion. So I think we could talk at the military level about intrusive inspections—intrusive may be the wrong word, but somehow verification by other than satellites alone. The Soviets believe that we push for intrusive inspections because we want to send some spies into the Soviet Union. With the proper dialogue, there are ways that we can have some sort of mutual inspection system without going beyond the bounds of that. A dialogue among the military people could be very, very useful in this regard. Since I left the military a couple of years ago I have had the opportunity to be a part of the Dartmouth group with Brent Scowcroft and have had a dialogue with some of the Soviet officials, both military and civilian, and I have found that very useful. It reinforces my belief that it is fundamental for both sides to agree that their military people quietly meet to discuss some of these critical issues that face our countries. I think this can help arms control a great deal in the long run, and also the broader issue of the differences within our country and many of the tensions that face both of our countries. Thank you, Mr. President.

President Carter: Those of you who are familiar with what goes on in the Oval Office and the Cabinet Room realize that the negotiations taking place between the leaders of the United States and the Soviet Union are not the only ones. Our first negotiations, at least on my part, had to be with the Joint Chiefs of Staff and with Harold Brown and with Cy Vance and the American delegation, who would go together many months later to negotiate with the Soviets. Of course that went along with constant negotiation with members of the Congress so that we would present a point of view that would be acceptable. When I went to Vienna to negotiate the final stages of SALT II, David Jones and Harold Brown and others here went along with me. You can see the quality of knowledge that they have, scientific and otherwise, but ordinarily when we got into a very difficult discussion the standard reply was: "We'll have to ask Bill Perry." And Bill Perry is here with us this afternoon. He was the Undersecretary of Defense for Research and Engineering, and is now a managing partner of H & Q Technology Partners. Bill, we are delighted to have you. Thank you for coming.

William Perry: Thank you, President Carter, President Ford.

In a well-ordered society it would seem that the proper order would be to decide what national security policy we desired and then, having decided that, determine what weapon systems would support that national security policy. In fact in this age of dramatic technological development it has not happened that way. We did not decide that we wanted to have a policy of assured deterrence and then go out to invent the atomic bomb to achieve that policy. It happened just the other way around, of course. In fact it was a good many years after the development of the atomic bomb that assured deterrence was articulated as a policy or strategy. Now, because of a variety of problems with that policy, some real and some perceived, it is being re-examined. The president has the view, for reasons that are easy to understand, that it would be better if we had a strategy or policy of assured survivability—if we had some way of protecting our population. Now—proceeding in the proper order—having determined that this is a desired policy, we are going to determine what kind of technology and what kind of weapons systems are appropriate to achieve that policy. That is the Strategic Defense Initiative program, which of course has led to a debate in this country, both as to the desirability and the feasibility of the Strategic Defense Initiative. This debate has been characterized primarily by confusion, and the confusion has arisen from a variety of factors, not the least of which is what Dr. Kissinger called "the manifold definitions of the Strategic Defense Initiative." But it has also been confused by the various opponents and proponents in the way they have argued it. I hope today that, instead of adding to that confusion, I would add some clarification to some of the issues.

It seems to me that the opponents of the strategic defense have confused the issue in several ways in their arguments about the desirability of the program. They have called into question the president's sincerity, saying that what he really wants is strategic superiority rather than this assured survivability. They have raised the question as to whether it is somehow fundamentally or inherently wrong to conduct a battle in space, and finally they have thought that the objective was not desirable because of the difficulty and the cost in achieving it. Now, my own view on those points is that I have no doubt that the president is sincere in this objective. I am totally skeptical of the people who are concerned about the sanctity of the heavens, as they say, for a battleground. If a battle has to be fought, I would rather it be fought in space than on the earth. I would hope, though, that we have a third choice between those two alternatives and can find a way of avoiding the battle altogether. In terms of the desirability of the objective, I believe that assured survivability is an exceedingly desirable objective, and if it were feasible, I would not be discouraged by either the cost or the time or the difficulty of achieving that objective.

So much for the opponents. Let me talk about the proponents and confusion factors. The proponents, it seems to me, have confused the issue of the strategic defense program as if it were synonymous with the feasibility of protecting the population from attack. Now I am a technological optimist, and my view today is based on my view of technological optimism. I believe that the strategic defense program as advocated by the Defense Department is indeed feasible; that is, if we look at the various technical objectives of that program—lasers and particle beam weapons, computers and communications and antimissile missiles—we can probably achieve each of those individual technical objectives. It may take longer, and it may cost more than anybody believes, but I think they are achievable. But even if all of those technical goals are achieved, in my opinion, it will not lead to assured survivability; it will not succeed in the policy objective of protecting the population against a nuclear attack, and I believe that, no matter how long or hard we work at it, or how clever we are.

Now inasmuch as the system is not defined very well today, it is hard to prove that point by looking at a specific system and arguing specific points of its feasibility. I would instead base my argument on the fact that throughout the history of weaponry there has been no perfect weapon. When you are dealing with a determined opponent, there are always countermeasures which, to some extent or another, can degrade your weapon, so you will not have a weapon system. Dr. Garwin already pointed out the jujitsu effect of the technological program in strategic defense. For example, the very same lasers that we can develop—the very same technical improvements we can make in lasers—to improve our ability for strategic defense, simply allow the person who is trying to penetrate a strategic defense to use that same technology to find ways of penetrating the defense. The same technology developments which will develop the communications and the computers necessary for a strategic defense system is the same technology necessary for improving the offensive force and managing the countermeasures that go with the defensive force. Therefore it is clear that technology is a two-edged sword. It can, indeed, be invoked by the side that is developing the strategic defense. It can be equally invoked by the side which is trying to defeat or degrade the strategic defense. So the question is not whether or not we are enthusiastic about technology, whether or not we're optimistic about technology, but recognizing that in a world of countermeasures, technology applies on both sides of the equation. This is not to mention the perhaps even more persuasive concern that, were we to be able to develop a strategic defense system totally capable of defeating ballistic missiles, the ballistic missiles are by no means the only means of delivering nuclear bombs; they can be delivered by bombers, by cruise missiles or, in the Lebanese style, by delivery trucks, or by satchels in covert ways. It is beyond imagination to think that we could stop all the different ways of delivering nuclear weapons that could be used by a determined opponent against a helpless civilian population.

In sum, then, I would say with certainty—with great certainty—that over the next decade we can and no doubt will make major advances in the technologies associated with strategic defense. It is probable that those defenses or that technology could lead to a defensive system which would be substantially more capable than any defensive system which is envisioned today. It is possible that that defensive system could be used to enhance deterrence, but in my opinion it is beyond the realm of possibility that this system could really provide assured survivability to a civilian population against an opponent determined to attack that population. My conclusion from all of this is that we should proceed with research and development in this technology. I think it is an important technology, but I believe the scope of the program that we proceed in, the commitment to testing and deployment, and most importantly the whole set of other measures we take relating to the other parts of our nuclear system—all should be considered in light of reality, of what could reasonably be achieved by this research and development program, rather than by the fantasy of what we think we would like it to achieve. Thank you.

President Ford: Bill, the kind of research that you believe we should proceed with—would that kind of research be in violation of the ABM treaty?

William Perry: It would be in violation of the present ABM treaty when it reaches the point of system testing, and therefore I would not recommend carrying it to that point.

President Ford: Do you feel that proceeding to that point is desirable to give us the option, not knowing exactly how we might negotiate or proceed otherwise, with an ABM treaty?

William Perry: I think it is a prudent hedge—we do not know what the Soviet intentions in this field are, and perhaps they will enlighten us on that to-day. What we do know is: (1) they have a vigorous research and development program in ballistic missile defense and (2) they have deployed a major strategic defensive system; it's their bomber defense system, which we estimate has had more than one hundred billion dollars' worth of resources devoted to it. So we have to take seriously Soviet interest and a commitment to strategic defense, and therefore it is prudent to have a hedge against their extending that ballistic missile defense.

President Carter: Bill, how long have we been conducting research on the same subject?

William Perry: The research on this program dates back to President Ford's and President Carter's administrations; the high-energy laser research, in particular, and the particle beam research, for that goes back ten years or more.

President Carter: We developed our initial deployment of the ABM system before that, right?

William Perry: Yes, with research associated with it. Our decision not to have a conventional ABM system deployed was based on a judgment of the ineffectiveness of that system, not on any other consideration.

President Carter: Isn't the significant change in recent months the implied assurance to the American people that it's possible to put an umbrella over us that would be totally protective, and also, in effect, the substitution of the "Star Wars," or Strategic Defense Initiative, for deterrence as a major role of the strategic capabilities?

William Perry: Yes, I think that it is misleading to believe that that could happen, and it is incorrect to think we should simply wait to see where our research and development takes us and that maybe it will achieve this result, because irrespective of how successful the research and development now underway is, it will not lead to that conclusion, in my judgment. It can lead to a system which could be built and deployed and which would be far more capable than any system we have ever built until today, but it could not provide the assured survivability of a population against a determined attack. I do not think that is a realistic objective.

President Carter: What is the range of cost estimates—I know they are very wide—to consummate the SDI as envisioned by the president?

William Perry: You mean the budgetary scope of the system for doing that? I do not think there is any intelligent way of making a real estimate on such a system as that today. It certainly will be measured in many hundreds of billions of dollars to build and deploy a system anything like the kind of systems that are indicated by the research and development program. In short, if we are going to build a system which involves many battle stations in space, it will be a very expensive system. But if—again, I would say if—I thought that that kind of a system could protect the population against an attack, I myself would be willing to consider that expense.

President Ford: I assume that following World War I, the theory of the Maginot Line was the same one: that if you built enough steel between France and Germany, that was the best way to resolve any threat from the Germans. But it was a total failure. They went over it, around it, and through it. That concept of total reliance on defense was misleading and a disaster—a catastrophe. Although I am strongly in favor of all the research, and maybe would go further than you, I fear that for us to assume in the interim that that will be a replacement for a deterrence predicated on offense is a mistake. I just don't think it would be wise for us to put all our eggs in the defensive basket. We have to have a twin capability, both offensive and defensive, until we have much more evidence than I've seen. Although I am for research to pick up that evidence, I believe it would be unwise, very unwise for us to change a policy of deterrence that has been pretty successful over a long period of time. [*Perry:* I agree.]

President Carter: We have had several references made to the scientific community and research community in the Soviet Union, and I would now like to call on Academician Velikhov, who is a designated representative of General Secretary Gorbachev. He is a deputy director of the Kurchatov Institute of Atomic Physics, a vice president of the Soviet Academy of Sciences, and also a professor of physics at Moscow State University.

Evgeny Velikhov: Thank you, Mr. President Carter. First of all I am not representing our government here. I am here only in a personal capacity. I think the presentation of General Scowcroft is very exact and comprehensive. I only wish to make some comments: first of all, about our understanding of the problem of and nature of nuclear conflict. To my knowledge we have a very wide consensus among the military authority of our country, and at the political level, and in the public, about the completely disastrous consequences of nuclear conflict. In this case I completely agree with Professor Brown: we need not study how to fight nuclear war; our main goal is how to prevent nuclear war. [*Dobrynin:* But he was doubtful about our position in this quarrel.] I will try to answer. I am very skeptical of any discussion of the nuclear option or nuclear war strategy, because for such a discussion we need knowledge, and we have only two choices: to have the exact knowledge and no people or to have people and not the exact knowledge. From the point of view of the arms race, in our working group President Carter raised the very important question: is there really a consensus in U.S. military circles and in the public that parity is satisfactory, or do they need some lead in the technology or in quantity of arms to feel themselves safe? This is a very fundamental question. Of course I agree with Professor Garwin: it is a very difficult problem because to define parity is itself a very difficult problem. But if the consensus is to wish to have some lead, we will never achieve the goal of stopping the arms race, either in quality or in quantity, because this lead mostly depends on technology development. It would use some achievement in new technology, and in such a case it is technology that would drive the arms race.

Another very important question is connected to modernization and reductions. I think it would be totally wrong to rely on "modernization" as a way to enhance strategic stability and mutual security without arms reductions. Let us mention the 5,000 Midgetmen; in my view it is a very unattractive goal. And I think Professor Garwin's point: we need a very drastic reduction first of all and after this, maybe—if it is really important after such reductions—modernization. On the question of antimissile systems—"Star Wars," I appreciate the remark of Mr. Lehman about our common sense, but I am not sure our sense today is common. Our sense tells us, in the case of the development of antimissile systems, that the most effective and simplest and cheaper reply is countermeasures, active and passive. Also, I think there is another peculiarity of this development connected with the SDI program. If we analyze the whole possible set of consequences of this kind of development we could find that the main possible result will not be the result which will lead to the more or less "impressive" antiballistic missile defense, but the first immediate result possibly will be the reaching of a weapons level which will be quite effective against any antiballistic missile system. Among them some technical means will be achieved which will be adequate for anti-space weapons but not weapons for the strategic defense system.

Another question which I think is very fundamental is connected with the development of a broad-scale antimissile system: how is it possible to rely on a very complicated, an extremely complicated, system without full system test? In such case I think we would face the same problems with nuclear weapons: we have no knowledge without testing, but after testing we would have nothing left to defend. But of course today we have a very misleading signal from the American side. What does the Strategic Defense Initiative mean? When we read the American publications we saw the five-year guidelines for development of defense, and in these guidelines the goal is to achieve the level of development of technological confidence, which would allow deployment of a full system in a very short time. And in such a case, of course, it is a very serious problem, because in any case it is in violation of the Antiballistic Missile Treaty, and in some ways it is like a very serious problem we faced in June of 1941 when Hitler did not violate any treaty before he concentrated his army on the border of the Soviet Union, but he did violate it in one night after this. In such a case, of course, we need to develop countermeasures. And my conclusion is this: for us it will not be very difficult and burdening to match this development, but I think the development of the Strategic Defense Initiative or "Star Wars" technology on such a scale would be a very big obstacle to achieving real reductions in nuclear arms.

My last comment is connected to the problem of a potential arms race in space. My understanding is that proposals not to put any weapons in space are broader and may be much more important than any discussion of the Strategic Defense Initiative alone, and I am surprised that it has such a low priority today on the American agenda for discussion. I think if we transform space into a new battlefield, we are going to have a very difficult situation, which is improper. I think the American people are very unhappy with this situation because the American public is sensitive to having weapons 1,000 miles from the American continent—from their home. But what if both countries go to a situation where we have some sort of weapons hundreds of miles up in the sky? If we lose time and do not prevent this development, it will be very difficult for us in the future to treat this problem in a constructive way, to go back, just as it is now with MIRVing. I think there is consensus today that the MIRVing was a mistake but it is very difficult to de-MIRV today; it will be the same with space. The conclusion of a treaty to ban all weapons in space is extremely important in this case, and the Soviet Union is paying great attention to this proposal. We already have had a moratorium for two years. Today the Soviet Union does not put into outer space any antisatellite weapons, and it would be very important if the American side will join our unilateral moratorium on such tests, and then we will go from moratorium to a ban of space weapons. Thank you very much.

President Carter: I would like to ask Brent Scowcroft, as chairman of the panel, to take a few minutes to summarize.

Brent Scowcroft: Thank you, Mr. President. Just a couple of very quick points. As to John Lehman: I am used to being a straw man for John Lehman. In the substance of what he said he has already been answered adequately; after castigating me for what he wanted me to have said, he went on to demonstrate the accuracy of what in fact I had said.

On the notion of deep reductions as mentioned by Dick Garwin: I think his focus is wrong and that the number of nuclear weapons is much less important than the character of those weapons. Indeed, as one gets down to numbers as low as 1,000, the premium on cheating and deceiving grows because a few makes such a difference. You put a perhaps unbearable strain on verification and actually accentuate instability.

On weapons in space I think again the notion, the emphasis, is miscast. I think it is far less important where the weapons are than what they do and what the political and military implications of the weapons are. The two sides appear to be at polar opposites on the issue of strategic defense, but I think it is important to note that the Soviet position is a political position, not a military position, as Bill Perry noted. They have spent at least $100 billion on a massive air defense system; they have probably outspent us so far since the ABM treaty on ABM research; and, a third point which he did not mention, they have an operational ABM system around Moscow which they have recently modernized. We abandoned ours because it was too expensive to keep up even for the lesson to be learned. So it is apparent that strategically the Soviets take defense very, very seriously, and if we can get beyond the rhetoric, it may be that an examination of technology might show some way that some modification of the ABM treaty could, in fact, enhance the security of both sides. Thank you.

Session 3
Negotiation and Diplomatic/Political Aspects

Howard Baker: President Carter, President Ford, my colleagues on this panel—and what a distinguished group you are, and an equally distinguished audience who will participate in this program as well. I am delighted to be here. President Carter and I served together, in a way. I was the Republican leader of the Senate of the United States; President Carter of course was a Democratic president of the United States. And I was called upon to introduce him once in my hometown of Knoxville, Tennessee, shortly after the opening of the World's Fair there. It was an unexpected pleasure that I was to introduce President Carter to my hometown group at this luncheon. I thought about it very hard, and finally I came up with this: I really admire and respect President Carter. We agreed on some things, and we disagreed on some things, but I must say to my fellow Georgian, the former president of the United States; he was the only president we have had in my lifetime who had absolutely no accent that I could detect.

But President Carter, I am delighted to be here and I am happy to have this opportunity to speak briefly at the beginning of this session of this significant, indeed historic, occasion. President Ford, it is a real pleasure for me to be with you once more. I remember so many occasions when we worked together in politics. We have known each other for many years since I was a young man—a condition from which I have now fully recovered. But I have an extraordinarily high regard for President Ford in a special and unique way, perhaps, because a part of my career in the Senate—and a happy part of my career—was involved in the trials and tribulations of the early and mid-1970s. There was a genuine political upheaval in this country, and I saw firsthand the special contribution that President Gerald Ford made to the restoration of stability, the restoration of respect, and the restoration of political institutions. I honestly wish to state that I do not know of another person who could have served our country as well under those circumstances as did Gerald Ford.

President Ford and President Carter, my concluding remark is this: I believe that in American politics, and certainly in the affairs of nations, there is an urgent requirement for civility, for an understanding of differing points of view, an understanding and appreciation of disagreements honestly made, and different points of view, honestly held. I believe that in our own country there is an urgent requirement for bipartisanship in foreign policy and in domestic policy as well. We have a long and distinguished history of bipartisan cooperation in the field of foreign policy in times of national emergency. It is not so well established nor so visible at times when the national emergency is not so acute or so apparent. I wish to express my personal appreciation to these two former presidents of the United States, one a Republican and one a Democrat, for coming together to sponsor this program and to present to the people of this country a bipartisan approach to what must be the ultimate question that is confronting public servants and officials in every country of the world; that is, survival in this nuclear age. It is my pleasure to be a part of this symposium; it is my pleasure to pay these tributes to two presidents of the United States who richly deserve them, and to say that I appreciate—as I believe the country will appreciate—the good example that they continue to set in their cooperation for the most lofty of all purposes. My friends, it is now my pleasure to yield to a former colleague, my friend from Georgia, Senator Sam Nunn. Sam and I have served together in the Senate, he since he went there in 1972—I went in 1966. I have now graduated to a higher estate; I am once more a civilian. But from the civilian perspective, I continue to have a great admiration for the statesmanship, diligence and intellect, and the special contribution that Sam Nunn makes, not only in the field of national defense and foreign policy, but the general conduct of the affairs of this nation. Sam, I am delighted to be on the program and I yield the floor.

Sam Nunn: President Carter, President Ford, my colleague and friend, Senator Baker, distinguished guests, ladies and gentlemen—I am particularly honored to be here on this historic occasion in the state of Georgia and on the campus of my alma mater, Emory University. I am particularly delighted also to be here with Howard Baker, a man who typified the bipartisan approach in his tenure in the United States Senate and in his leadership of the majority, and before that, the minority of the United States Senate. Howard not only had vast experience in that regard; he also served on the Foreign Relations Committee for many years and acquired a very strong background and knowledge in national security affairs, foreign policy, and military affairs, and particularly arms control. So Howard, I am delighted to co-chair this conference with you today.

President Carter, we thank you for what you've done for our country and what you are doing here with your center. This program is certainly not the beginning but is, from my perspective, the highlight so far of your endeavors, and they are going to pay dividends, not only for our state but for our nation and for the world for years to come.

President Ford, thank you for coming to Georgia. We appreciate the exemplary and unprecedented fashion in which you and President Carter are embarking on numerous joint ventures together in the bipartisan spirit that is required and necessary, as Senator Baker said, to solve the very difficult problems facing our nation. We particularly note that you have made the supreme sacrifice by being on the campus of Emory University rather than the greens of Augusta, Georgia, this weekend. We hope you will have time to take in another Georgia event before the weekend is over.

I was pleased to have a chance to be here for most of yesterday, and without any doubt as far as I am concerned this was the most distinguished group of panelists that I have ever seen in one group on one occasion, in one location, discussing national security and arms control. I think our panel this morning was outstanding, and I have read the report that was put together by Ralph Earle and his panel. I look forward to hearing the vigorous discussion this morning. I believe that the report is a real masterpiece, concise and simple enough for even politicians to read. I did that last evening. I think that it is going to stimulate a great deal of meaningful and useful discussion.

Napoleon was once reported to have said, "Men can do anything with bayonets but sit on them." With nuclear weapons, I do not know what Napoleon would say, but I think somewhat the reverse is true. We must make certain that nuclear weapons are not used in the world. I was particularly delighted to see several references in this report and in other reports to some of the mutual interests that the United States and the Soviet Union have, and certainly right at the forefront of them is making sure we never have a war of any kind, and certainly not one that is inadvertently started, by accident, or by miscalculation, or by terrorist groups or by Third World countries. Sometimes I think we get so carried away with debating the differences that we superpowers have that we overlook some of our fundamental mutual interests, and I would put avoiding accidental war right at the top of that list. So I hope we're able to discuss that this morning. Senator Baker, I hope we can run this as much as possible on time. I know that the panelists have been asked to stay between seven and ten minutes; if President Carter and President Ford will permit me to do so I am going to slip the panelists a note when they've gotten to the seven-minute mark. It will not be intrusive intervention, Mr. Dobrynin, and others, but it will be a reminder that we have a distinguished group here. We have a distinguished audience here that I hope can participate, and Senator Baker, I will play that role with your permission. Thank you for allowing me to be here.

Howard Baker: President Ford, President Carter, at this point, ladies and gentlemen, it is my pleasure to present to you Ambassador Ralph Earle, who is known to all of you who have an interest in foreign policy. As the program indicates, he is the former director of the Arms Control and Disarmament Agency and was the chief negotiator for SALT II in Geneva. He is now a managing partner of Baker & Daniels. My first experience with Ralph Earle came in Geneva when he tried to lead me through the labyrinthian negotiations and rationale of negotiations between the United States and the Soviet Union at that time, which led to the document referred to as SALT II. It is my pleasure, then, to yield at this point to Ralph Earle, who will make the presentation of the report.

Ralph Earle: Thank you, Senator Baker. President Ford, President Carter, Senator Nunn, I would like to make one personal comment. In the summer of 1979 I spent what seemed like five years testifying in front of Senator Baker, and it's nice to be on the same side of the table finally.

Our panel dealt with the subject of negotiations, and political and diplomatic aspects of arms control and international security. It was largely composed of American representatives, but there was a Soviet representative, and a representative from West Germany. We began and proceeded throughout our discussions of international security and arms control with the premise that the single most important goal that negotiations and diplomacy can hope to achieve is the avoidance of war, both conventional and nuclear. As I say, that was a given that we maintained throughout the proceedings.

The first thing we did was to seek common ground between the sides. And we concluded, that in connection with this goal of avoidance of war, the United States and the Soviet Union do have a number of parallel objectives, including survival, security, equality, and curtailing military expenditures. At the same time, we bore in mind that the two nations differ in a number of respects, both regarding the means by which their objectives—even these common objectives—can or should be achieved and, indeed, regarding the meaning of those objectives, even when the same words are used; for instance, equality may mean something quite different to the Soviet Union than it does to the United States, and vice versa. Having found those comon objectives, we then obviously had to turn to the differences. And the most natural and obvious one was the political aims of each side, which differ widely. Not only do the two superpowers espouse widely different political philosophies, but they also have highly divergent interests throughout the world in practical nation-state terms. Thus, unfortunately, but inevitably for the foreseeable future, the state of competition at best, or hostility at worst, is virtually unavoidable.

Arms control negotiations and agreements are an integral part of efforts to avoid war, as are many of those other goals I mentioned, but arms control by itself cannot prevent war and must be treated as one element, albeit an important one, in an overall strategy for assuring national and international security, strategic stability, and a peaceful world. In connection with negotiations, we did note that there are several going on right now. In Vienna, the negotiations on troop reductions in Central Europe;* the Stockholm Conference on confidence-building measures;† and the multilateral negotiations in Geneva, dealing particularly with the problem of chemical weapons; and of course the bilateral negoti-

---

*The Mutual and Balanced Force Reduction negotiations.

†The Conference on Security and Cooperation in Europe, begun in Helsinki in 1975 and renewed in Belgrade, Madrid, and, since January 1984, in Stockholm.

ations in Geneva,** which began last month. We also noted that there are some negotiations that are not going on that had been going on in the past such as antisatellite weapons negotiations, conventional arms transfers, and some others. The different systems of the two countries produce their negotiating policies and positions at the table in different ways. We spent a little bit of time on that issue, but concluded that it really didn't matter how we got there; it's where we got that counted.

We addressed the question of external pressures, and it is clear in that context that domestic politics play a particularly significant role in Western countries. The United States Congress has become increasingly involved in arms control. One beneficial result of that involvement is that I met Senator Baker. In the United States, public opinion has often been steadier than government policy over time, but in recent decades it has become increasingly difficult to keep foreign policy nonpartisan, and I would like to join Secretary Kissinger and the senators today in congratulating the two presidents here on this bipartisan effort.

And, somewhat surprisingly, we addressed the media's role in these matters. It was not surprising we addressed it; rather, the conclusion is somewhat surprising. We concluded that the media have not been primarily responsible for the swings in views on arms control and security issues. Public opinion has emerged as a major factor, particularly in Western Europe, as reflected in the debates of the past several years over deployment of American intermediate-range missiles. Both the American and the Soviet negotiating positions and public postures have been substantially affected by the consideration of the reaction of Western audiences, and this, in the view of most members of the panel, has led the superpowers to play to the grandstand. In this connection I should note a disagreement by our Soviet colleague, as well as by our NATO colleague, concerning this characterization of American negotiating positions. We also noted that as the Geneva negotiations have dealt increasingly with weapons systems affecting the military situation in Europe and elsewhere, in addition to the direct confrontation of the superpowers, consultation with our allies has increased proportionately. This has been a necessary and helpful development, and we expect it to continue and urge that it be continued.

There is a difficulty in making arms control policies consistent with military procurement and production decisions. General Scowcroft and his panel addressed this yesterday. Both sides tend to try to limit the other's modernization while keeping its own options open. The future impact on arms control is not always considered (very infrequently, from my experience) when research and development decisions are made. And the problem is further complicated because both sides' military modernization programs are out of phase with each other. One conclusion that the panel reached is that agreements with longer terms might

---

**The Talks on Nuclear and Outer Space Arms.

help deal with this problem, since five years, roughly the term of previous strategic offensive arms limitation agreements, is simply not long enough to affect research and development decisions over the long term.

The panel then turned to the problems of compliance with existing agreements and verification of existing and future agreements. The more complex and wide-ranging arms control negotiations become, the more important will be the issue of treaty compliance. In the past both sides have admittedly committed technical violations of a few agreements (such as inadvertent venting of radioactive material into the atmosphere from underground nuclear tests) and there have been problems in interpreting the terms of treaty requirements as well as in determining the facts of questionable events. To date this has not been a major problem (well, until very recently) because, first, it was not clear that such cases were deliberate; second, in general they have been dealt with satisfactorily in discussions of the Standing Consultative Commission, which was set up by the SALT I agreements and which continues to deal with just such questions; and, third, none of the violations or alleged violations went to the heart or the purpose of the treaty involved. However, most members of the panel believe that over the last few years there has been increasing evidence of Soviet violations of existing agreements, both ratified and unratified. Because of the nature of recent questions about compliance as well as other factors, the issue of verification is becoming much more politicized.

Turning to a specific agreement, the panel was in accord that the Antiballistic Missile Treaty of 1972 is a requisite for maintaining a stable deterrent for the foreseeable future, and should be reaffirmed. Research on ballistic missile defense is allowed by that treaty, and in any case is basically not subject to monitoring. It was also noted that it is uncertain how research programs could be controlled by negotiated agreements and that this issue will be more significant in the future if the United States and the Soviet research programs begin to identify promising technological possibilities. Most of the participants on the panel agreed that while strategic defense may occur, both superpowers' strategies will, for the foreseeable future, continue to depend upon offensive retaliation. The panel agreed that the serious negotiation of arms control, negotiation of arms control agreements in itself, provides an important channel for dialogue, and thereby can contribute to the reduction of misunderstanding and the increase of unilateral confidence. Arms control is not only a matter of immediate and practical importance in avoiding war, but it can also be a significant part of a long-range process of creating a structure of peace.

Given those matters that I have just reviewed, we have drafted, for your consideration, a number of recommendations:

We recommend that the United States and the Soviet Union continue to adhere to the Antiballistic Missile Treaty and the Outer Space Treaty, which bans nuclear weapons and other weapons of mass destruction in outer space, and that no steps be taken contrary to the terms of those treaties without negotiation.

We recommend that the United States and the Soviet Union continue their existing policies of not taking steps to undercut the provisions of treaties agreed to but not formally in effect, including the 1972 Interim Agreement on Limiting Offensive Arms, the Threshold Test Ban Treaty, and SALT II. And with respect to SALT II, we recommend that the definitions and other noncontroversial provisions of that treaty be carried forward into any future agreement. We recommend that the United States and the Soviet Union pursue negotiations to reduce and further limit offensive nuclear arms, both intercontinental and intermediate-range, taking into account, but without letting the possibility of future developments in strategic defensive systems inhibit, such reductions and limitations. I would like to come back to this subject in a moment.

The sides should take more constructive and imaginative steps regarding verification of compliance with future agreements, including cooperative measures as appropriate and necessary to enhance such verification. In this connection, issues of compliance should be dealt with by both sides in a manner which is aimed at their resolution, not their exploitation for political or propaganda purposes, and the same criterion should be applied to the negotiations themselves.

We recommend strongly that the United States and the Soviet Union address, with the utmost priority, the question of establishing mechanisms aimed at crisis prevention and crisis management in order to avoid misunderstandings or miscalculations which could lead to conflict.

We recommend that current and future negotiations continue to take into account the interests of allies and other countries, and that current and future negotiations, while not conducted in a vacuum, should at the same time not be held hostage to linkage with other unrelated issues between the sides.

We recommend that neither side seek to achieve real or apparent superiority through negotiations.

We recommend that in the future both sides move more ambitiously in limiting and reducing offensive arms without excluding limited steps in the short term. And we recommend that the public in both countries be educated to the fact that the issues are complex and that both sides enter the negotiations with major asymmetries, many of them immutable.

Finally, the panel is greatly concerned about the danger that the new negotiations in Geneva are heading for an early stalemate. The Soviet side appears to be unwilling to consider deep reductions in strategic offensive weapons as long as the possibility of new strategic defensive deployments is not definitively foreclosed. The American side, on the other hand, wishes to negotiate precisely such deep reductions while holding open the strategic defense option, pending completion of research to establish its feasibility. The panel believes that negotiation must proceed with full account of the strategic offensive-defensive interrelationship, exploring both offensive and defensive arms limitations. We further believe that an unregulated competition in both offensive nuclear weapons and strategic defenses would be disastrous, and that a cooperative transition toward deployment of extensive strategic defenses may not be feasible on either technical or political grounds, even if desirable in principle; therefore, our final recommendation is that the two sides now begin to examine what kinds of more far-reaching arms control agreements limiting offensive forces might be sufficient to stabilize the competition in a manner that would minimize or eliminate the incentives of either side to deploy extensive strategic defenses. Thank you, Mr. Chairman.

Howard Baker: Ambassador Earle, I thank you very much for the presentation of the report. The panel consists of men who are well versed in every aspect of this report and who are all qualified to speak first. I would choose, however, to ask Ambassador Dobrynin, who is the dean of the diplomatic corps in Washington, to make whatever comments he may wish at this time.

Anatoly Dobrynin: I have here a very good friend from Moscow, and he is eager to speak, so I yield the floor to him.

Sergei Tarasenko: Thank you, Senator Baker. I would like to begin by saying that it is a great honor for me to speak before this distinguished audience. In my view, the work of the third panel may serve as a model for successful arms control talks. Here in Atlanta the American side was represented by an extremely strong team. Frankly speaking, we in Moscow did not suppose that this administration had in mind Carter's seminar when it named its negotiating team for the Geneva talks. Here we have one more example of how good intentions can be misread by another side. We did not assume that the people in Washington knew beforehand that President Carter would need the best arms controllers here, the negotiators who in the past successfully withstood pressure from such experts as Mr. Semenov and Mr. Karpov of our side. The lonely Soviet member on this panel could hardly stand a chance. But the U.S. representatives of the panel used their "position of strength" very wisely, I would say, and the Soviet constructive position and attitudes are well known, for that matter. Ambassador Ruth acted as a skillful mediator and moderator on the panel and helped the work of the panel greatly. But it was the intervention of President Carter and Secretary Vance that saved the day. That proved once again that decisions on the political level are crucial for the success of these kinds of negotiations.

On a more serious note, I would like to stress most emphatically that we cannot afford a situation where arms race while talks crawl. Yesterday's discussions showed too clearly that technology has an ominous lead and may make talks obsolete even before they can gather speed. A practical way out, albeit a temporary one, would be—I would use the word "freeze," but knowing how deep aversion runs in some circles here against this very word, may I suggest another term, say, a "cooling-off period" or some "standstill arrangements" agreed upon between both sides. We are not suggesting that because we are ready to say "uncle" (as someone else has been invited to do). In our view it is absolutely necessary, if we are serious about arms control at all, to have such arrangements. And frankly speaking it is hard for us to understand why the American side does not want to have this "cool-off" opportunity. Even if we could agree to stand still for a day or a week or a month it would be of great importance for our negotiators and for the arms control process as a whole. Why not try that way? Again, it must be clear enough that it is difficult to try changing horses in midstream, specifically if the stream is so fast. So if we are to move to more stable deployments, we must create a more favorable environment for our negotiators in Geneva, and I think that beginning with a "standstill" or "cooling-off" period would be a great help to them. Thank you.

Howard Baker: I would propose now to yield to former secretary of state Cyrus Vance, who has served so well and so ably in many positions over the years, and who is now a distinguished practitioner of the law as well.

Cyrus Vance: President Carter, President Ford, Senator Baker, and Senator Nunn—first, let me say that I am very pleased to have been able to join in this set of discussions. I think, as other have said, that President Carter and President Ford have rendered a great service to all of us in bringing about this meeting, and I believe that it can come up with conclusions and some suggestions that may be of help to the parties in their negotiations. Let me say at the outset that I agree with the basic conclusions and recommendations of the study panel. I had very little to do with the drafting of that report, having come in at the very end of it. I feel that Ralph and his group have done an excellent job in winnowing out a set of principles to guide arms control negotiations. It is a wise and, I believe, practical set of recommendations.

Before addressing one of the most important recommendations contained in the report, I want to make a few general observations about the importance of arms control and the use of negotiations and diplomacy to help manage the political and military competition between the United States and the Soviet Union. I realize, sadly, that it is very popular these days to run down arms control as an effective and outdated political instrument. I do not agree with this view, and I do not believe that a majority of the American people share that view either. I start from the premise that a fundamental goal which all of us share is the avoidance of war—especially nuclear war. In order to achieve this goal it is necessary for the parties to apply a combination of firmness, realism, and a willingness to negotiate agreements that will cap the military competition and over time move us toward a more stable and less threatening posture on both sides. In the absence of such negotiations the arms competition will continue to spiral upward. Contrary to the assertion of some critics of arms control, I believe that neither side will let the other side achieve a significant military advantage by outspending the other. Whatever is required to maintain rough equivalence will be spent by both sides. Moreover, it is equally wrong to believe that either side has greater technological capabilities than the other. History teaches us that once one side gets a technological lead, it is soon matched or outdone by the other. We only have to look back and witness the development of the intercontinental ballistic missile, the development of the hydrogen bomb, the development of the MIRVing of missiles, and a host of other weapons. If this continues, then, I believe that the arms competition will continue to be ratcheted upward. And this leads me to the conclusion that the most effective way to turn down the arms competition is through painfully negotiated arms control agreements that are both fair and verifiable. As we all know, this is not an easy course to follow. It takes infinite patience, perseverance, imagination, and a willingness to strike a fair bargain, and I underline willingness to strike a fair bargain.

As Henry Kissinger pointed out yesterday, however, in the current circumstances it is not enough to confine the dialogue between ourselves and the Soviet Union to a discussion of arms control matters. I fully agree with Henry that it is critically important for the arms control negotiations to be accompanied by quiet and broad-ranging political discussions at a very high level, preferably at the foreign minister level. Discussion of political issues has been postponed too long, and I was happy to hear Anatoly Dobrynin say yesterday that a round of such talks is likely to take place in the near future between Secretary Shultz and Foreign Minister Gromyko. I hope that these talks will be pursued on a continuing basis. There is much to be discussed about a large number of subjects. In saying this I am not suggesting that the arms control negotiations should be linked to the political talks—quite the contrary. As the study panel suggests, the arms control negotiations, while not conducted in a vacuum, should, at the same time, not be held hostage to linkage with other unrelated issues between the two sides. As a matter of fact, there is a chance that political discussions can create a more positive climate for arms control negotiations.

Finally let me turn to a few brief comments on the last recommendation in the study panel's report. In this recommendation the panel points out (as Ralph Earle has indicated in his summary) that it is greatly concerned about the danger that the new negotiations in Geneva are heading for an early stalemate. I share that concern. The panel points out that the Soviet side appears to be unwilling to consider deep reductions in strategic offensive weapons as long as the possibility of new strategic deployments is not definitively foreclosed, and the American side wishes to negotiate precisely such deep reductions while holding open the strategic defense option pending completion of research to establish its feasibility. How do we deal with this problem and prevent the talks from getting bogged down at the outset? The panel suggests that the two sides now begin to examine what kinds of more far-reaching arms control agreements limiting offensive forces might be sufficient to stabilize the competition in a manner that would minimize incentives for either side to deploy extensive strategic defenses. I want to go a bit further than that and suggest that two specific steps may be helpful. The first is to seek further definition and clarification of what kinds of research are permissible under the Antiballistic Missile Treaty, i.e., define the dividing line between prohibited testing and development and permitted research and, second, to couple that action, as the panel has suggested, with a reaffirmation by both sides of their adherence to the ABM and Outer Space treaties and to the proposition that no actions will be taken by either side contrary to the terms of those treaties without negotiations between them. If the specific steps I have described are taken, there may be a chance of getting around the SDI problem, which could otherwise bog us down at the very start. I hope that the suggestions of the panel will be given serious thought and attention, because I think they are wise and sensible. Thank you, Mr. Chairman.

Howard Baker: Thank you, Secretary Vance, Senator Nunn, if I may at this point, I would propose a list and sequence in which panelists may be recognized. If a panelist has a different preference, if he will express it, I am sure we can rearrange it, but it would be my intention next to ask Mr. Ruth of the Federal Republic of Germany to be followed by Mr. Hyland, to be followed by Mr. Brzezinski, to be followed by Mr. Adelman, by Mr. Schlesinger, and by Mr. Bundy. If there is no objection to that order, then I will proceed now to recognize Mr. Ruth of the Federal Republic of Germany.

Friedrich Ruth: Thank you, Mr. Chairman. President Carter, President Ford, senators, ladies and gentlemen—the Carter Center has made it possible for me to return to my alma mater, to Emory University, and I am extremely happy to be here.

I would like to attest to the constructive spirit which we experienced in the panel discussions, and especially to the role that our Soviet colleague was playing. That made it possible for us to formulate the report you have seen. This report reflects the substance of an interesting discussion which was very valuable for us and gave us an opportunity to hear a variety of views worth pondering.

Let me make a few remarks from a European, a German, and, I would say, an alliance point of view, about some of the problems which we have addressed during the last few days. They will be of a rather general nature. The thrust of them is that although arms control is a difficult and complex task which has its ups and downs, and which is not as satisfactory as we would want it to be, it has become an indispensable instrument of practical politics. How important arms control is can be recognized if you would only imagine for a moment that all the channels of security communication which arms control provides would break down at the same time. The world would be in a very poor and very dangerous state, and for that reason, arms control—imperfect as it is—is an important contribution to peace. Look just for a moment at the ongoing negotiations. The Geneva talks between the United States and the Soviet Union opened on March 12 with an agenda and a mandate which is far-reaching, substantive, and conceptual, and we feel in Europe that this mandate and these negotiations offer a challenge and a chance to the two great powers sitting at the negotiating table to really make a contribution to enhance stability, which is the aim, the stated aim, of these negotiations. As Secretary Vance pointed out, we have no illusion about their complexity, but at the same time, we are aware of the intrinsic potential of these negotiations to make a contribution to the security relationship between East and West in the direction of more basic and more extensive cooperation in the security field, and we are convinced that it would be in our common interest if that cooperation would be taken up. This is, however, not the only ongoing negotiation, albeit the most important at the present time. For me as a European it is important to point out that multilateral negotiations where European states from East and West are participating directly at the negotiating table are equally important. And if I run down the spectrum of negotiations you will see that there is the potential of a very comprehensive arms control approach to the security relationship between East and West: in addition to the bilateral negotiations, we have, as Ralph pointed out, the discussions in Vienna, which are manned by both alliances in East and West.* NATO and the Warsaw Pact are negotiating with each other in Vienna.

The next forum is the Stockholm Conference on Confidence-Building Measures and Disarmament in Europe, where thirty-five states are participating— all European states—the members of the NATO alliance and the Warsaw Pact, as well as the nonaligned and neutral states of Europe. And of course the United States and Canada are participating in both of these negotiations.

The third large forum to be taken into consideration is the conference on disarmament in Geneva. Forty states of all regions of the world participate in that conference, covering a range of subjects but in particular negotiating about a complete ban on chemical weapons. This extends the East–West relationship to a global dimension—a dimension which is becoming increasingly important. And that, of course, brings us into the overall framework of the United Nations, where disarmament and arms control subjects are also discussed.

The debate at the negotiating table requires a great deal of organization, of consultation among the various groups. We on the Eastern side see the need for harmonization of the views with which we want to go to the negotiating table, and one of the tasks of the Atlantic alliance has become to serve as a clearing house of negotiating positions in the multilateral as well as the bilateral field where our interests are immediately concerned. Thus the task which the Atlantic alliance had been founded to achieve, namely, the maintenance of its security through effective deterrence and defense capabilities, has been complemented by a second important element, namely, the readiness for dialogue, the readiness to negotiate and to add to the competitive relationship between East and West the readiness and capability to cooperate. Consequently, one of the most important principles guiding the Western alliance is contained in the statement that, as far as we are concerned (and this is a position that is shared by all in the Atlantic alliance) deterrence and defense, arms control and disarmament are integral parts of our security policy. This underlines the importance that we attach to this endeavor.

---

*The Mutual and Balanced Force Reduction negotiations, begun in 1973.

I would like to close by saying that the Atlantic alliance, based on the solidarity between North America and Europe, based on the cohesion of our common positions, is capable of and willing to make a negotiated contribution to a more stable peace between East and West. This is a task which is a challenge, and gives perspective to our common cause of maintaining security and preserving peace. A panel like ours has shown that it is possible to move forward. I can assure you that we, the European allies, who are very much aware of the need for stable and peaceful relations between East and West, not just in terms of arms control but in the other areas of security and cooperation, will make our contribution to that cause. Thank you, Mr. Chairman.

Sam Nunn: Mr. Chairman, if I could assume the prerogative of the chair just for a few minutes, I'd like to give a very brief view of the report that we have been discussing this morning from at least one senator's point of view. On the critical side, I would take a somewhat tougher line on the allegations of Soviet violations. I believe the Soviet Union needs to understand the seriousness with which the Congress of the United States, and I think also the executive branch, view these alleged violations. We do have the forum which has been alluded to, the Standing Consultative Commission, that is empowered to undertake discussion of these violations. And the Soviets may very well have complaints on their side, and of course if that is the case we ought to address those very serious complaints if they have them. But the radar that we have talked about, the Krasnoyarsk radar, to us appears to be a very serious violation, not of an unratified treaty, but rather of a treaty, the ABM treaty, that is ratified, that is in force, in effect. I cannot overemphasize the importance of that, I believe, not only for the Congress of the United States but also the public opinion of the United States. The same can be said of the allegations about coding or encrypting telemetry, which, if they are correct, violate the SALT I agreement as well as, specifically, the SALT II agreement. To me, addressing those serious issues is a prerequisite for any kind of agreement to be forthcoming at Geneva.

Second, I want to express some concern about the Geneva negotiations themselves. I am not quite ready to say that they are in grave difficulty. I think the report indicates that they may be already bogged down. I am not prepared to go that far. I think it is going to take a lot of patience, but I do believe that the negotiators have adopted a rule of confidentiality in Geneva among themselves, and they need to adhere to that rule. We have seen several statements come out about the Soviet position in *Pravda*; we have seen television interviews by Mr. Karpov. I believe that it is very important that both sides recognize that if these negotiations are to succeed and if the negotiators themselves have the rule of confidentiality, that a breakdown of that rule could break down the confidence that's necessary to proceed on substantive issues.

There is one final point I would make about the report. The report seems to finesse the question of SDI by saying that SDI should not be allowed to inhibit negotiations. That does not completely address the rather obvious fact that SDI may be the central issue of the negotiations, from both the Soviet side and, to some extent, our own side. As the report states, the Soviets clearly have the goal of stopping SDI; the United States clearly has the goal of having a cooperative transition to a defensive-type system on both sides. Now, on the positive side, I completely agree, Ambassador Earle, with the report and its emphasis on nonpartisanship or bipartisanship. I think that is essential in arms control from an American point of view; it is absolutely necessary that we develop together—Democrats and Republicans, as a united nation—not only a coherent arms control policy but a patient arms control policy. I must say that I was interested in the dialogue between President Ford and Secretary Lehman yesterday about the origin of strategic nuclear programs, because I have had similar dialogues in public hearings with members of this administration. Ambassador Adelman and I have discussed this before, so I am not saying anything I have not said before, but I think it needs to be said again: if we are going to have a bipartisan approach, then the spirit of that bipartisanship has to be exemplified by top administration officials, and they have to recognize the history of weapons development and arms control, rather than engage in what I call revisionist history. Just to give you one example that is rather specific: last year Secretary Weinberger stated, in a hearing before the Arms Services Committee (and, Mr. President, you will note here this has a similarity to what we heard yesterday)—and I quote directly from the public transcript—"We should have modernized and strengthened the triad all through the preceding years, but we did not start on it till 1981." Continuing the quote, "We're now well along on the program that won't be finished until 1989; the Soviets have not paused." Continuing the quote in another part of the dialogue, "There had been no developments of the kind that would bring strength to the strategic program except for some proposals." Now, you note not only was the Ford administration excluded, and the Nixon administration, but also the Carter administration in that quote. It was bipartisan in the sense that it recognized no progress in any respect in any administration for a number of years; it ignored such programs that we consider important on the Arms Services Committee, such as the cruise missile, the advanced cruise missile, the advanced-technology bomber, the Trident program, and the MX, all of which were started by either the Nixon or the Ford or the Carter administration. So I say to our friends in the administration, a good point to begin bipartisanship is to recognize that public statements of this nature can greatly increase the tendency of other parties and other people even from the same party to engage in the same kind of very irresponsible conversation.

Two or three other points, very quickly or I am going to run over my own time limit here, Mr. Chairman. It is very important in this country that we recognize, as the report did, that no matter what happens with SDI research we're going to continue to rely on the ability of our nuclear forces to survive and to respond to a nuclear attack on the other side. That is the ultimate deterrent, and we are going to rely on that for a long time to come—in Jim Schlesinger's words, "for at least the lifetime of our children and perhaps our grandchildren." That is, even with a very successful SDI research program. Therefore, when the administration uses terms to describe our current posture and our current deterrent posture such as "flawed," "simplistic," "disproven," "discredited," and "immoral," it raises very serious questions about how we are going to continue politically a consensus for deterrence when this deterrent policy has already been attacked from the left in previous years. If we have a convergence of the left and the right in considering what we have to rely on, at least for the foreseeable future, as immoral, simplistic, and outmoded, we are really in trouble in the long run, and we're laying traps for ourselves. I took more than my time, Mr. Chairman.

Howard Baker: President Ford and President Carter, I must say I feel right at home because my principal experience as majority leader of the Senate was to begin each session of the Senate by announcing an agenda and then seeing it turn into ruins and shambles. As far as I can see, Senator Nunn has posed issues that may require an answer by our friends from the Soviet Union. It might require an answer from other members on the panel, and you might even get President Carter and President Ford in on the act, to say nothing of the sole defender of the administration who may be sitting here at this table. But I am going to do something also that is a chairman's prerogative—I am going to reserve my statement until the very end, at which time I will take a potshot or two. But I would like. . .[*Dobrynin:* Mr. Chairman, excuse me for interrupting your beautiful agenda but I have a few words in connection with statements made by Senator Nunn.] You can indeed, but may I make one statement first, Mr. Ambassador, I would like to do this; I would like to say that, while the agenda provided for the recognition of Mr. Hyland next, I have also one other problem. I have been advised now that the distinguished ambassador of the German Democratic Republic is in the audience, and I think it would be appropriate to call on him as well, so what I would like to do, if the panel will agree, is to call on Ambassador Herder after we recognize Mr. Hyland, and then after Ambassador Herder is recognized, I am going to turn next to Ambassador Dobrynin, and then we will note any other requests by panel members who wish to comment as well, and at that point I hope we're back on our agenda and can proceed to conclusion, but now, as Ambassador Dobrynin pointed out, or his colleague did, a "cooling-off" period is pretty good; I declare a cooling-off period and now recognize Mr. William Hyland, who is the distinguished editor of *Foreign Affairs* magazine, a former member of the National Security Council staff who has served both Republican and Democratic presidents and a distinguished expert on foreign policy. Bill Hyland.

William Hyland: Thank you, Senator Baker, President Carter, President Ford. Let me turn to the negotiating situation. It is worth stepping back a bit and recognizing where we have been over the past several years. In effect, we have lost five years of valuable time in the dialogue between the United States and the Soviet Union. When President Carter met with President Brezhnev in Vienna in 1979, he proposed that in addition to the SALT II treaty they had signed, that there be a five percent reduction in forces for each year over the next five years. Had President Brezhnev accepted that rather straightforward and easy proposal, the missile forces of both sides would now be below what President Reagan is proposing as the current target for the present negotiations, and substantially below what the Soviet Union is now proposing as the outcome of the negotiations. So, that illustrates what happens when dialogue breaks down.

Now, why did that occur; why could Brezhnev not accept a fairly simple proposal? I think it illustrates the difference between the United States' and the Soviet Union's approach to negotiations, especially on arms control and strategic matters. The Soviets, frankly, prefer to keep what they have. Most of their record in the strategic arms talks has been proposals that preserve their forces roughly intact. There was the case in SALT I when they favored a simple freeze on the number, not the characteristics of ICBMs—that eventually was broadened—but basically that was the approach of SALT I. That was also true, as President Ford will remember, at Vladivostok. Brezhnev, at Vladivostok, had the opportunity to go into a much more detailed and stabilizing proposal but he preferred, in the end, to take a level of strategic forces that was roughly what the Soviets had and to rely on the next phase.

Now, the United States is not blameless, of course. Our approach also complicates negotiations. We tend to be very erratic, frankly, because of politics. Changes in administrations inevitably raise the question: "Shouldn't there be a new approach?" or, as Sam Nunn has said, "Wasn't the past approach flawed? Hasn't there been a decade of neglect?" and so forth. Our proposals sometimes are very confusing, and we tend to go back and forth for political fluctuations. We also, as the panel report noted, get involved in domestic politics. It is a strange situation where the main argument for the MX missile, which five years ago was to be the backbone of our new strategic forces, is that we need it to trade away in Geneva. This leads to erratic negotiating performance and, given the faults on both sides, we have had a very long and tedious, and not terribly productive, period. It has been ten years since President Ford met with President Brezhnev in Vladivostok and set forth what was to be the framework for a negotiation and an agreement which then took five more years to finish and now is about to run out, and we have no replacement.

The situation is not alarming, but it is not terribly encouraging. I think we have to recognize one other fact. I welcome the fact that Ambassador Dobrynin and his colleagues are here. That is a good spirit, and it is good that they are here to have a dialogue, but we have to face the fact that the burden for the failure of the past ten to fifteen years must rest very squarely on the Soviet side. Let us not forget that in 1979 we had a treaty, which, despite a great deal of carping and quarreling in the Senate (as Ralph Earle has just mentioned), probably would have been ratified had it not been for the invasion of Afghanistan, and in my view President Carter was correct in withdrawing that treaty at the time because the United States has to recognize that there is a limit to the behavior of the Soviet Union. The fact is, also, that the Soviet Union walked out of the strategic arms talks because of their belief that our putting some shorter-range missiles in Europe had upset the balance, and so they made a linkage between those two talks, and we have had more than a year without any negotiations, and that too, I think, has to rest on the Soviets' side.

In any case we have a new ball game. It is wrong to think of the present talks as simply picking up where we left off in 1983 or 1979. In these talks for the first time we have a radical new element—the "Star Wars," or Strategic Defense Initiative. This changes the framework of those talks radically. For ten years we have been arguing about how many reductions could be possible. President Carter had proposed five percent and the Soviet Union has proposed roughly ten to fifteen percent from the levels that were reached in SALT II, but now we have to consider that in relationship to the defense.

The offensive/defensive equation is now the dominant one, and frankly I do not believe either side has a good notion of how to solve this equation: how much offense, how much defense. That is going to be, as Ralph Earle said, a problem, and it could lead to a rather dangerous stalemate.

I do not have any problem with the report. It is adequate and, if followed by both sides, would be a good step forward. But, frankly, it is a report that emphasizes continuation of the status quo: continue SALT II for a little while longer, put off any major decisions on SDI, and so forth. I am not sure that is good enough. It has been almost twenty years since President Johnson had the idea that turned into the SALT talks. We do not have a great deal to show for it. If the American public begins to get the notion that these talks are simply play-acting—the going through the motions of arms control—while both sides are in fact building up, we could find ourselves in this country in a major political quarrel; because there are, frankly, very strong elements in the United States who believe arms control, as Cy Vance mentioned, is a failure and should be discarded and that we should not worry about it, simply take care of ourselves, and rely on our own defenses. I can see some major problems if we cannot go beyond simply what we have on the table with slight marginal changes. I do not have a formula for breaking this loose; I do not know that anybody at this early stage of a brand-new negotiation can see his way out. I do think we are obsessed with the notion of reductions. Frankly, at levels of 10,000 strategic warheads a reduction of twenty percent at this point would not be much, except in political symbolism. We need to get at the root of the matter, which is the destabilizing character of certain weapons as opposed to other weapons. It may be time for the United States to give more serious thought to a freeze on ICBMs. We've been opposed to that. I am not so sure it was a good idea when it was proposed, but now it may look a little better. The Soviet Union is producing two new ICBMs. Our

MX program is dwindling away, and frankly, a freeze looks much different now than it did a few years ago.

As for SDI, I have no idea how to get out of it. There has to be something better than preserving a free hand under the rubric of research, which could lead—and almost certainly will lead—to some kind of developmental testing and deployment, or the Soviet position, which is a complete ban, which I think is now no longer feasible. Defense is back on the agenda; strategic defense is on the agenda. I do not think we can put that particular genie back in the bottle. So these negotiations are much tougher than we generally realize. We welcome the fact that they are back in Geneva, and both sides are talking. We have to understand that this is a much tougher negotiation than the preceding ones.

Finally, let me say that the dangers of failure of this negotiation are much greater and could have far greater consequences than its predecessors. When President Carter withdrew the SALT treaty in 1980, it turned out that his successor, President Reagan, agreed to abide by the treaty, which was something of a surprise, but I think it was a welcome move. So we have been operating under a treaty, even though it's not ratified; therefore, when the Soviets walked out of the talks in December of 1983, it was not the catastrophe that it might have been. We still had a framework. Frankly, the Soviets were waiting for the presidential elections. We were waiting for them to settle their leadership problems. Now both of those events have passed, and we are back at the table, but if these talks fail, there is no alternative. We cannot wait for a successor to Gorbachev—that is simply not a policy. (We could, but it might turn out to be a rather long wait.) We are not going to have another election for another three and one-half years, although I suspect the campaign will start fairly soon.

In any case, I just would like to sum up by saying that we are now at a crucial point. These talks are not simply a continuation of what has been happening for the last twenty years, though there is a clear linkage. The pressure to succeed is much greater, but, in addition to the dangers I have outlined, it is a major opportunity. We have a president elected with a very strong mandate who now seems to be willing to entertain some ideas that he had rejected earlier. We have a Soviet leader who seems to have a tenure ahead of him and, before it is too late, we still have a framework for negotiations, but after December we will be in the situation where the treaty that was signed by President Carter will have formally lapsed. Even if we are abiding by it, we will be in the bizarre situation of abiding by a treaty which we claim is being violated but which has already lapsed. Thank you.

Howard Baker: Thank you very much. Once again, the agenda, I think, is going to have to be changed. It has been called to my attention that Ambassador Dobrynin must leave the platform shortly, so I would propose, Mr. Chairman, if you agree, that at this time we yield to Ambassador Dobrynin. If there is no objection to that, I yield now to Ambassador Dobrynin.

Anatoly Dobrynin: Well, I did not intend to participate right away in the discussion because we have our ambassador who was on the panel, who participated in preparing this recommendation, and who made some remarks. I think we would like to make a very brief comment because of something that was said right now.

Well, I do not really want to be involved in your domestic affairs, but I should say that you have an outstanding senator from Georgia in Washington, Senator Nunn. I knew him quite well when he was just a beginner, and now when he is a foremost expert on security affairs. I mean, as dean of the diplomatic corps, I have authority to testify that he is one of the really few in Congress—I do not want to exaggerate—who knows the problems very well. And it is not easy to argue with him, because he knows the subject, not in generalities, but the subject matter, and I welcome this knowledge in the Senate.

He mentioned the violations. He was careful now, diplomatic now, when he spoke about serious alleged violations. This is the point: if you read all the special government reports—American reports—it is always said: "maybe," "it seemed to us," "except for a few exceptions," "so to speak," "maybe"—variations—so when I sometimes go to the State Department and begin to ask about specific violations, they say, "Look, Mr. Ambassador, we don't have exact proof, but we strongly suspect that this is the case." I think that when you politicize the suspicion this does not do any good for the negotiations. These remarks I would like to make right now. We have a Standing Consultative Commission. By the way, this commission is now in session. We both have complaints. I'm sure Mr. Adelman could testify to it. We complain to you. You complain to us. I don't know—probably fifty-fifty in the long run, from the very beginning of this commission. It is fifty-fifty. We have never complained publicly. It does not mean that you are right. During the last three years you have been complaining almost every day (we have so many reports I do not have time to read them), so it is a different approach. If you have something, come to the commission, discuss it, and try to get an understanding. In most cases I should report we do understand each other. It is not a bleak picture, with nothing positive. No, it is a useful organization, a useful commission. And unfortunately it was not given credit, as a joint venture. On the contrary, everything on the negative side is emphasized by Americans—not the members of the commission but officials. I think the commission deserves some credit, because it is doing useful work. Speaking about encryption, for instance, one of the two issues that were mentioned by Senator Nunn. We discussed this with him in private two or three weeks ago at lunch with a group of senators. I should say about encryption: first of all, if you look at how it was written in the SALT II treaty, it is rather an ambiguous description that was agreed to by both sides. So it is not exactly something you could pin on someone. Then, because the American side began to complain about our behavior, we asked the American side: "Please give us what exactly you want, what kind of data you want from us, exactly." We didn't receive any. This is the situation. We understand why maybe they hesitated to give us this data, but why then blame everything on us? We do not violate the provision of the treaty dealing with encryption—on this we are prepared to defend ourselves before any international court. But then they put us in the category of violators, permanently, every day.

On other things, for instance, on this Krasnoyarsk radar: It is not finished; it is just in the middle of construction, probably. General Mikhailov may have a chance to tell you a little bit more. I am not an expert on military things. But it should look after our Sputniks, and I'm sure that when it is finished in two years, I don't know, but we may even invite you, at least I know that academicians have this idea—maybe to invite some of your skeptics to see this—how it works, because it will be very easy for you, from the lengths of waves to determine what the real purpose of this particular radar installation is. In our minds you have some violations too. Just take the SALT II treaty. There is an article saying that there will be no circumvention of this treaty. It means that the strategic parity which was arrived at during the talks in Vienna between President Carter and then President Brezhnev would not be changed. We had rough parity, and both sides took an obligation not to change this rough parity. When you introduced Pershing and cruise missiles into Europe (yes, you say, "in reply"), in our view it was strategic weaponry, because it can hit our territory, including Moscow, also Leningrad, Kharkov—the most important parts of my country. Within Europe it is one thing, but between us—the two nuclear powers—it was an addition, so we considered this is a real violation. We did not make much fuss about it, because we understand there are some other negotiations. Recently, you made a test; a warhead was hit over the Pacific by a Minuteman. This is a violation of the treaty—the ABM treaty, by the way. You have some mobile radars for ABM. We consider these violations. You have some now that look towards the West and the East, which, really, though they are on the perimeter, still cover most of your territory from both sides, in our opinion, so in a way it could be at least a small violation. So it is really not a matter of specific charges and countercharges. What I really appeal to you for here is, let us give instructions to those people who are very knowledgeable, those sitting on the Standing Consultative Commission, to look at this matter and try to solve it in a peaceful and mutually satisfactory way.

Senator Nunn mentioned the confidentiality. I agree with him, it is very important. But, frankly speaking, now there is nothing to reveal there, nothing specific, nothing happening there, so there is nothing to reveal—really nothing that is top secret. I hope there will be. But it has been only four weeks and they are just beginning to talk. You understand it is a very difficult subject and it is very difficult to expect them to make any basic progress. There will be a recess on the 24th of April; they have only just gotten acquainted, so to speak. We are not discouraged. I'm sure Americans are not discouraged either. But for the time being there is no really big secret they are discussing there. Confidentiality is important if necessary, and it should be kept.

Well, Mr. Hyland blamed everything on the Soviet Union. I just want to quote his former boss, Kissinger, who says that statistically you could not say that the United States is always right in this situation. [*Hyland:* It is not always wrong] I prefer to say it my way. [*Hyland:* That's the problem] And now coming to the SDI. We mentioned it yesterday, and I would like to say some words about it today. I find this very interesting—this report, mostly I agree with it; I think it is serious, not in everything, but mostly I should say I accept it. The question here is about the interrelationship between offense and defense in the situation when we have this SDI. Well, you have to understand what you are facing now in the negotiation. I hope it will change. There is nothing under discussion with us, as they mentioned yesterday. Up till now, the U.S. position is that they are not going to discuss anything specific with us about space until after the research period. We understand that this is only the beginning of the first four weeks. They have had a preliminary discussion, but after the recess they may come with some ideas. But up till now they simply don't discuss it with us, because they say: "Well, our position is that after the research we will discuss it"—not in the sense that they do not want to discuss the subject at all, but nothing specific is said. Everything is deferred until when this period of research will be over—five years according to Mr. Adelman; five years or more, maybe ten years. And so we have to wait—wait until what? Until a new administration comes and then another new administration? With whom are we going to negotiate then? Unfortunately history shows that sometimes in your country one president signs an agreement and the other will consider this a big window of vulnerability. So we Russians sometimes do not quite understand what is going on. Maybe when you spend some years here you begin, little by little, to understand, not all but still something.

So this is the situation, and in this case I rather like what my good friend Vance proposes. I understand it was a preliminary thought when he said, look here, these are two opposite things—one thing is we can see that of course it couldn't be just reduction of offensive weaponry without doing anything on SDI. This is our rather clear position. It is not an ultimatum, because we have three panels there. Secretary Shultz and Minister Gromyko agreed (I was there and Mr. Adelman was there) that there should be three panels which would discuss and try to come to a solution more or less simultaneously. It doesn't mean there is a veto if they find something very good on offensive systems—it will be no problem to deal with offensive. But we are not prepared to put aside one thing, not discuss it until you finish research, but concentrate on the other thing. This we are not going to do. This is our position. But you should understand that we are not saying that it should be simultaneously everything. That is why we have three groups of panels, three teams, three men dealing there who are very experienced from both sides. If they could move on the offensive—it will be within possibility—we are prepared to do it on the European missiles; we are prepared to do it. But at the same time we are not prepared, for instance, to go very drastically on offensive when we have nothing—even ideas—what we are going to do on SDI. This is our position. It's not a secret that was what we discussed for two days between Gromyko and Shultz. We made our position very clear. Mr. Shultz, after consultation with your delegation, the experts (you have many more experts than we have) came to the conclusion that this is a good joint statement. It is specifically said in the joint statement that these things should be considered in their interrelationship—that the objective of the negotiations will be to prevent an arms race in space and to end it on earth, and to start to drastically reduce nuclear arms, strategic as well as European. This is the common position. It is not only our position; it is your position as well. That is why we are addressing this. Mr. Hyland was trying to present the case that he does not want to discuss SDI because it is another story. We cannot do it. So it is a question, really, of addressing all the areas: the SDI—maybe you will convince us, I don't know, by presenting your idea during the comprehensive negotiations. We are open-minded; we are prepared to look into this case. So, in general I think it was a very instructive discussion, at least for us Soviet participants. We will carry some ideas away with us. We will think it over, I promise you. It is not necessary to accept everything, but we will give it some deep thinking. So I thank you very much.

Howard Baker: The next to be recognized on the panel, according to the much-revised schedule, is Dr. Brzezinski. Dr. Brzezinski, of course, is former National Security Advisor to President Carter. He is now Senior Advisor at the Georgetown University Center for Strategic and International Studies, among his other accomplishments. He is also expert in this field, and I yield now to Dr. Brzezinski.

Zbigniew Brzezinski: Thank you very much, Mr. Chairman. Let me say that I read the report of the panel with much admiration. I found the report to be much better than I expected it to be, and I found that rather gratifying. I also enjoyed listening to Ambassador Dobrynin lay out the case for the Soviet perspective on these complicated issues with his usual charm, good humor and intelligence, and I thought that given the case that he had to make, he was quite persuasive. In fact I think that his presence here added enormously to the value of this deliberation and consultation, and I hope that it has established a useful precedent so that at some point in the near future a similar meeting can be held in Moscow with a similarly large audience of interested citizens, with the American ambassador and American experts given the same opportunity to lay out the American perspective, and with these proceedings being carried to the interested Soviet citizenry by Soviet television. I think such a development would be most welcome. And my hope is that our Soviet visitors will convey this hope of ours to their colleagues in Moscow and that at some point in the future, such a very positive development will come to pass.

With respect to the report itself, I would like to limit myself to four general points. First, I do feel that one has to face the probable reality that for some time to come we are not going to get a new comprehensive arms control agreement between the United States and the Soviet Union. This is regrettable, but in all probability it is a fact. And there are some good reasons for this. First of all, the question of verification, given weapons developments, has become far more complicated than it used to be in the case of SALT I and SALT II, and therefore more far-reaching arrangements need to be made than have been possible in the past, if the verification problem is to be resolved to mutual satisfaction.

Second, there is the problem of compliance, to which reference has been made. As long as one party to the agreement, or both parties to the agreement, entertain doubts as to the compliance of the other side, that too will continue to inhibit the reaching of greater and more comprehensive agreements. Ambassador Dobrynin stated that the facility in Krasnoyarsk is not a military facility, and he may well be right. On the American side, of course, there are strong suspicions that this is not the case, and perhaps one very constructive outcome of this consultation will be to arrange for some group of private experts, many of whom are present here today, to be permitted to visit the Krasnoyarsk facility to establish to our mutual satisfaction that what Ambassador Dobrynin was telling us is in fact true. And I think that would be extremely reassuring and would tend to diminish American suspicions, which, as he has indicated, may be unfounded.

Beyond that, what complicates the negotiating process is two further considerations. One is that we have the obligation to keep our Far Eastern allies and friends fully abreast and to be cognizant of their interests—as well as of the interests of our West European allies—and this means first of all Japan and China. Some aspects of Soviet deployments in recent years have certainly affected their security, and we could not be indifferent to their concerns in any comprehensive agreement. But that, to be sure, complicates the process of reaching that agreement.

And finally there is the complexity of trying to reach some understandings in three separate panels, dealing with three separate but important sets of issues. I found it very encouraging to hear Ambassador Dobrynin say, if I understood him correctly, that agreements in all three are not necessary for an agreement in one of the three to be consummated. And if that is the case, then, indeed, it is an important step forward and one which should be registered and underlined. If, on the other hand, we require agreement in all three for an agreement of a comprehensive type to be consummated, then I think the question becomes far more complicated.

My second point is that in addition to the intrinsic complexities of negotiating a comprehensive arms control agreement (which leads me to a somewhat pessimistic conclusion as to its likelihood) there is the larger geopolitical problem and the reality of serious political disagreements between the United States and the Soviet Union. In my view it is highly unlikely that a comprehensive agreement, which requires a certain degree of mutual trust and accommodation, is likely to be possible if the tragic invasion and occupation of Afghanistan is continuing at the same time. We have to find some formula for resolving that issue, and I would think that with good will and serious negotiations by both sides, some formula for the restoration of a genuinely neutral Afghanistan, but one within which the political arrangements correspond more to the desires of the people, should prove possible. And if it did, it would greatly improve the climate of American–Soviet relations. Now, to be sure, there is no formal negotiating linkage between that issue and issues negotiated in arms control. But even if there is no formal negotiating linkage between the two, it is a political fact that there is an unavoidable interaction between these two issues, particularly insofar as a democracy such as ours is concerned. Our public opinion and our congressional attitudes are bound to be affected by either the presence of an accommodation or its absence on a sensitive geopolitical issue that will condition their attitudes and their receptivity to accept arrangements and to ratify them. Therefore, political interaction between geopolitical issues and arms control negotiations is a fact, even if one wishes somewhat arbitrarily to compartmentalize them, and even if one denies a formal linkage between these two sets of issues. And obviously the Afghan problem is not going to be easy to solve. It will require some patient negotiations, and it is, therefore, important that an American-Soviet dialogue on this issue be launched. It does not yet exist. There was a preliminary probe in the context of the recent American-Soviet Middle Eastern exchanges, but that probe was very limited and it has not been succeeded by an ongoing discussion, which at some point would lead to negotiations.

My third point in view of the foregoing, too (and my sense that we might as well face up to the reality of the difficulty of obtaining a comprehensive agreement soon) is that, in that context, therefore, some limited arrangements may be desirable and they may serve as catalysts for stimulating movement toward a wider agreement. And I have two aspects particularly in mind, which in my judgment could be helpful in that regard. The first is to emulate the example set by President Ford and Brezhnev in Vladivostok and see if in the absence of a comprehensive arms control agreement we cannot initially reach a limited interim agreement, confined perhaps to very narrow broad categories—narrow categories in the sense of the totality of the issues, but broad in terms of their characteristic. More specifically, I mean an arrangement which would wed the Soviet proposal to reduce the number of launchers with a parallel limit and reduction in the number of warheads. A formula along the lines of, let us say, 1,800 launchers and 7,500 warheads would go a long way toward beginning to modify the arms control equation. It could be a catalyst for further agreements, though it would not deal yet with some of the underlying difficulties of the arms control negotiating process, particularly as it pertains to the increasing proliferation of essentially first-strike systems. Nonetheless, it will be a beginning, an important beginning, and one which I believe could be reached in the course of a political encounter, and not necessarily the highly complicated, expert negotiations in Geneva. For example, if there is a summit meeting between Mr. Reagan and

Mr. Gorbachev, I think that would provide an appropriate venue for such an essentially political, not overly complicated, limited interim agreement, which would serve as a catalyst. Along the same lines, I, for one, would advocate a somewhat more flexible American attitude currently in the MBFR [Mutual and Balanced Force Reduction] negotiations. While I know that there are very good reasons for not accepting the Soviet proposals as lately formulated, on larger, broader grounds of verification and access to data and so forth, I would be inclined to take a somewhat more flexible attitude as a beginning step to the recent Soviet proposal—subject to some verification—for the removal of 20,000 Soviet troops in exchange for the removal of 13,000 American troops. I do not believe that this formula, in the long run, is adequate for dealing with the MBFR problem, but as a starter, and as an effort to launch the process into motion, I think it would be a useful catalyst again, and I make these two points particularly because I stress my general view that reaching a comprehensive agreement, a more ambitious version of SALT II, which is even a more ambitious version of SALT I, is going to be very difficult.

And my final point is that in the above context (and preferably in the context of an agreement, but if necessary, in its absence) some movement, first by the United States, or possibly by both the United States and the Soviet Union, toward the enhancement of the respective retaliatory arsenals with some limited, essentially counter-first-strike SDI, would be stabilizing. And the reason for that is that weapons are becoming so increasingly accurate and so time-urgent that they in themselves introduce a new factor of instability and precariousness into the strategic relationship which was not present in the 1960s. I am an agnostic when it comes to President Reagan's overall population defense, and I think perhaps some aspects of it have been overstated, and I think that the Soviet attitude in general on the SDI has been propagandistic and deceptive, given the reality of Soviet research on that issue. But a more limited and realistic focus on a limited deployment of an SDI system, either by an amendment of the ABM agreement or even in its absence, and combined with greater reliance essentially on retaliatory forces and not concentration on the deployment of more, essentially first-strike systems, would, in fact, contribute to the stability of the nuclear relationship and reduce some of the precariousness which has manifested itself in recent years. I believe steps along these lines, based on the recognition of the inherent complexity of the overall problem, could help to stabilize the American–Soviet relationship in the arms control area. Thank you.

Howard Baker: Dr. Brzezinski, I thank you very much for your very excellent and very lucid presentation. As I announced earlier, following on after Dr. Brzezinski it is the intention of the chairman to recognize now, from the floor, Ambassador Herder of the German Democratic Republic, who is in the audience.

Ambassador Herder: Mr. Chairman, President Carter, President Ford—as a diplomat who has had the honor to represent my country as arms negotiator at the Geneva talks on disarmament and the conference on disarmament for about nine years, I would like to make a few remarks on certain aspects of the high importance my country attaches to negotiations and a broad dialogue, in the overall effort to maintain peace, international security, and achieve disarmament agreements.

As a small socialist country located on the dividing line between NATO and the Warsaw Pact, the most powerful military alliances in the world, we cannot remain indifferent in the face of the continuing arms race and its manifold consequences. On the eve of the fortieth anniversary of the victory of the Allied nations over Hitler's fascism we are still, in my country, acutely aware of the death, suffering, and destruction the war inflicted on our continent, including my country. We therefore fully agree that the only way to prevent a nuclear holocaust (in which we, situated in Central Europe, would certainly become the first victims) is by seriously conducting an intensive dialogue and by serious negotiations with a view to achieving a radical reduction, and if possible the total elimination of nuclear weapons. We join with all those of you who yesterday and today said that a nuclear war should never be fought. And therefore we welcomed the agreement on the beginning of the U.S.–Soviet talks in Geneva, which should lead to halting the arms race on earth and the prevention of a new arms race in space. Guided by a sense of good reason and good will, everything should be done to create an atmosphere favoring the achievement of such badly needed results. As an expert in disarmament, I felt that very often our experts overlook the broader aspect of disarmament, the general atmosphere which is absolutely necessary to produce concrete results. My own experience has shown that under conditions of tension nothing can be done, but where there is a will, there is a way. I am not sharing the sort of pessimism which has just been expressed by Dr. Brzezinski with regard to the possibility of coming to agreement, at least on limited measures like a comprehensive test ban and others. Of course, there cannot be immediately an overall arms agreement between the Soviet Union and the United States. But first steps could be made and should be made, and therefore we welcomed the Soviet decision on a moratorium and also on halting strategic armaments, a moratorium on space research, even if they are small steps and even if they are regarded by a few people as propaganda tricks. But could not such steps—these or others—have a positive impact on improving the general atmosphere to facilitate the achievement of tangible results at these armaments negotiations? There can be no doubt that if these space weapons programs continue, progress in other areas will be either considerably diminished or even made impossible. I recently was reminded of an Indian maxim which says, you cannot smoke the peace pipe with one hand while loading your gun with the other. We believe to promote negotiations, good will should be demonstrated by actions—sometimes if necessary, even bold actions. Furthermore, in my view, nothing should be done to provoke or to deepen the mistrust as, for instance, questioning the existing borders or postwar agreements in Europe which have become the basis for maintaining peace in Europe for more than four decades now.

To sum up: for successful negotiations on disarmament an environment should be created, by concrete demonstrations of good will and by exercise of a maximum of restraint in international relations by all parties involved. Finally, I would like to thank President Carter for having initiated this very interesting dialogue. I would also like to thank him for having extended the invitation to my country, which gives me the chance to be here and to enjoy your hospitality.

Howard Baker: The distinguished ambassador from East Germany is most welcome, and we appreciate his appearance. There is one other ambassador here who has made his presence known. He has indicated that he wishes to speak very briefly, and I would now disgress once more from the announced schedule to ask Ambassador El Reedy of Egypt to address the group.

Ambassador El Reedy: Thank you very much, Mr. Chairman. I am very grateful to you for giving me the opportunity, and I would like to begin by thanking President Carter and President Ford for addressing an invitation to President Mubarak to send a representative here. I happen to be his newly appointed ambassador in Washington, and I think it is a great opportunity, to have the opportunity to come here and to listen to such a distinguished group of American politicians and intellectuals.

The reason I wanted to speak, aside from this, is to give support to the idea that has been articulated by Secretary Vance, and yesterday also by Secretary Kissinger, related to the importance of having political discussions or consultations on political issues parallel to arms control negotiations. We think this is a very positive idea. While we believe that arms control and disarmament negotiations stand on their own feet and must not be hostage to other political issues, we believe that the environment would be certainly improved by negotiations on political issues. That is why in Egypt we have supported the consultations between the United States and the Soviet Union on the Middle East. These consultations can be very useful. There is no contradiction between these consultations and our view that the United States' role in bringing about peace in the Middle East is pivotal and central. Having said this I would like to propose, for the consideration of the panelists and for the conference, the idea of including in the report a reference to our proposal—which we bring year after year to the United Nations General Assembly—on the establishment of a nuclear-free zone in the Middle East. We think that the establishment of such a zone in the Middle East would contribute immensely to peace in the Middle East and to the cause of nonproliferation. We know that both the United States and the Soviet Union support the resolution that we take to the United Nations General Assembly in this regard. The idea is also supported by Middle Eastern countries, including Israel, but we feel the support coming from both superpowers for the idea, not just voting for the resolution, but actually making a commitment to work for this idea. This would be a great achievement for the cause of nonproliferation and for the cause of peace in the Middle East, and I would request President Carter and President Ford to give their support to the inclusion of this point among the recommendations which will finally appear in the report. Having said this, I would like once again to thank you, President Carter, and you, President Ford, and to thank the people of Atlanta for their great hospitality and compliment them on safeguarding the beauty of their land. Thank you very much.

Howard Baker: Mr. Ambassador, we thank you very much. We especially appreciate your recommendations and your participation in this meeting. Next on the agenda is Ambassador Kenneth Adelman, who is the director of ACDA—the Arms Control and Disarmament Agency—the man most under the gun at this time, and I yield now for his comments.

Kenneth Adelman: Thank you, Senator Baker. It is a pleasure to be here today and to be part of this bipartisan exploration of arms control. For a long time I have thought—especially in this position that I am in today—that we needed to spend less time negotiating with one another as Americans and more time negotiating with the Soviet Union, and the kind of bipartisan consensus that we have been talking about today is critical to success in arms control in particular. There is no reason that there should be a Republican arms control proposal or a Democratic arms control proposal; there is every reason in the world why there should be an American arms control proposal. Senator Nunn, I think that some of the points that you made along these lines are absolutely right. I think there is a tendency, in this administration but in recent administrations as well, to think that the earth was created on inauguration day, that things going on before it were just no good and had to be changed radically; and then, inevitably, there is a move back to see the wisdom of what went on before.

I thought that in that spirit of bipartisanship it would be good to go through a few of the things on which we could all agree and then face very frankly some of the things on which there is disagreement between the administration and others. I think we could all agree, as Secretary Vance said, that arms control is part of a bigger role in East–West relations that are fundamentally based on diplomacy, deterrence, and arms control. It has to be a three-legged stool to really support the structure of the world as we would like to see it. I think that we would all agree that deep reductions in nuclear weapons is a focus of arms control and should be among the foremost foci of arms control. It is absolutely true, as has been pointed out in this panel, that President Ford and President Carter made a heroic, dedicated effort to have the Soviets engage in deep reductions in strategic nuclear weapons. This is not something that was invented by the Reagan administration at all. Presidents Ford and Carter were basically thwarted in those attempts, by and large, by the Soviet refusal to do anything but make arms control legitimize a defense buildup that had been planned for some time. So this has been the story of arms control since the dawn of the strategic age: that we have wanted deep reductions and the Soviets, by and large, have not. We should look at deep reductions, in the strategic nuclear realm and in the intermediate nuclear realm. as an answer to the threat facing us today: that the world is in a situation where both sides have over 7,500 missile warheads—far too many for what we need for a deterrence posture. We can have deterrence at a much lower level. The INF [Intermediate Range Nuclear Forces] situation in Europe is similar: the Soviets have some 1,300 warheads in place now, threatening the military forces and facilities, and the capitals and the main cities of our NATO allies and of our friends and allies in Asia. We can really reduce or eliminate an entire class of weapons systems as, again, we have been trying to do for a good number of years. It is fair to say that the objective of deep reductions of nuclear weapons is an objective that, by and large, is agreed to within all American circles. I think that you can make a very potent case that deep reductions make sense with or without any kind of SDI program.

I think that all would agree also that compliance is critical to arms control. To be serious about arms control is to be serious about compliance issues. Otherwise, we are not engaged in arms control at all but instead are engaged in unilateral disarmament under the guise of an arms control agreement. I think that Ambassador Dobrynin knows well that the two reports on Soviet violations the president has sent up to the Congress in the last two years have not found ''alleged'' or ''so-called'' or ''maybe'' violations or the other euphemisms that he (Ambassador Dobrynin) used, but very serious and very definite Soviet violations of the ABM treaty, in terms of the Limited Test Ban Treaty, in terms of the political commitments undertaken in the Threshold Test Ban Treaty and certainly the Biological and Chemical Weapons Convention. The SCC, the Standing Consultative Commission, has been a useful device to better understand the positions of the United States and the Soviet Union. That is why we spend a great deal of time preparing for the SCC. That is why when the Krasnoyarsk radar was first discovered by the United States in the summer of 1983, the very first thing we did was talk to the Soviets, to Ambassador Dobrynin in particular, about holding a special session of the SCC to talk about the radar, and the reply at that time was that the Soviets were not going to give us a special session of the SCC. We then laid out our case in the diplomatic channel, but our first tendency here, as always, was to use the SCC to try to resolve this problem. I look forward to the possibility—if Ambassador Dobrynin made the offer with any specifics— that we could have some kind of inspection of the radar in the future. I think that holds some promise for resolving the situation. I have been quite surprised over the last year and a half that there have been very significant changes in the United States' public perception on the question of compliance. When I first testified on the first report in the early part of 1984, it was very much a question of whether or not the Soviet Union was violating the arms control provisions. At that time, I visited both President Ford and President Carter, separately, to talk to them about the compliance report, to lay out the facts, and they spent a great deal of time on it with me to determine the facts of the situation. A year and a half later, when our second report was issued (and, Senator Nunn, you were there at the Arms Services Committee) in the testimony, to the best of my recollection, there was no question at all by any senator present about whether or not the Soviet Union was in violation of these treaties. The questions were: "What do we do about it? How do we get them to stop these violations? What does it say about the integrity of the arms control process?" This is critical, and the radar, again, is a very good illustration. The fact is that the radar must have been planned, if construction was not actually begun, in the 1970s, at the time when expectations were high for detente. Hopes were high for successful arms control within the same decade that the ABM treaty was signed. The Soviet planners of the radar, which is as large as several football fields, must have known it would be seen by American intelligence operations, national technical means, and I do not think that there could have been any person in the Kremlin who thought anything else but that the United States would call this a violation. So it raises a question, not just about the radar: if you are going to plan so flagrantly to violate and to be in violation in the future, what does that say about your seriousness on arms control?

As Ambassador Dobrynin mentioned, we are bothered by the encryption of Soviet telemetry (that is, the scrambling of the signals that are given off by missiles during missile tests) because I believe that President Carter had—and should have had—as one of the prime goals for SALT II, the opening up of information from both sides on strategic arms through arms control agreements. One of the promises and one of the hopes that people had for SALT II was that we would know more about each other's systems; we would have more information because of the provisions of SALT II. Since that time, by any measure, Soviet concealment and deception practices have increased, and we know less about Soviet programs today than we did at the time of SALT II, and I think that is something we would agree on.

Let me say that the definition of confidentiality that Ambassador Dobrynin gave us (when, Mr. Chairman, you raised the very good point that to be serious about arms control we had to have a confidentiality rule) was, to tell you the truth, bothersome to me. It was a rubber yardstick definition of confidentiality, namely, that the Soviets will decide when anything important happens in the negotiation and if they do not deem it important then they can go on television and have their negotiators in Geneva say whatever they want about it. If that is the standard of confidentiality that we have come to use, then it must erode the whole process of arms control. To be successful, it has to be quiet; it has to be serious and confidential.

Quite clearly we do not agree—the administration and its opponents—on the importance of SDI as a concept, as a research project, as an activity that the United States should engage in, at least at the level that we are engaging in it right now. It is important, at least, to have people understand what drove the president and the administration to think that an SDI was worth the research program that we are engaged in right now.

First, to pick up a point that was made this morning, but which has been overlooked very much in the history of arms control, is the question of accidental or unauthorized attacks by ballistic missiles. This is a situation that received a great deal of publicity with the novels of the 1960s and for a time was of great concern. Right now there is nothing a president of the United States could do about an accidental or unauthorized launch but withstand it or retaliate in kind.

Second, I believe that deterrence has always had both a component of protection and a component of punitive action. What SDI promises to do is to look toward a situation where deterrence would have a greater component of protection and less of a component of retaliation or punishment. In the situation today, a president of the United States has no choice but ultimately to keep the peace by the threat of mutual annihilation. Further, if nuclear winter research is to be taken seriously (as I take it), then that is a very awesome responsibility, as these gentlemen well know, for any human being. SDI research is also a prudent hedge against what the Soviets have been doing for a good number of years, and which, as most of you know now, has been greater than the level of the effort that the United States is now making. While all the discussion has been on how to treat SDI in the negotiations, contrary to what Ambassador Dobrynin said, we are discussing it in particular; we have a group in Geneva doing nothing else but discussing the movement toward a more defense-oriented deterrence posture and stopping the erosion of the ABM treaty. In January we discussed at great length how the United States and the Soviet Union both agree that a ban on research on defense capabilities could not be verified; that both sides were engaged in the research; and that the Soviets, throughout their history, have engaged in a lot of defensive efforts.

Let me end by saying—back to the areas of agreement, many of which were summarized by Bill Hyland so eloquently—that we have a chance now, with a new mandate for our American president and with a new Soviet leadership, both of them saying (at least on the level of rhetorical grand policy) that they want real or radical reductions in nuclear weapons. We have new negotiations going on now, and conditions may be far more favorable to concrete negotiations and results from those negotiations—if the Soviets are more willing—than they have been in the past. I thank you.

Howard Baker: Ambassador Adelman, I thank you very much. Next we have a most distinguished member of this panel who is former secretary of everything and also the former chairman of the Atomic Energy Commission. He is a distinguished American by any measure. I refer, of course, to Dr. James Schlesinger.

James Schlesinger: Thank you, Mr. Chairman, President Ford, President Carter, Mrs. Carter, honored chairmen, ladies and gentlemen.

I bow to no one in support of bipartisanship or of arms control, but the pursuit of that Holy Grail is beset with practical difficulties, to which I turn. There has been much discussion of strategic defense this morning, and properly so, because it is now the central element in the negotiations, as has already been observed. No negotiations can proceed without grappling with the interrelationship between offense and defense. I myself have been a skeptic about the Strategic Defense Initiative—its pace, its prospective military utility, and its costs, particularly in the more ethereal versions of strategic defense—but as one surveys the possibilities in the strategic defense area, one is reminded of Wellington's remark as he observed his own British forces: "I do not know whether they frighten the enemy, but by God, they frighten me." Nevertheless, as we look at strategic defense, there are three things that our Soviet guests should fully understand first. Since 1972 the Soviets have maintained a large, indeed a vast program in strategic defense. Now, imitation is the sincerest form of flattery, and consequently, the Soviet Union should feel flattered by the United States' imitation of this program. Why is it legitimate to invest immense sums in deployment around Moscow, building on the original Galosh system and working on elements like lasers in Soviet laboratories, while it is illegitimate for the United States to pursue these same goals?

Second, research cannot be precisely monitored in this area. If the Soviet Union is working on strategic defense, the United States must do research in that area just to be aware of Soviet progress and also to hedge against the possibility of a Soviet breakout.

Third, the primary reason that the United States has been forced to reconsider the ballistic missile defense issue has been the development of heavy counterforce capabilities by the Soviet Union in violation of the spirit and the understanding at the time of the agreement in 1972—a subject to which I will turn later. And perhaps there is a fourth point regarding strategic defense: if the Soviet Union continues indiscriminately to attack strategic defense, many people, Americans and others, will come to support strategic defense for that reason alone.

Let me turn now to the broader sweep. If what the Soviets say today is true, if they are now eager to negotiate a general agreement, then the pattern of relationships is but another example of the lack of simultaneity in the timing of interest in negotiations—a problem that has evolved since the death of Franklin Roosevelt, forty years ago yesterday. In 1945 the United States was not only prepared to discuss disarmament, it was prepared to disarm without any discussion; it disbanded its forces; it abandoned the draft; it brought the boys home. Perhaps the monumental achievement of the late Joseph Stalin (whose virtues have been so eloquently etched by Nikita Krushchev) was that he brought the United States back from its semi-isolationistic state and brought about the return of the U.S. forces to Europe through a series of incidents in the late 1940s that I need not recount. It was indicative, however, that when the Americans were most passive or when the Americans were most inclined to accept the fundamentals of "peaceful coexistence," the Soviet Union tended to overplay its hand. Throughout the 1950s and 1960s, the massive Soviet forces facing Western Europe were rationalized by many of us as holding Europe hostage, as a way of neutralizing the American advantage in strategic nuclear weapons. That American advantage has disappeared. The Soviet forces directed against Western Europe have not been reduced; they have been strengthened. After 1972, the American attitude was reflected in the atmosphere of detente and captured by the principles of "peaceful coexistence," and after 1972, there was the immense buildup of Soviet counterforce capabilities, embodied particularly in the SS-18 and -19, to which I referred earlier. The buildup of those counterforce capabilities was inconsistent with the spirit of the 1972 agreement and has undermined one of the premises on which the ABM treaty rested.

In addition, there was the Soviet decision to continue the support of "wars of national liberation." Americans felt deceived by this; they felt wrongly deceived. Throughout the period the Soviets were quite blunt in saying that Soviet support for "wars of national liberation" would not waver, and indeed that detente required an intensification of the ideological struggle. That was not an appropriate response, at least in the American version of detente. Now, these are examples from the past in which the simultaneity of the timing of interest in negotiations fell awry. Today the Soviet Union suggests that we should proceed with a broader agreement. The Soviet Union suggests—and there is some logical justification for this—that the deployment of strategic defenses of a general nature would create a structural imbalance. If the Soviet Union feels strongly about that structural imbalance, if the Soviet Union feels that we should move toward a comprehensive agreement, then the Soviet Union might elicit a response from the Americans regarding strategic defense by suggesting or offering to eliminate one or both of the two imbalances in the structural situation that have been created by prior Soviet policy: one, their massive conventional capability that threatens Western Europe, or two, the development of monumental counterforce capabilities since the 1972 agreement. Is the Soviet Union prepared for deep reductions in her own offensive forces? If so, I believe that a way can be found to deal with what the Soviet Union regards as the threat of the Strategic Defense Initiative. Thank you.

Howard Baker: Dr. Schlesinger, we thank you very much for a very excellent statement. The last participant on the panel today is Dr. McGeorge Bundy, who has the distinction of having been national security advisor to two presidents of the United States. He is also a former president of the Ford Foundation. We are delighted to have him with us, and I yield now to Dr. Bundy.

McGeorge Bundy: Mr. Chairman, I want to begin by joining with all of those who expressed appreciation to President Carter and President Ford for their initiative in this enterprise. I do think that their joint sponsorship has made possible a level of seriousness and an absence of party spirit which are absolutely critical to the consideration of these issues, and I have to say that, having spent five arduous years in Washington being lectured and admonished by two presidents (only one of whom had an accent) I find it a great opportunity to be able to lecture and admonish two presidents at once. It never occurred to me, even in my fondest dreams, when I was in Washington that—as a university type—I might one day find myself on the lecture podium with two such distinguished targets in the front row.

I am going to come out about where Jim Schlesinger did, and really, about where the admirable report of Ralph Earle and his panel came out, with the belief that there are the makings of a grand bargain in Soviet fear of SDI and our fear of Soviet excessive deployments of both intercontinental and theater missiles. But I want to get there by a slightly different road.

I think our problem in both countries is that we have doctrines which drive procurement, and fears which drive those doctrines to drive procurement. Both countries have war-fighting doctrines, and this is not as new as some people assert, although the direction of efforts in the last ten years in several administrations has moved progressively toward the reassertion of war-fighting doctrines and even an intent to prevail in nuclear war. This gives me some cause for personal regret, because it was the Kennedy administration which removed—I think correctly—the word prevail from the doctrines of the United States government on the sound and continuing belief (so well expressed by President Reagan) that a nuclear war cannot be won and must never be fought. Military planners necessarily proceed on the basis of the instructions they get and in large measure on the traditional basis of an expectation that their mission is to achieve victory. They measure the requirements—as is in some measure their duty—by what they perceive as what the other side may be able to do. In the main they are not able to form their judgment on the basis of the correct and, I think, deeply important perception which General Jones shared with us yesterday—that senior military commanders are among the most prudent of men with respect to the risk of nuclear war because they know better than the average man what manner of weapon it is with which they have to deal. Nonetheless, on both sides we have proceeded—the Soviets more steadily, we more by fits and starts (with a major fit in progress right now)—to build up and modernize and change and expand our inventories and our capabilities. No president has been able unilaterally to put a lid on it, and neither has any Soviet leader, and we are now in a period of prospective intensification made graver, and not less dangerous, by the Strategic Defense Initiative.

One way to get a handle on this risk is to take hold of an insight which President Ford expressed to us all yesterday. He remarked that he had known many presidents, had negotiated intensely with one most important leader of the Soviet Union, and that in his experience none of these men (and certainly not he himself) had ever been unaware of the nature of nuclear war, unaware of his supreme responsibility for seeing to it that no act or deed of his should bring his nation or any nation closer to that catastrophe. That presidential understanding in both superpowers has been demonstrated in many moments, one of which I saw at close hand in the Cuban missile crisis. It is not merely a moral and personal conviction, it is a prudential one. One way of stating it is as General Eisenhower did back in April, 1954, describing the prudence of the men in the Kremlin: "The very fact that those men, by their own design, are in the Kremlin means that they love power. They want to be there." And he explained the point further in a conversation with his biographer, Mr. Ambrose, "There is nothing in the world the Communists want badly enough to risk losing the Kremlin." Presidents feel the same way about the White House. And that gave President Eisenhower a certain serenity in the face of a certain amount of nuclear bluster from the Soviet leader of that time, which leads me to suggest to you that when we hear about the prospect of atomic blackmail we should take those fears with a very large grain of salt. I found it very instructive and helpful yesterday when Hal Sonnenfeldt reminded us that in the last five years we have had no serious crisis—that in the troubles we have had (and there have been some, and not trivial ones, with Marxist-Leninist regimes of one sort and shape or another) there has been no hint of atomic blackmail; that we have had no crisis comparable to those of earlier years in places like Berlin or Cuba. Yet as he spoke I found myself recalling the hearings on SALT II in 1979, in which a battery of witnesses of great distinction, one now a very senior arms control advisor, explained that we were entering a period of a window of vulnerability in which the prospect of atomic blackmail would be high or, in the language of a former secretary of state, that we would have five years of maximum danger. It did not happen. The fear was unreal. The strategic balance has been robust throughout that period. It is robust today. And we are entitled to approach these matters, therefore, with a certain self-confidence and to be cautious when we are asked to proceed on the basis of fear.

Now, let me comment very briefly on SDI, because most of what I want to say has been said by others. I found Mr. Adelman's description of it remarkable, because not one of the explanations he offered us was the explanation the president gave us in March of 1983. And if you compare the dream of making the weapons impotent and obsolete with the more practical question of whether it reinforces deterrence, you see that we are talking about "Star Wars I" and "SDI II," and they are not the same. And that is how it happens, in my view, that Dr. Kissinger is wrong when he tells us that a plan cannot be both infeasible and destabilizing. The president's dream is infeasible; Mr. Adelman's substitute is destabilizing, and that is why I believe the right course is for us to recognize that the Soviet fear of what we might do in strategic defenses is genuine and to ask in return that they recognize that our fear (whether or not in the end it is soundly based) of their wholly excessive deployments of both intercontinental and theater missiles is genuine, and that we trade out those fears in a grand bargain at Geneva.

Howard Baker: Dr. Bundy, thank you very much.

I have a challenge before me now, President Ford and President Carter, that I am sure I will not manage to address successfully; that is, I have allowed myself two minutes to make a closing statement, but following on after the good example set by all of my colleagues in that respect, I will have a minimum regard for that discipline.

I do, however, wish to say these things. First, I thank President Carter and President Ford for inviting me to participate. I thank Senator Nunn for permitting me to co-chair this panel, and I thank my fellow panelists for a very excellent presentation in every case, without exception.

I would observe that throughout this presentation (or at least that part of it, of this symposium, in which I have participated) as far as I know, we have avoided the real, underlying reason for these conversations. That is, we live in an era that is unprecedented in the history of civilization. We have had other times of stress and conflict. We have had other nations set against each other, diplomatically and in warfare. But we have never before, except in the last few decades, had the undoubted ability to incinerate this planet. It is against that new imperative that we must address the question of how, by civil, diplomatic, and nonmilitary means, we will preserve civilization. The alternative to military might is diplomatic initiative. The precedent and the record of success for diplomatic initiative and preserving the peace over the last several millennia is not good; it has never succeeded for very long. But the real challenge before this group— before this nation and before civilization—is to invent a way to resolve our disputes, to allay our fears and concerns, to live together and to avoid mutual annihilation. That is the reason we must find ways to reduce the risk of nuclear war. That is why we must pursue the question of arms control negotiation. That is why we must understand each other and express a decent respect for differing points of view. That, my friends, is why we must try to de-politicize this greatest of all challenges before humanity. How do we survive in a nuclear age? I know of no way to do that except the way we are doing it now and that is to hear each other's points of view—to test those ideas and theses in public debate and to try to formulate a general consensus on the approach that we must take. That is the real requirement for bipartisanship. It is time now, in my opinion, to disregard the past, to resolve at this moment, and in the future, that we are going to try to go forward together because there are some issues that are so important that they simply cannot be resolved in the realm of adversarial politics within our great exquisite system of democracy. It is time that bipartisanship be more than simply notifying the opposing and minority party of a decision previously made. It is time that we consulted with our adversaries, with our antagonists, and that we involve them in the process of making future decisions for the welfare not only of this country but for this planet. It is time that we involve the Congress, especially the Senate of the United States, and this country, in full consultation as we progress toward the time when we can offer to the Senate and to the American people a structure, a charter, a document, which may be the next step in trying to reduce the risk of nuclear war. It is time, my friends, that we work together, because we dare not fail in inventing this new technique of substituting negotiations and diplomacy for the horror of war and incineration.

I have two specific proposals that I would like to add to the already very excellent set of recommendations that have been made to this group. We are now involved in watching the unfolding and developing of a new summit talk, perhaps between the president of the United States and the new leader of the Soviet Union, and I applaud that. I believe it is appropriate. It is perhaps essential and indispensable that the leader of the United States meet with the leader of the Soviet Union to understand each other and explore ways to try to reduce the conflict between our two nations. But I also observe that it is a great media event, this upcoming meeting between President Reagan and the new leader of the Soviet Union, and I think that the value of face-to-face contact is so great that it should not be so extraordinary. I proposed once, and I repeat today, that this and future presidents of the United States should consider asking their counterparts in the Soviet Union to meet regularly, on an annual basis, without a predetermined agenda, simply to discuss the general welfare of our two nations.

I believe there is one other recommendation I would put before this group. It is not new, certainly, and has been discussed many times and has been received with varying degrees of acceptance or rejection by administrations here and abroad, particularly in the Soviet Union. At the very dawning of the nuclear age, it was once suggested that the only sure way to control the destruction of nuclear weapons is to make sure we believe each other. I believe there is no substitute for verification, and that there is no verification unless we can have on-site inspection in our two countries—the United States and the Soviet Union. I believe that must be the cornerstone of a future, believable, workable arms control agreement between the two superpowers of the world. President Carter, President Ford, I thank you for permitting me to say these things. I congratulate you once again for this very excellent meeting.

Session 4
Overview: Options
and Recommendations

President Carter: We are going to begin this afternoon with a brief summary of the recommendations that have been derived from four full days of study and consultation, discussions, and sometimes debate and argument, and what I would like to do in order to expedite the afternoon's proceedings is to read the recommendations with President Ford, as we have concluded them. They will be divided into two parts: one part, which I will read, basically is related to U.S.-Soviet relations and specifically to arms control, and the other part, which President Ford will read, will relate to alliances and to nonproliferation and the other questions of that nature that do not apply directly to negotiations between the two superpowers. Although it might be better if we had two or three days to have a debate on each recommendation, we will not do that. I am going to read all the recommendations, and then after President Ford reads his, we will call on the panelists on the stage to comment on any matter that they would like to raise, and also to comment on any of the recommendations or suggest a change.

I might say quickly that these recommendations that I shall read form a consensus, quite interestingly, among me and President Ford, Senator Baker, Senator Nunn, the three panel chairmen, and the Soviet delegation. Secretary Vance was kind enough to act as our scribe or secretary during our meeting, and he participated as well.

First of all: That the United States and the Soviet Union continue to adhere to the Antiballistic Missile Treaty and the Outer Space Treaty, and that no steps be taken contrary to the terms of these treaties without negotiation. Parties should clarify the terms of the treaty to distinguish between development and research. (That last comment applies to the Strategic Defense Initiative or, as some refer to it, "Star Wars," in that we should not go beyond the research phase to the development phase without defining, between the United States and the Soviet Union, where one ends and the other commences. As we go into the development stage, that is the time at which the Antiballistic Missile Treaty would have to be abrogated or violated.)

Second: That the United States and the Soviet Union continue their existing policies of not taking steps to undercut the provisions of treaties agreed to but not formally in effect, including the Interim Agreement on Offensive Arms, the Threshold Test Ban Treaty, and SALT II. The definitions and other noncontroversial provisions of the SALT II treaty should be carried forward into any future agreement. In other words, to leave in effect existing agreements which do not have legal status because they may have expired or may shortly expire without negotiations between the two superpowers.

Third: Based on the U.S.–Soviet agreement of January, 1985, which established the Geneva negotiations now ongoing, that the United States and the Soviet Union pursue negotiations greatly to reduce and further limit nuclear arms, both intercontinental and intermediate, taking into account but without letting the possibility of future developments in strategic defensive systems inhibit such reductions and limitations. Any such agreement should create a more stable balance at lower levels of weapons and contribute to overall strategic stability.

Fourth: That the sides should take more constructive and imaginative steps regarding verification of compliance with negotiated agreements—with agreements, including cooperative measures as appropriate and necessary to enhance such verification. In this connection, issues of compliance should be dealt with by both sides in a manner which is aimed at their resolution, not their exploitation for political or propaganda purposes. That the same criterion be applied to negotiations themselves.

The purpose of this recommendation is to cover the serious and growing problem concerning confrontations that arise from allegations about violations of the agreements. And there is a growing belief that the allegations of violations have substance. But the purpose of this is to recommend that the Standing Consultative Commission be used—diplomatic procedures be used—and that on-site inspections not be excluded. In other words, after you exhaust the Standing Consultative Commission and diplomatic measures to resolve allegations of violations, then to include on-site inspections, if necessary, to determine whether or not a violation has occurred.

Next: That the United States and the Soviet Union address with the utmost priority the question of establishing mechanisms aimed at crisis prevention and crisis management in order to avoid misunderstandings and/or miscalculations which could lead to conflict. Frequent meetings of senior political and military leaders would be desirable. I think all of you remember that General David Jones pointed out the extreme benefit, at the conferences in Vienna to conclude the SALT II treaty, when he and the Soviet military leaders were able to talk privately for just a few hours.

Next: That current and future negotiations continue to take into account the interests of allies and other countries in the avoidance of war and enhancement of stability. We asked the Soviet delegation if they would take into consideration the interests of their allies, and they said they would do the same as we.

Next: That current and future negotiations, while not conducted in a vacuum, should at the same time not be held hostage to linkage with other, unrelated, issues between the sides. In other words, it is our opinion—the whole group that I described to you earlier—that if there are those inevitable differences that arise because of regional conflict or allegations of violations, this should not prohibit or interrupt the highly crucial arms negotiations.

Next: That neither side seek to achieve real or apparent superiority through negotiations. This was an item which seemed to be very important to the Soviet participants.

Next: That in the future, both sides move more ambitiously in negotiating comprehensive arms agreements without excluding limited steps in the short term. What this means is that in the present negotiations in Geneva, which may go on three or four years—no one knows—that as the two parties reach agreement on a significant item, even though a final treaty is not signed, that that agreement be put into effect whenever possible. It may be that both sides agree that a particularly destabilizing weapon or system ought to be eliminated or reduced, and not wait until the final signed agreement before putting that interim agreement into effect.

Next: That the public in both countries be educated to the fact that the issues are complex and that both sides enter the negotiations with major asymmetries, differences, many of them unchangeable. The hope here is that not only the leaders of the two nations but others in positions of authority will not take a simplistic approach which highly distorts the complexities that do exist but will make sure that the general public understands that there are inherent differences between the two countries and that we should try to find a peaceful way to live with those inevitable differences. One of the steps toward that, of course, is this consultation, which is why it is being publicized.

The next one is long, but we think it encapsulates extremely well what was presented this morning about the basic differences that exist between the United States and the Soviet Union in the control of strategic weapons, weapons with limited range, and the Strategic Defense Initiative. I will read it for your consideration:

At the Geneva negotiations the Soviet side appears to be unwilling to consider deep reductions in strategic offensive weapons so long as the possibility of new strategic defensive deployments is not definitely foreclosed. The American side wishes to negotiate precisely such deep reductions while holding open the strategic defense option pending completion of research to establish its feasibility. The panel believes that negotiations must proceed taking full account of the strategic offensive-defensive interrelationship, exploring both offensive and defen-

sive arms limitations. The panel believes, further, that an unregulated competition in both offensive nuclear weapons and strategic defenses would be disastrous, and that a cooperative transition toward deployment of extensive strategic
defenses may not be feasible on either technical or political grounds, even if
desirable in principle. Therefore, they recommend that the two sides now begin to examine what kinds of more far-reaching arms control agreements limiting offensive forces might be sufficient to stabilize the competition in a manner
that would minimize the incentives of either side to deploy extensive strategic
defenses. All of us understood that this is complicated and difficult to understand,
and we tried to think of a simpler way to express it, but I have to point out to
you that the conflict that exists at Geneva at the negotiating table—one of the
things that kept the people from going back to Geneva for so long—was this basic
point. Anyone on the panel who wishes to discuss it more may do so, of course.

The next recommendation is: that parties should consider as an interim goal
a relatively small number of single warhead missiles, 2,000 as a suggestion,
deployed as invulnerably as possible, in deep silos on the southern side of moun-
tain ranges where they could not be hit by incoming missiles, or in ocean-safe
havens. The exact number is not as important as survivability and assured deterrence. We should seek agreement from other nuclear powers, like Great Britain, France, and China, to make comparable reductions in their nuclear arsenals.
This was a suggestion discussed quite extensively in the panel sessions but not
covered so well in the public sessions. And this is what you might call the next
step before total elimination of nuclear weapons from all arsenals, that is, to have
a fairly small number of single warhead missiles deployed as invulnerably as
possible—maybe about 2,000. But if the two superpowers reduce their arsenal
from 25,000 down to 2,000, then the importance of the other nuclear powers'
arsenals becomes very great, and they would be asked to join, for the first time
really, in reducing their own arsenals in an appropriate way.

The next one is: to ratify the Threshold Test Ban Treaty, steadily lowering
explosion limits commensurate with technical ability for verification, ultimately
to achieve a comprehensive test ban agreement. It was the opinion of all our
group that a comprehensive test ban was desirable. This is not feasible in the
immediate future because of political considerations which I need not describe.
So we thought the best approach to this was to take the Threshold Test Ban
Treaty, which now puts a 150-kiloton limit on tests, and to reduce this limit as
rapidly as possible, always being sure that we can verify the limit (which is more
difficult to detect as the limit gets lower) until we finally reach a point equivalent to a comprehensive test ban agreement.

The next item is to renew negotiations to ban any deployment of offensive
weapons in space. As most of you now know, at least, weapons of mass destruction are prohibited in space. This is not to recommend specifically the banning
of all offensive weapons in space, but to renew negotiations between the two na-

tions with the goal of banning the deployment of offensive weapons in space.

The next one is: we recommend that United States–Soviet consultations include the question of nonproliferation, and we also advocate regional agreements involving nuclear-free zones and their encouragement whenever possible.

Some of these recommendations are quite innovative; some of them are there because we feel that their adoption should be re-emphasized; some of them are briefly expressed, and there are nuances we have not been able to cover adequately; some of them are inherently complex, and we tried to express them in the simplest terms. But in a few minutes, after President Ford presents another group of recommendations—those not related directly to U.S.–Soviet arms negotiations—then we will call upon our panelists on the stage to comment on these particular items, add others as they choose, or make comments as they prefer. President Ford . . .

President Ford: As President Carter indicated, the recommendations that he has read relate almost exclusively to U.S.–Soviet relations. The ones that I will read are more in the line of recommendations that cover relations between the United States and its allies, with some broader implications. The Soviet Union had no participation, in effect, as far as these were concerned, because of the focus of what we are recommending.

1. The United States, as the leader of the West, will have to pay greater attention to the views and the interests of its allies in order to maintain the cohesion and effectiveness of both the Atlantic and the Pacific alliances.

2. The active involvement of allies will continue to be needed in all major dimensions of the East-West relationship—political, military, economic, and social. Allied participation in these areas has often been important in the past, but even greater efforts will be called for in the future if East–West relations are not to be permitted to drift into areas of greater danger. These recommendations came exclusively from the panel headed by Bob O'Neill, and they were much longer, but were cut down to be significantly reduced in length.

3. The West should develop and allocate the resources necessary to implement longer-term strategies for preventing or limiting regional conflicts. In most cases leadership must come from the United States, but in some situations, as in the past, individual allies must be prepared to play a leading role.

Next, the development of regional initiatives and organizations to enhance security, both nationally and collectively, should be encouraged. With the ever-increasing threat of terrorism, short- and long-term remedies must be urgently sought unilaterally, bilaterally, and multilaterally.

Next, nuclear proliferation remains a very potent threat to world order. New technology and increased concern by potential nuclear powers about regional threats require renewed vigor in dealing with this problem. Firm controls on the transfer of nuclear technology must be maintained, and new ways for thwarting the clandestine diffusion of this technology must be devised. The cause of nonproliferation must be kept high on the international agenda. Those are the recommendations that basically came from the O'Neill panel, and we submit them along with the others for your consideration.

President Carter: As you all know, in the previous three sessions, we have read out the panel reports and then called on the Soviet delegation to make a comment. We will continue with that policy, so now we would like to hear from the Soviet delegation on these specific recommendations.

Sergei Tarasenko: First of all, I wish to thank you all for the very interesting and very important discussion; I think the report very exactly reflects our discussion, and I have no major comments on the report.

One thing worries me a little; that is, the words "offensive weapons in space," because I think it would be possible to have a long discussion about what is offensive in space and what is defensive. I would be much happier if we just ask for the prohibition of any weapons in space. Thank you.

President Carter: President Ford and I have decided that we will delete the word "offensive." The recommendation was that we renew negotiations towards the goal of banning any deployment of weapons in space, and the negotiations would have to decide the character of the weapons or how to define the weapons, but we have no objection to that. Do you all have any other comments?

Sergei Tarasenko: Well, I guess the audience noticed that the Soviet contingent has moved a bit closer to the chair. There is a real danger that if you give us a couple of more days maybe we will take over. But really, on behalf of all my colleagues, I would like to say that this seminar, this meeting was very educational, very useful, both on technical, political, and human levels, and we do appreciate the kindness of President Carter and the Carter Center in organizing this very complicated and logistically difficult thing. Our thanks go to everyone who helped to hold this meeting and helped us and took care of us here in Atlanta. We felt that we lived in a very hospitable climate and—believe me, I have lived in the United States for several years—rarely have I personally met with such good feeling towards the Soviet representatives from the public and from all the participants, and for that, our deep and sincere thanks to all of you. We certainly feel that this endeavor and endeavors of this kind are extremely useful, and if we find ways to continue or make a tradition of this kind of meeting, that will be a very good thing to do. Thank you very much.

President Carter: We are very grateful this afternoon to have the panelists who have come here sometimes at great sacrifice, not just these but others who have participated. We have a very favorite place in the Virgin Islands that Rosalynn and I immediately went to when I left the White House—a tiny place that we do not want too many people to know about—called Cinnamon Bay. The next speaker, Senator Ted Stevens from Alaska, has left his wife and family down in the Virgin Islands—on St. John's—to participate with us. I think this is a sacrifice beyond the call of duty, but we were very eager to have him here because of his background and knowledge in this subject. I would like to call on Senator Ted Stevens from Alaska to comment next.

Ted Stevens: Thank you very much, Mr. President. We are indebted to you and President Ford for this invitation. Those of us who are participating in the negotiations in Geneva, at least those of us in the Senate as observers, are becoming acutely aware of the need in our open society for a greater discussion about what is going on over there, where on the basis of confidentiality the discussions are necessarily closed. Your forum, your consultation, here, is a very meaningful one at this time, to bring before the American public a greater knowledge of the subject matter that we are pursuing there in Geneva, and I think you are to be credited also with having CNN (Cable News Network television) here to take this out throughout the country.

The Senate leadership, mindful of the fact that three recent treaties in the arms control area remain unratified, has appointed a group known as the Senate observers group to monitor the discussions in Geneva. As Senator Nunn mentioned today, one of the great problems in the Senate has been these isolated issues, such as both presidents have discussed here now. The most significant one now is the Krasnoyarsk radar, and I might say that I share with our friend from Russia, Mr. Tarasenko, the feeling of having been able to participate while we are here in terms of just personal relationships, of having conversations at dinner. We do not raise subjects like this at dinner, but our Soviet friends should realize how significant this issue is in the Senate. Representing Alaska, I think I realize more than anyone here the difficulties of building a radar in the Soviet eastern zone of the Arctic, and I understand, perhaps, why the decision was made to put it where it is. But the difficulty with this circumstance is that the Soviets did not take the occasion to discuss those reasons of geography and cost and maintenance, which we would find very valid. Along with Senator Nunn, I probably pay more attention to these negotiations than any of the members of the Senate at the present time, I think, because of our role as co-chairmen of this observer group (along with Senator Gore—pardon me, he is also with us). We are trying to find out what stumbling blocks there might be for an agreement if one is achieved now. This radar is one of the most significant stumbling blocks I have seen in my 17 years in the Senate, and I would say to my friends from the Soviet Union that I think that this is the time now to think about on-site inspection. Mr. Brzezinski mentioned it this morning, and I see no reason why a group such as ours, the Senate observer group or representatives of a group like this, should not be invited to come take a look at this radar if it is indeed totally a civilian radar. Its location and its ability to be synchronized with other developments that we know are going on in the Soviet Union leave many of us with an increasing fear of the meaning of this radar, in terms of territorial defense. It is a very significant development in our relationships, and I would hope that the comments that have been made here by both Senator Nunn and myself and comments made by others in private would not go unheeded by our friends from the Soviet Union. I think it is at meetings like this that we can have exchanges that may lead to some step being taken by one side or the other.

The confidence-building measures that we all talk about in connection with these negotiations require us to identify potential roadblocks ahead and to urge that the other side take some action to help us eliminate those roadblocks as the negotiations continue. I am not as pessimistic as many of those here concerning the progress in Geneva nor the eventual outcome in Geneva, in the sense of some meaningful agreement coming out of those negotiations. Our negotiators are extremely capable. I think they have a wide latitude. We have been impressed with the Soviets on a similar basis, and while we do not discuss what is actually being said, under the agreement of confidentiality, I would say that all of the members of the Senate who went there recently to observe the beginnings of those negotiations came away with greater hope than I have seen before in negotiations in the past. I think what you are doing here, as I said, is a meaningful adjunct to those negotiations, and I hope that we can keep these up and keep on a positive basis among ourselves as we try to seek a solution with our friends abroad. I thank you for inviting me.

President Carter: It was not exactly clear to me this morning, but I think it is very significant that Senator Nunn made the same comment about the Krasnoyarsk radar, and my interpretation of the Soviet response was that the best way to address an alleged violation is not to go public with it, not to have a political confrontation, which, in effect, damages the prospects for cooperation and arms control, but to take it first to the Standing Consultative Commission. If this does not prove to be successful in resolving the questions, then try to resolve it by diplomatic means—I presume at the top level, at the foreign minister level or even higher. And then I understood Ambassador Dobrynin to say that even onsite inspections might be permissible as an alternative to a breakdown in negotiations or further disharmony. I wonder if Mr. Tarasenko or Professor Velikhov would state if I have expressed it correctly.

Ted Stevens: I am not sure that the depth of the misunderstanding on this subject is recognized. We do not understand the motivation for this radar... [*Carter:* Yes, I think coming from both you and Senator Nunn this has been doubly emphasized to the Soviet delegation, including Ambassador Dobrynin, before he had to leave at noon.]

President Carter: Kenneth Adelman has already been introduced to the group this morning. As you know, he is head of the Arms Control and Disarmament Agency, and he is intimately involved in the preparation of American positions and in the pursuit of better relations with the Soviet Union in overall reduction in the threat of nuclear arms. I would like to call on Dr. Kenneth Adelman to comment at this moment.

Kenneth Adelman: Thank you, President Carter, and thank you, President Ford. Let me say that I thought the conclusions of the report were by and large very sound, and I had just a few comments. To pick up where Senator Stevens left off, I think the question of compliance is a question that is separate from the question of verification, as we all know. There are some provisions in arms control proposals that are very easy to verify, such as the provision in the ABM treaty that deals with phased array radars, but the question comes up about Soviet noncompliance. I agree with the thrust of the report that these should be handled in the SCC [Standing Consultative Commission] or in the diplomatic channels. This is what we have been trying to do, as we have on the other compliance issues, even though I personally believe that the radar is the most important. There are the issues of encryption (about which you, President Carter, felt so strongly, and rightly so, before); the issues of the new SS-25; the issues of venting; and the Helsinki Final Act and other issues. So I think that it is important to realize once again that arms control just cannot get anywhere unless both sides adhere to the agreement.

Second, let me say that while the Standing Consultative Commission is the main thrust, we have at times gone outside the SCC because of Soviet violations, and this has at times proved successful. Let me give you one example that I felt particularly strongly about when I was at the United Nations for the first two years of the Reagan administration: yellow rain. Many people in Southeast Asia were dying from chemical weapon attacks in a brutal kind of way, choking on their own blood, etc., because of yellow rain attacks. To the best of our information it is in part because of the attention that we brought to this issue (and the fact that innocent Hmong people were dying), that for the past two years there have been no confirmed reports of chemical weapon use in Southeast Asia. I have visited refugee camps high in the northern part of Thailand and spoken to Hmong people who had been subjected to chemical weapons attack, and it is a gruesome story. I believe it is very beneficial that there have been no confirmed reports of recent chemical weapon use in Southeast Asia: beneficial, not only to arms control but obviously to the U.S.–Soviet relationship and to the future of the Hmong people.

My second general point is that I believe the thrust of the recommendations for a lower level of offensive nuclear weapons is entirely right. These high levels are the crux of the problem today. They are the danger of today. That has been what arms control has concentrated on since 1969, when the process really began. That should be the concentration now and in the future. SDI, as the report acknowledges, is an element there, although it was not the element that drove the Soviets away from the talks or prevented them from coming back to the talks. We know that what drove the Soviets from the talks was the NATO fulfillment of the 1979 dual-track decision on the Euromissiles. But they did come back, and we are eager to get on with the business. I think that the kind of questions that the report mentions on the gray areas of what research would be allowed and what would be banned are the kinds of discussions we should be having in Geneva, and they are precisely the kinds that we hope to have in Geneva. I, for one, was a little disappointed when Ambassador Dobrynin said this morning that this is not being discussed; we are not talking about SDI, although there is a big Soviet delegation there that is doing little else but talking about SDI, and we are talking about the issues such as the gray area issue. President Carter, I think you are absolutely right about what General Jones said, that the military-to-military discussions are very beneficial and could be more beneficial. Like President Ford and your administration, we have tried to talk to the Soviets about that as one of the initiatives. The president, taking the bipartisan approach that both of you had recommended, announced this in a United Nations speech, and we have gone back to the Soviets repeatedly about it, but they have just not taken it up. I think that the emphasis on the report that President Ford read on regional conflicts is absolutely key to this initiative.

Let me end by saying that when I think about the problem we are discussing in this good conference about the—God forbid—possible use of nuclear weapons at any time in our lives I think that could take place in one of two ways only. One is an escalation from a regional conflict, a repeat of the Cuban missile crisis, the 1973 Middle East crisis, or the crises we have had in Southeast Asia or Southwest Asia since that time. The fact is that in the last five years the main conflicts in the world have been three: the Falklands, Iran–Iraq, and Lebanon. And I think it is remarkable that none of these has had any direct East-West friction to them, in contrast to these kinds of conflicts that we have had in the past. I think there is, by and large, a better understanding between the United States and the Soviet Union on acceptable behavior, and that is due to a great number of factors that I do not have time to get into. The second way that nuclear weapons could ever be used in the world is by the spread of nuclear weapons to additional countries, particularly if nuclear weapons got in the hands of some irresponsible leader somewhere in the world. This, let me say, is the one area of arms control where we have had more success than most of us had any right to expect. I recall that in 1963 President Kennedy said that by 1975 the world would have 15 to 20 nuclear weapons states. At the time he made that remark, there were five nuclear weapons states, and today there are still five nuclear weapons states. India tested a nuclear explosive in 1974, but did not create a nuclear weapon. And of course, many other countries bear close watching. But more than twenty years after his statement, there is certainly nowhere near the 15 or 20 that he so ominously warned against. One reason for this is that the United States and the Soviet Union recognize their common interest in stopping the spread of nuclear weapons, and we have had a dialogue on this important subject. We have decided to regularize it in the Reagan administration by having twice-annual meetings. These meetings have been underway for a number of years with the Soviet Union, to talk about nonproliferation issues only. These meetings are not widely publicized. I do not think they need to be. Next week in Helsinki we are going to resume that dialogue and go over problem areas that we and the Soviets have and strengthen the international institutions that deal with nonproliferation. We are going to cooperate; I believe that the Soviet Union has been involved in this issue and is as serious about this issue as we have been, and I applaud them for that. We have been cooperating on the Non-Proliferation Treaty review conference that will begin in late August. It will be of critical importance to keep the treaty together. If we could find a way to cooperate with the Soviet Union on controlling our own nuclear weapons in the same way that we cooperate on preventing others from getting nuclear weapons, then I think we would have a very much better future and a much more hopeful world. I thank you.

Sergei Tarasenko: I would not like to go into it, but I will have to raise a question about something that may cause some confusion among the audience: about this yellow rain. I really resent that on an official level this falsehood is repeated, and I can give you every assurance, and can cite you all the assurances of the Soviet government, that on no occasion have we used, nor has there been any use of, chemical substances. And I specifically resent it when the accusation comes from the people who are not too generous in settling the suit of the Vietnam veterans who were subjected to Agent Orange.

President Carter: Now we will have Senator Albert Gore comment on that subject or others as he sees fit. And I might say that Senator Al Gore is a neighbor of ours, from Tennessee. He was one of the members of the House of Representatives whom I greatly admired for his intense interest in and knowledge of these issues that we have discussed this week, and I would say that the loss of the House of Representatives is the gain of the Senate. We are very delighted to have you with us—Senator Albert Gore.

Albert Gore: Thank you very much, Mr. President. I would like to extend my thanks to you and to President Ford for the invitation to be here and for the excellent discussions that we have had during these several days. I have been to many discussions of strategic policy, and I can say without reservation that this is the best that I have ever had the chance to participate in or to see. I think our country is extremely fortunate to have two former presidents with the kind of dedication that you both have. I want to make certain the country realizes the tremendous assets that you can bring to a discussion like this, and I personally appreciate it.

Drawing from the conclusions that you have outlined, I would like to limit my remarks to a few of them that concern stability and two specific systems: the single-warhead missile and the Strategic Defense Initiative. I do not know if there is a procedure for modifying any of the recommendations that you have outlined, but I want to agree in large part but to suggest some slight modifications on both of them.

First of all, the goal of stability has now become our principal strategic goal in the United States, and there seems to be a broad agreement on the part of the Soviet Union that this is the preeminent goal which both nations should seek in arms control talks. But after all of the time that has been spent discussing stability, perhaps not enough effort has gone into thinking through the precise meaning of the word in terms that can be translated into hard policy, about the numbers and types of weapons that we should procure and the kinds that the Soviet Union should procure in conformity with agreements that we seek together.

The core of the problem of stability for the United States has been—and remains—the survivability of our land-based ballistic missile force, and the degree to which we should exert ourselves to resist the trend toward increasing vulnerability. The Scowcroft Commission gave impetus to the idea of a single-warhead missile as a means of reducing the value of targets in the United States and simultaneously reducing the perceived threat on the part of the Soviet Union. But I do not think that we have yet gotten far enough in our specific recommendations about what the single-warhead missile force should look like. The recommendation you read, which discussed extremely large numbers and deep silos on the south of mountains, is something that is somewhat removed from the emerging consensus about how these missiles should be deployed. Specifically, I think that thinking has converged on a system that depends upon limited mobility within an area of 5,000 to 10,000 square miles, with a reasonable degree of hardness, in a mode that is verifiably contained in these zones so that if you find even one outside of a restricted zone, then you know that that is a violation (Mr. Adelman is familiar with these concepts in depth). I believe that this method of building and deploying the single-warhead missile is far preferable to the kind of idea that was included in your specific recommendation. Extensive mathematical studies have recently been completed indicating that a Midgetman force in mobile hardened launchers deployed on government property within a 10,000-square-mile area will yield either a significant force of single warhead missiles untouched after a Soviet attack, or cause the Soviets to expend such a huge number of their own warheads that they have no advantage to be gained in such an attack, particularly if the fractionalization limits of SALT II are kept. I believe that this particular approach is something for which it is very important to maintain the bipartisan consensus that was formed around the Scowcroft Commission report, and I hope that we can continue in that direction.

Now, I would like to move on to the Strategic Defense Initiative and its implications for stability. And, again, I think the recommendation that you outlined is essentially sound. But I think that it would be improved if it reflected the distinction, that McGeorge Bundy and others have spoken of, between the two different strategic defense initiatives. I think it is important to realize that the political support in the country for the Strategic Defense Initiative derives by and large from the popular belief that a leakproof population defense system is possible. It is not possible, and we should say so forthrightly. It is a fantasy. It cannot be done. There is a point where one must distinguish between realism and idealism. Some truths are sad truths, but they are truths nonetheless. Deterrence is going to remain our mainstay as a policy throughout this century and well into the next century for as far as we can see. I believe that there are some who know that a leakproof population defense is a fantasy and yet have been reluctant to say so. I believe they should say so, and I believe they should—those who are in a position to do so—should tell the president, if he does not know it already. I have the feeling, that for some this "first" SDI is a kind of stalking horse for the "second" SDI—building a running interference, as it were, and building political support for the second version of SDI, which is ballistic missile defense.

Now, the second version of SDI—to defend missiles—is feasible, and indeed there are even some arguments that can reasonably be advanced in support of the concept, but in my view, it is unwise because there are two kinds of stability. One kind is crisis stability. Most of our discussion has focused on crisis stability, as is appropriate. But there is also arms race stability, and although it is theoretically feasible to attain a kind of crisis stability with the introduction of limited ballistic missile defenses on both sides, it will destabilize the arms race, and I think the recommendations of the panel are clear on that point.

This is why the principles undergirding the ABM treaty must be renewed and we must rededicate ourselves to them. That is why Krasnoyarsk is so potent as a political obstacle: because it appears to be, clearly, a violation when the radar is turned on. I would say, with all the due respect to our Soviet colleagues here, it is not a space tracking radar. But it is not really that, and it has been discussed in the SCC, it has also been discussed in diplomatic channels, and the United States has been stonewalled. Now, I think there is a very important argument about its military significance. It may not be all that significant in a military sense, but—and this is my point—when the argument in the United States shifts to ballistic missile defense and we talk about this second version of SDI, the debate will be profoundly affected if those in favor of SDI "II" are able to say that the Soviet Union evidently does not feel strongly enough about the principles embodied in the ABM treaty to refrain from violating that treaty.

Now, I would like to say that there are two developments that we are likely to see occurring in the near future. I have just alluded to one. The domestic debate on SDI will shift toward a debate which mimics and revisits the 1969 and 1970 debate over the Antiballistic Missile Treaty. The Soviet Union can affect the outcome of that American decision-making process in a positive and constructive way by offering seriously deep reductions in offensive missiles in order to remove the real underlying pressure that has been pushing SDI "II" forward.

The second development, I fear, will crystallize in Geneva around the United States' reluctance to discuss space and defense weapons in great detail. If the Soviet Union comes forward with a meaningful version of the grand trade-off that several, including McGeorge Bundy and Secretary Schlesinger, have referred to—offering deep offensive cuts in return for stalling deployment options on SDI—at that point the United States may well face a moment of truth. Between now and then, those of us here at this conference and others who are vitally concerned with these issues must find a way to accelerate the maturation of our government's view of the Strategic Defense Initiative. The criteria outlined by

Paul Nitze offer a graceful way to change direction if this system is re-evaluated in a serious way. Also, I believe that there is a way to draw a distinction between research and development and deployment, which is alluded to in the recommendations which you and President Ford presented. I would like to recommend for your consideration a more specific version of what that line could be, to temporarily forestall not only the deployment of the Strategic Defense Initiative, but to forestall it at a point that falls short of a serious breakout threat while nevertheless permitting research and experimentation to continue—which, after all, cannot be verified on either side.

There are three specific elements: (1) no experimentation with hypervelocity rail guns in space, (2) no experiments with high-energy-level, directed-energy systems in space, and (3) no experiments with large-array mirrors in space, operating cooperatively with energy sources on the ground, and no high-energy sources directed from earth at such cooperative mirrors. I believe that such a distinction, were it acceptable as a boundary on SDI developments, could be coupled with offensive missile cuts and, of course, compensating U.S. reductions in cruise missiles and bombers, to form the outlines of the kind of broad agreement which may be the only feasible outcome of these complicated negotiations that we are now in in Geneva. But of course, I also concur with your recommendations that we continue the SALT II limits and continue abiding by the other treaties. Thank you.

President Ford: President Carter and other members of the panel, I very strongly concur with the recommendations that we have made as a group involving SDI, etc. I firmly believe that we should proceed with responsible research, and I must say to the senator from Tennessee that he should be a bit cautious about saying our scientists could never do this or do that. I served in the House of Representatives when his father was a member of the House, and subsequently in the Senate, and both of us at the time were, I suspect, very, very dubious right after World War II that some of our scientists could do the things that subsequently we now have in hardware and are fully operational. I as a layman (and, I believe, you are also, Senator) do not have the competence to pass judgment on what our scientific community as a whole can achieve. I would question the technical recommendations that have been made, primarily because, in the first place, those are projects or terms on which I believe people in scientific disciplines ought to pass the judgment, not a group of politicians who are basically not qualified for such judgments. I only say that we should proceed with the research, and I have made no commitment beyond that, and I am not going to give an open rein to any scientist of any discipline to proceed beyond a responsible position. But to say categorically as you did, Senator, I think is a bit unwise, because some of our scientists have a pretty good track record of surprising laymen, particularly, and even other members of their own scientific community. When we are dealing with things of this magnitude, I do not think we should take the extreme view that some people in the administration have taken that we can abandon deterrence and put all our eggs in the defensive basket. I vigorously oppose that point of view. On the other hand, I do feel that we have an obligation—in a responsible way in conjunction with a continued deterrence policy—to proceed with a responsible research program.

Albert Gore: I wholeheartedly agree that we should continue research. I also believe that since that view is unanimous, we need to give some thought as to whether or not we are locking ourselves into a course that leads inexorably toward development and deployment. And in advancing a set of ideas on how one might draw a boundary line between research and development, I do not recommend that such specific items be included. It would be inappropriate. I say I advance them for consideration. They are not originating with this layman; they are the result of discussion with people active in the field.

As I said, I think that the second kind of SDI is feasible. Is the first kind—a perfect defense—possible? I chose to make the statement that in my opinion a leakproof population defense is not possible because I have been frustrated with the continuing sort of wishy-washy statements from people who really know better, and I think that there are some scientists in that category who know better and who will tell you, off the record, "Look, it's 99 to 1." At some point, we have to be willing to say that this is unrealistic. And if we are in a situation where holding out the possibility that a 99 to 1 shot is going to be vigorously pursued and that possibility is preventing progress in arms control, then I think we have to be willing to reassess whether it is realistic 'or not and shift the debate to whether we really want a ballistic-missile-defense kind of SDI, and I think there is a reasonable ground for debate and difference. I am on one side, but I see the arguments on the other side.

President Carter: I think one of the comments that Senator Gore made earlier is worthy of repetition here. Among some of the very knowledgeable people who have attended, some of whom are still in the audience, including Secretary Harold Brown and James Schlesinger, there is a consensus that it is practically impossible, certainly fiscally infeasible, to develop an umbrella that would totally protect the population of the United States. But I think the presence of the Soviet delegation here has made some of the American spokesmen a lot more cautious in defending the proposals of our own government. As you can see, a former secretary of defense, in taking this strong position against the SDI as originally described by the president, in effect you are aligning yourself with the Soviet delegation and attacking the American government. And it makes it very difficult. But I think that many of you are knowledgeable enough to have read the very carefully prepared speeches and documents by people like Harold Brown, who is a notable physicist, a former president of Cal Tech and a very knowledgeable person. There are some in the audience here in the second and third row who are smiling to note that what I say is true. Nobody knows for sure. But there has been a great de-escalation in the description of "Star Wars" since the president's first speech on the matter, when it was implied that a beautiful umbrella would be placed over the American people to protect us from any number—thousands really—of simultaneously incoming nuclear weapons. I think that that concept has now been basically abandoned. I would like to call now on Congressman Norm Dicks from... [Soviet representative Sergei Tarasenko requests the floor] Okay.

Sergei Tarasenko: Just to help you in this situation the Soviet delegation switches its position in support of SDI. (audience laughter)

Harold Brown: That would help.

President Carter: I might say that several have commented that the Soviet Union is very dedicated to protecting their own forces with defense mechanisms, but you apply your prohibition to SDI just to the United States.

Kenneth Adelman: I would hope, that if the Soviet delegation was going to switch its position like that, they would redirect their efforts to switch them right in Geneva on Tuesday. That would change the nature of the game and would be very welcome indeed.

Harold Brown: Welcome aboard.

President Carter: Congressman Norm Dicks from Washington is recognized in the House and Senate and by all who know him as an expert on the subject. We are delighted to have him here this afternoon. I will minimize my introductions in the pressure of time.

Norman Dicks: President Carter, President Ford, Mrs. Carter, distinguished members of this panel. It has been a great personal honor for me to be here. I have learned a lot, and as a member of Congress, it has been good for us to have a chance to meet with the most able people, not only in this country, but from around the world, including our Soviet colleagues. There has been an outstanding two-day effort here by those who were here before, working on these papers. When one considers the fact that we may be at an impasse in Geneva, as some have suggested today, I would just hope that President Reagan would avail himself of the kind of talent that has been brought here to these meetings by President Ford and President Carter. I hope he will consider various options that might help us work our way out of this possible impasse in Geneva. I really believe that the great work that Brent Scowcroft did with a bipartisan approach, on his commission, could be emulated again to come up with a series of recommendations for this administration. By the way, the statement made by Secretary Vance, I think, is very important in trying to come up with a way to resolve the possible impasse in Geneva.

As one of those who did support the Scowcroft Commission's recommendations, I will just make this comment. The support for it, Brent, is waning a little in Congress on one particular item known as the MX missile. (I have been at the center of that debate along with Congressmen Gore and Downey and others from the House and the Senate.) Part of the reason for that, of course, is budgetary pressure. Another concern—I would point out to my good friend Ken Adelman—is that one part of the Scowcroft Commission's recommendations was a serious commitment to arms control. I for one will be very disappointed if the opportunity for a grand bargain is missed in Geneva because this administration will not consider making SDI negotiable. I think there is an opportunity for an agreement, and I think those of us in Congress who have provided bipartisan support expect the administration to take a hard look at that particular option. I would also point out that I think there will be a deployment limitation imposed by Congress on the MX missile of somewhere between 40 and 50 missiles, for a variety of reasons. I also believe that it can be a positive sign of a legislative pause. I hope the administration will go along with it, because I think most of the people who have been the so-called group of moderates will be supportive of that limitation as we get to the '86 funding.

I also think you are going to see a significant reduction of funding for the Strategic Defense Initiative. I concur with my friend Al Gore, with whom I have worked over the last several years, in thinking that the big problem has been that SDI has had so many different descriptions. I am not sure from one day to the next exactly what the administration is talking about. I think it is very useful for us to have a debate right now in this country about what we are considering. I agree it is a research program: we all support the research. We are not troubled by that. But what we are troubled by is that the prospect of SDI, looming as it does, is going to force our Soviet colleagues here and the people in the Kremlin to make decisions now, not four or five years from now, when this research is over. They are going to have to decide now whether they will ever consider deep reductions, or else what kind of new offensive systems they must have to overcome a strategic defense initiative if we should go forward with it. I would predict that in the House, at least, there will be significant cutbacks in the $3.7 billion requested by the administration. I, for one, believe that it is absolutely essential.

I was very pleased to see a strong statement in the recommendations about the necessity to maintain and keep the launcher limitations of the SALT II agreement, particularly when the Trident submarine, the *Alaska*, is deployed. This issue will be at the forefront in the next several months. My view is that we should make the reductions in other forces necessary to keep within the SALT II limitations. That issue, by the way, has not been resolved by the administration. But I can again state that those people who have tried to provide bipartisan support in the Congress are very dedicated to seeing those limitations maintained.

I would also say that the commitment to the ABM agreement should be reaffirmed. When we talk about stopping erosion in the ABM agreement, I think the first thing we must do is to come straightforwardly to the issue that Secretary Vance raised: how do we mark the point, moving from testing into deployment, where we clearly violate the agreement? I, for one, believe that violation would be a serious mistake. We need to see if there is a possibility for an agreement before we move in that direction.

I would also state that our House members are very concerned about the Krasnoyarsk radar. We are also concerned about the massive level of Soviet conventional forces and Soviet counterforce capability as demonstrated by their SS-18s, SS-19s, and their new SS-24. And we would like to urge our Soviet colleagues to exercise some restraint in these areas as well.

I think there is a chance for an agreement in Geneva. Some of us in the House—Tom Downey and I, for example—think there is a chance for an agreement, but we must take some steps right away or I am afraid an impasse will result because of the prospect of the Strategic Defense Initiative.

Again, I want to say to President Ford and President Carter that this nation owes both of you great thanks for the work you are doing. I believe in bipartisanship. I do not think we are going to make progress in this, the most significant issue of our time, without it, and you two clearly demonstrate what all Americans want to see, that is, good people working together for solutions to our national problems. Thank you.

President Carter: In June 1979, after six and a half years of negotiation under President Nixon and President Ford and me, we finally reached agreement with President Brezhnev and the Soviet delegation and then walked into a beautiful hall in Vienna to sign the SALT II treaty. I looked up and there in the front row sat a very young congressman from New York who had paid his way over there to witness this historic event, and I have had a special feeling in my heart for him ever since then. I might say that as president, both before and after SALT II was concluded, I had a steady stream of memoranda and advice from him on how we might better conclude the agreements. I am very delighted now to introduce that congressman—Tom Downey.

Tom Downey: We political people spend a lot of our time in effusive and false praise, and I don't want this to sound like that. I want to add my voice to those who have come before me to say to you, President Carter and you, President Ford, that this is an extraordinary conference. It is historic, and I hope that conferences of this sort take place in Ann Arbor and again at Emory on this and other subjects, because I think the country needs a strong dose of bipartisanship after five years of some very hard rhetoric on both sides.

Let me say that I am in substantial agreement with the recommendations that have been made. I want to comment briefly on one of the areas that I have always felt strongly about and that we talked about, Mr. President, in 1979–80; that is, this whole question of how we achieve stability, at least in one leg of the triad. You offered (I think Secretary Schlesinger talked about it) this idea of safe zones in the ocean where submarines could lurk without strategic ASW [Antisubmarine Warfare]. I think it is a good idea. I think it is a way to guarantee the survivability of one leg of the triad for both the Soviet Union and the United States, and it is something I hope we can explore a little more in detail.

Second, I would add a corollary to that safe zone concept: that we could also establish prohibited zones for submarines. I do not like the idea that Soviet submarines in the future will have the ability to combine short warning and high accuracy against both bomber and missile bases. Keeping them distant from U.S. shores would increase our warning time and also increase our stability. I offer those as recommendations to the panel.

As a House member I suspect that I will be a little suspect in this next recommendation, which I will label Category Three. As much as I love the Senate of the United States, it has taken my best friend from me, so I have some doubts about it. I believe that treaties (we have negotiated very few of them historically as compared to executive agreements) have outworn their usefulness. The president of the United States could decide that an agreement he reaches with his Soviet counterparts, if and when that happens, becomes an executive agreement. I feel that way for a couple of reasons, not only because I want to play a role in this process in the House of Representatives, but because I believe that a willful one-third of the Senate in 1919 did not help this country, and a potentially willful United States Senate in 1979 would not have helped this country either. The idea that you will have both the House of Representatives and the Senate participating and explaining the process of the treaty to our constituents is something that is good for the United States, good for the world, and helps to improve our relations with the Soviet Union, providing a little more stability, and, I hope, a somewhat more rational policy in terms of ratification.

Lastly, let me just say one thing about this notion of bipartisanship. I am a partisan Democrat. I am proud to be a Democrat. I have not agreed very often with this administration. But I believe the great admonition of Mark Twain about the truth—that you should always tell it: it will please some people and astound the rest—that is something we should not forget. I am prepared to go forth on this April afternoon as a bipartisan player. I will no longer simply rail against SDI as being both destabilizing and stupid, or that the MX is a profound waste of money in my view, and that I have deep, deep suspicions about my own government's interest in arms control—if the administration will meet me halfway. I do not ask for much from them. I would just like the SALT II treaty presented to the Senate, and President Reagan to say that he was wrong when he called it fatally flawed, and that the Threshold Test Ban Agreement was a good idea when it was negotiated. It is still a good idea. It is something that this administration should talk about. And lastly—and I think Senator Nunn and President Ford have put this issue to bed, and I hope it is soundly asleep—that the decade of the 1970s was a period of strategic neglect. This is fantasy. It is the same fantasy that Al talked about, with an umbrella over the United States. You cannot go from 3,000 warheads in 1970 to almost 9,000 in 1980 and call that a decade of neglect. You cannot build the Trident submarine, a cruise missile, and modernize every single leg of the triad and call that a decade of neglect, because it isn't. So I would be happy to go forth and become bipartisan. All I would like from the other side is a little more ingenuousness on the question of strategic stability, on the question of what is real, what happened and what didn't.

I hope that President Reagan is watching, and if he is not, I hope that he will invite these former presidents to explain some of the fine recommendations that you have come up with today. Thank you.

President Carter: Now, I would like to ask Brent Scowcroft, the chairman of one of our panels, as you know, to make the final comment from the stage. Then I would like to summarize, and if anyone from the audience would like to make an additional comment, I will call on you if we have time. Brent Scowcroft. . .

Brent Scowcroft: Thank you, Mr. President. President Ford—just a couple of very minor points or observations on some of the details. First of all, I would like to support Senator Gore's comment about the small missile, and not simply because I'm hostage to him on the MX.

I would like to thank Congressman Dicks for pointing out that the MX is in jeopardy—I had not noticed.

On this exchange about the SDI (which has illuminated many of the complexities and in a sense the slippery nature of it) I will only add that there is a lot of space between a perfect population defense and point-defense of missiles. So it is much more complicated than even the exchange up here indicates.

On the comment about continued adherence to the ABM treaty (which I support), I would just note that in its assent to the ABM treaty the United States made the unilateral statement that its continued adherence could be jeopardized if there were no accompanying arms control agreement which adequately dealt with the problems of offensive forces, and I would hope that our actions at Geneva, on both sides, would ensure that that reservation remains or becomes a dead letter. It is not necessarily so at the moment.

On the issue of the relationship of arms control negotiations to other elements in the U.S.–Soviet relationship, I certainly agree that arms control negotiations should not be played with as an element in the vicissitudes of this larger relationship. But I would like to point out that significant or real arms control negotiations depend on some minimal level of civility and confidence, and that simply sitting down at the same table does not constitute negotiations. I think we would all have to be realistic about that.

As I indicated in my comments yesterday, I think the goal of banning weapons in space is misdirected. I think our efforts should not really be where the weapons are but what they do and how they do it, and—in line with what Senator Gore said about stability—I think we ought to underscore that in every case where we are analyzing the effect of weapons.

Mr. President, President Ford, as somebody who has participated in the conference from the outset, I would like to say that I think you two have taken a significant step in convening this conference. The opportunity to discuss issues like this with Soviet representatives, with our allies, with friends, and with representatives of nonaligned countries in this manner is an innovation which I think is obviously valuable, and I especially applaud the bipartisan nature of the

American representation (even though most of us may be has-beens), and the executive-legislative nature of the discussions as well. To me it is vitally important that the American approach to these issues be on a bi- or a non-partisan basis, not least so that we give the Soviets no incentive to try to paralyze the American domestic process rather than to negotiate the issues at Geneva. Thank you.

President Carter: We have had discussions about some items where many of us in the group agreed, but we were seeking a consensus of near-unanimity among a wide range of participants. I will give you just two or three to illustrate what I am talking about.

There was a proposal that we advocate the banning of further antisatellite tests—a proposition with which I agree, but there was some concern expressed that this might give away part of a very valuable bargaining chip at the negotiating table.

There was another proposal made to me that we endorse the freezing of strategic nuclear weapon deployment, and some advocated that we trade what I consider to be a relatively useless deployment of MX in fixed silos for the formidable Soviet new weapons, the SS-24s and SS-25s, and this has some merit, but it can get so directly involved in the negotiations in Geneva that we decided not to include those. I have a fairly substantial list of such proposals that I need not pursue any further.

I might add that President Ford and I both agreed that in many cases, Tom Downey's proposal that the usefulness of treaties has passed is a very accurate assessment. We have many treaties that have been concluded by presidents with the full knowledge that a third of the senators can veto a treaty, that if they vote it down it is dead, or the treaty is kept in the bosom of the Foreign Relations Committee of the Senate and is never brought to the floor. I never withdrew the SALT treaty. It was in the Foreign Relations Committee, and I advocated that it not be brought to the floor of the Senate, because after the Soviets invaded Afghanistan, it would surely have been killed. I think it is one of the defects, one of the few defects of a profound nature, in the United States Constitution that after an agreement is negotiated by a president it only needs one third of the Senate to kill it.

Well, these have been some very significant comments that our audience has been able to hear but were not thoroughly discussed—I think they are very important. I might add another point at this time. I think that the decision by the Soviet leaders to participate and the performance of their delegation while they were here has been a very fine addition to our consultation. I have already expressed my appreciation to Ambassador Dobrynin, who had to leave at noon; he stayed half a day longer than he had originally anticipated, and I have asked him to express my thanks on behalf of all of us to General Secretary Gorbachev, because it was not until after he became the leader of the Soviet Union that we had a firm commitment for a Soviet delegation to come (certainly not in this high level that has been represented here) and that's been important to us.

I would like to call on Dick Garwin, if he would, to make a comment.

Richard Garwin: Mr. President, I wanted to pick up something that Brent Scowcroft said. It is not sitting down at the table which is important, it is not even reaching an agreement, but doing something effective. For instance, we have the problem of agreeing to reductions in such a way as to achieve stability, in a world in which one side inevitably values one aspect of weapons more than the other side values that particular aspect. What we have been doing over the years is having long discussions to try to come to the same point of view as to which weapons are the most threatening, and then to reduce them. A professor at the University of Edinburgh, Stephen Salter, has picked up this recurrent theme of the last ten or twenty years and has pointed out that if the two sides have different views as to the degree of threat or the degree of value, then that may help the implementation of reductions. Let me give an example. Two children faced with the problem of sharing a cupcake may, for a while, argue about how they should go about it—eventually there will be a shriveled cupcake that nobody is interested in anymore. But the two children really should learn—and it is a revelation (I remember when I first learned it)—the "you cut and I choose" proposition: One child cuts the cupcake; the other chooses. You have never seen such accurate and careful cutting as when the one who cuts knows that the other will get the first choice.

So the proposition is, if there is an agreement to reduce by five percent per year, then each side assigns military utility weights to each part of the force. And the other side then chooses that five percent which is to be eliminated. After the first year, each side can reassign weights because it is always the other side that gets to choose. In this way there is a great advent of realism into the military assessment of one's own force. In fact, the greatest criticism I have heard of this proposition is that we are not yet ready for that realism.

President Carter: I would like to ask first if there are any other of the members of our group on the stage who would like to make an additional comment. If not, are there any panelists who have participated in the evolution of a recommendation who would like to make a comment? I think what we have seen here is some sharp focusing of both attention and understanding on the obstacles that we face in achieving the goal of arms reduction and greater stability, national security, and world peace, and I have been able to learn a lot. It is a subject to which any president must devote a great deal of intense study, and one of the good things about being president is you have available the finest advisors in our nation—all eager to present their views when called upon. There are some very significant recommendations that we have made, and I think it is impossible yet to ascertain or to even estimate how far-reaching their benefits might go. For instance, I have a feeling (which the audience might share), that Ambassador Dobrynin and the Soviet delegation have spoken with great authority because of the structure of their government and society. It would be inconceivable to me that Ambassador Dobrynin would make a statement that was in contravention to the basic policy of the Soviet Union. So I think that what we have heard from the Soviet delegation on this stage is a very carefully comprehended and prepared assessment of Soviet policy. One can always judge how much weight to put upon it from an American point of view or European point of view, but these statements have not been made lightly from the scientists, military people, and also the directors of the American section in the Soviet foreign ministry. I think you have seen a wide range of views also expressed by the Americans at this forum, on a bipartisan basis. We have also been very delighted to have had representatives from Japan, China, Great Britain, East and West Germany, Pakistan, Egypt, and there are a number of other nations who sent representatives here but have not yet been called upon to make a statement.

We have advocated that there be continued adherence to the Interim Agreement on Offensive Nuclear Weapons, and to the SALT II treaty in all its provisions; that we should not abandon, or damage, or abrogate the Antiballistic Missile Treaty, now endangered by the Strategic Defense Initiative; that we should work toward a comprehensive test ban by taking the threshold treaty, still being observed by both sides, and constantly lowering the levels of explosions permitted. We have advocated that negotiations be recommenced to strengthen the prohibition against weapons in space. I think it was a very significant statement by the Soviet Union that unresolved allegations of violations (which all the members of Congress have emphasized are important) might be resolved by onsite inspections—quite a departure from previous Soviet prohibitions against this concept at all levels of government. I was impressed by General David Jones's hope that there not only be a continual series of meetings of top political leaders at the summit, but also that military leaders on both sides have frequent meetings. When we were in Vienna again in 1979 we asked that this be done. At that time, the Soviets immediately said no, this will not be done. But I think there has been a much more positive reception to that proposition at this session. We have also advocated a minimized linkage between continuing arms talks and the inherent and inevitable disagreements that we and the Soviet Union are going to experience in troubled areas of the world because of common ambitions to extend our spheres of influence, and a different perspective on how we should deal with those troubled areas. I also thought significant the recommendation that in the long and laborious process of negotiations (it took almost seven years to complete SALT II) that when the two negotiators reach an agreement on a significant point, that agreement concluded on that particular portion of the negotiations be immediately put into effect, and not wait until the final signing date, postponing some very beneficial results that might have been achieved earlier.

Well, at this point, I want to express my thanks again, especially to President Gerald Ford. It adds a dimension of effectiveness (not only in recruiting people to come but in raising the level of their participation) to have him here with us. It is a delight for me personally, and at this time, I would like to turn over the chair to President Ford and ask him to comment, then to adjourn the session. President Ford...

President Ford: Thank you very, very, much, President Carter. Let me say with emphasis at the outset that it has been a great pleasure and privilege to work with you personally on this project that took some time and which has culminated in the fine sessions for the last two days here. We initiated it, to a degree, at the Ford Library in Ann Arbor, Michigan, on the University of Michigan campus. There it was not as comprehensive as this, but it was a forerunner of the excellent results that we have seen here at Emory. May I express to President Laney our appreciation and gratitude for the facilities here at Emory. I congratulate you, not only on your facilities but on the atmosphere. It has been a delight to be in your community. I would be very remiss if I did not express my very deep personal appreciation for the opportunity, not only to work on this project but on others, with President Carter. He has come to the Ford Library on two occasions—one time on three economic issues and about six months ago for the preliminary meeting towards this occasion. It has been a delight and a pleasure to compliment you on the fine organization that you set up here at Emory and especially to Dean Ellen Mickiewicz and Roman Kolkowicz and to Ken Stein, who deserve a great, great, deal of credit. To all of those who have led in providing the background, the logistics, the administrative side: we are very, very grateful.

As I have sat and listened for the past two days, participated in each of the public sessions, I have been tremendously impressed with the talent of the people who have appeared on the various panels. The academic representation from many disciplines has been superb. The members of Congress who have been here, I believe, are excellent representatives of our legislative branch, and I compliment them on their knowledge and on their participation. I am also equally complimentary to the people from the Reagan administration who have come and participated—Ken Adelman is one. The various guests from overseas, the several ambassadors and others, have added significantly to the discussions, the dialogue, that we have had for the last two days. I would be very remiss if I didn't compliment all of you in the audience who have been here to listen to what has transpired. It has been an excellent audience.

It is a very deep feeling on my part that the Soviet delegation here has added significantly to this conference. I want to compliment Ambassador Dobrynin, Professor Velikhov, Mr. Tarasenko, and General Mikhailov for their participation. I can say, from my observation, it has been a very high-level group representing the Soviet Union, and what they had to say, in my judgment, is the most forthcoming observation of any Soviet delegation I have ever heard on the number of occasions where I have been and Soviet spokesmen have participated. I congratulate you for being here and thank you for the constructive contribution to what we have discussed for the last several days.

I go away from this two-day seminar with one or two observations to make. I cannot definitively tell you the impact of what we have said and what we have decided, but I have a very distinct feeling that, to a greater degree than what we might imagine, we will have an impact, and I certainly hope so. We have had top people, Democrats, Republicans, legislators, people from the executive branch of the government, members of the press, foreign leaders, especially those from the Soviet Union. You cannot assemble a group of people with all of this background and talent and not have an impact on one of the most crucial issues of Soviet–U.S. relations and particularly arms negotiations. I believe we have discussed (as much in depth as one could in public) some of the substantive differences and issues. In addition, we have highlighted, in a responsible way, some of the avenues that, in my opinion, may lead to success in the negotiations between the representatives of the Soviet Union and the United States. If we have taken any significant steps in assisting our people here to understand the complexities and the controversies, that is a step forward. If we will have an impact on our leadership, both here and in the Soviet Union, that would be incalculably beneficial, so I leave here with a good feeling that it has been worthwhile, and I thank everybody who's contributed so tremendously to what I think is a great effort and I thank you, President Carter, for giving me the opportunity to join you in making it possible.

APPENDIX:
REPORTS OF
STUDY PANELS

Study Panel Participants

1. ALLIANCES, PROLIFERATION, AND REGIONAL CONFLICT

Chair: Robert O'Neill*

Rapporteur: Christopher Makins, former First Secretary of the Political Section of the British Embassy in Washington, now Director of the Institute of Security Programs at the Roosevelt Center for American Policy Studies.

Desmond Ball, Senior Fellow and Head of the Strategic and Defense Studies Center of the Australian National University, Canberra.

Karl W. Deutsch, Director of the International Institute for Comparative Social Research, West Berlin, Stanfield Professor of International Peace, Harvard University; and Ryoichi Sasakawa, Professor of International Peace, Carter Center, Emory University.

Josef Joffe, editor for foreign affairs for the *Suddeutsche Zeitung* (Munich).

Pierre Lellouche, Associate Director of the Institut Français des Relations Internationales (IFRI), Paris.

Makoto Momoi, Director of the Momoi Research Institute and Guest Research Fellow at the *Yomiuri* Research Institute, Tokyo.

Kinya Niiseki*

Joseph Nye*

Qian Jia-dong*

---

*Identified in Contributors, p. viii.

Leonard Spector, former Chief Counsel to the Senate Non-Proliferation Sub-committee, now a Senior Associate of the Carnegie Endowment for International Peace.

2. WEAPONS, STRATEGY, AND DOCTRINE

Chair: Brent Scowcroft*

Rapporteur: Dennis Ross, Executive Director of the Berkeley-Stanford Project on Soviet International Behavior.

Lynn Davis, formerly Professor of National Security Affairs, the National War College, now at the International Institute of Strategic Studies.

Richard Garwin*

Amoretta Hoeber, Principal Deputy Assistant Secretary of the Army for Research, Development, and Acquisition.

Bobby Inman (Adm. USN, ret.), former Director of the National Security Agency and later Deputy Director of the Central Intelligence Agency, now president and chief executive officer of the Microelectronics and Computer Technology Corporation.

Michael May, Associate Director-at-large of the Lawrence Livermore Laboratory.

Edward Meyer (Gen., USA, ret.), formerly Chief of Staff of the Army.

K. F. Mikhailov (Lt. Gen.), serves on the General Staff of the Soviet Armed Forces.

Kosta Tsipis, Senior Research Scientist and Director of the Program in Science and Technology for International Security at the Massachusetts Institute of Technology.

E. P. Velikhov*

Herbert York, Professor of Physics and Director of the Program in Science, Technology and Public Affairs at the University of California, San Diego. He was ambassador to the Comprehensive Test-Ban Negotiations and special representative at the Space Arms Control Talks.

3. NEGOTIATIONS AND DIPLOMATIC/POLITICAL ASPECTS

Chair: Ralph Earle II*

Rapporteur: Richard Betts, Senior Fellow of the Brookings Institution.

Harold Berman, Professor Emeritus, Harvard University, and Woodruff Professor of Law at Emory University.

Raymond Garthoff, former Ambassador to Bulgaria and SALT I negotiator, now a Senior Fellow at the Brookings Institution.

Arnold Horelick, Senior Political Scientist and Director of Soviet and East European studies at RAND, and director of the RAND–UCLA Center for the Study of Soviet International Behavior.

Samuel Huntington, Eaton Professor of the Science of Government at Harvard University.

Friedrich Ruth*

S. P. Tarasenko*

---

*Identified in Contributors, p. viii.

Study Panel 1

Alliances, Proliferation, and Regional Conflict

The panel, composed of analysts from North America, Asia, Europe, and the Pacific, sees major problems ahead in terms of the security of vital interests, the management of East-West relations, the limitation of regional conflict, and the control of the spread of nuclear weapons.

A CHANGING WORLD

Any serious prescriptions for improving international security must rest on an understanding of the major social, economic, and political changes which have occurred in recent years. Levels of literacy and urbanization have increased dramatically. Mass mobilization in the political process has spread, often in radical forms. The economic gap between the richest and the poorest countries has increased. Modern weapons are increasingly widely available. These and other changes in the past 40 years have helped create a world in which the ability of the major powers to shape events in other countries has steadily declined. At the same time, terrorism, often supported by governments, has increased in scope and scale. The net result is that the world has become less manageable and that the risks to its safety have multiplied.

There are grounds for believing that some of the major challenges to the world community in the coming years—such as the problems of food production for a rapidly growing population and of social and economic development— can be successfully met. But this success may be uneven, and some countries or regions are likely to face critical problems and serious instabilities. The temptation for more countries to look to nuclear weapons and other mass destruction weapons as a source of security in this situation will remain strong. So will the likelihood that outside powers will be drawn into regional disputes, thus increasing the risks of wider conflict.

This broad outlook provides the context for considering the role of alliances in the coming years and the prospects for the management of regional conflicts and of halting and reversing the spread of weapons of mass destruction. There are different views as to how major a change in the international system of the post–World War II era these trends foreshadow. In all probability, the basic structure of that system will not change substantially within the next decade. The competition between the United States and its European and Pacific allies, on the one hand, and the Soviet Union and its allies on the other, will continue. The People's Republic of China will continue to follow a course independent of both major alliance systems. Nonaligned and neutral countries will chart their courses in accordance with their interests, though they will remain subject to conflicting pressures from the major powers. But within that structure, significant changes, deriving from problems that are already on the horizon, may affect the international system.

THE ROLE OF ALLIANCES

For the United States and its friends, the alliances built up after World War II served to protect against the threat of further Soviet expansion and to provide the political structures within which they could rebuild their economies and societies after the war. Among these alliances, the North Atlantic alliance has continued to occupy the strategic center of gravity in the East–West confrontation, and is likely to do so for a long time to come. For the Soviet Union, the Warsaw Pact provided a political and economic shield which has served as a source of reassurance as to its security.

The United States and its European and Pacific allies all see a strong interest in maintaining and enhancing the strength and cohesion of their alliances. But they face difficult problems in their relationship. Some of these are social and economic. A generation is coming to power in all these countries that had no direct experience of World War II and the relationships and attitudes which it formed. Western European countries also have a need to accelerate the pace of economic and technological change, which creates difficult problems for their internal policies. Other problems are political. Aspirations for ending the division of Europe created by World War II remain strong in Western European countries. But the means of achieving this objective are elusive, which gives rise to a growing sense of frustration.

The context for the Atlantic alliance has been changing in recent years, notably as a result of the continued strengthening of the nuclear and non-nuclear forces of the Warsaw Pact. In the view of some people, this change in the military situation has already brought NATO to the point at which, de facto, it has a no-first-use policy concerning nuclear weapons because the threat to use nuclear weapons has become increasingly self-defeating. Moreover, changes of public attitude toward NATO strategy are increasing the desire to move away from the traditional reliance on the threat to use nuclear weapons early, if at all, in the face of a Warsaw Pact attack.

Among the Pacific allies of the United States, some similar trends can be seen. In Japan, concern about growing Soviet military activities in the region is real. But there is also anxiety at what many Japanese see as an exaggeration of the Soviet threat by the United States. As a result, confidence in U.S. military judgment is weakened. In Australia, and even more New Zealand, concern at the allies' reliance on nuclear weapons as a central element in security policy has grown. The fact that recent disagreements between the United States and New Zealand on the subject of nuclear warship visits have not been contained, as they have been in the past, has gravely threatened the fabric of the ANZUS alliance among the three countries, though the alliance remains of great importance to the United States as well as to Australia and New Zealand.

None of these developments has affected the importance that all allied governments continue to attach to nuclear deterrence as the prime element in their security policies. But there has been a growing desire for a diminished reliance on the threat to use nuclear weapons, especially in the early stages of a war. It has been accompanied by a growth of concern among the Western European allies about the degree of their reliance on U.S. military assistance. There have been some signs that the allies are prepared to increase their capacity for self-reliance. Within the Western European Union (WEU) and in bilateral relations between France and Germany, some important steps towards greater collaboration in defense policy and production have been taken. In Japan, there is a greater recognition of the need for a more equal division of labor in the security field, with Japan taking broader responsibility for defense of the approaches to the Japanese islands and for some intelligence and logistics functions. Australia and New Zealand are also moving to increase self-reliance. But it is still by no means certain that these steps will lead to a substantial increase in allied defense contributions. In NATO, there is support in principle for the introduction of new nonnuclear forces within the overall context of a strong nuclear deterrence. But new non-nuclear weapons are more expensive and labor intensive, while the manpower available for European defense is declining for demographic reasons. The absence of progress toward closer political integration also remains an obstacle to a stronger European pillar in the alliance. At the same time, pressures within the United States Congress are once again raising the possibility of a cutback in U.S. support for NATO.

Alliance problems are not confined to the West. The life of the Warsaw Pact will undoubtedly be extended this year. But it is showing the weaknesses to be expected of an alliance held together by Soviet force. Unlike the Atlantic alliance, there is no thriving spirit of community among its partners. International divisions remain as important as ever in Eastern Europe. Nationality and ethnic problems are rife. Eastern European states look to increased trade with the West to boost their prospects of growth much more than does the West to the East. Eastern Europeans are not permitted the human contact with the West that they so strongly desire. The sad series of upheavals, such as in Hungary and Czechoslovakia, continues in Poland today.

The Warsaw Pact remains a powerful and substantially effective military alliance. But it can never hope to be the political community based on free association that the Atlantic alliance represents. We would, however, be foolish to underrate its strategic power, which is being rapidly modernized and extended, and which casts a long shadow, even in time of peace.

The development of the U.S. Strategic Defense Initiative, or SDI, popularly known as "Star Wars," has further complicated relations between the United States and its allies. Considerable doubt has already been expressed in the scientific community about the technological feasibility of defending populations in the foreseeable future. But even should strategic defenses prove feasible, they will undermine the credibility of the NATO strategy of flexible response. If defense of population centers against strategic nuclear attack proves feasible for the United States and the Soviet Union, Western Europe would still be exposed to conventional attack against which there could be no nuclear response or deterrence. Should strategic defenses prove feasible only for key military installations, Western responses to aggression based on first use of nuclear weapons against such targets would become increasingly difficult and unlikely. For these and other reasons, including opportunity cost and problems of technology transfer, America's allies see many questions which must be examined before any attempt to deploy strategic defenses is made.

At the same time, the allies acknowledge that a program of prudent research should be pursued by the United States because the Soviet Union is already active in this field. Allied public opinion is puzzled, however, that such high priority should be given to the SDI at this time. The recently resumed arms control negotiations in Geneva have to grapple with formidable problems that were not resolved in the 1981–83 negotiations on strategic and intermediate nuclear systems. This array of issues is made even more difficult to settle by the additional requirements posed by the possibility that strategic defenses might be deployed both on earth and in space. Chinese and Japanese members of the panel recalled an old maxim of both nations: "There is a sword for every shield and a shield for every sword." Strategic defenses will foster new forms of offense. Military competition will continue. Nuclear weapons cannot be disinvented, nor can their destructive power be wholly negated.

With careful management, these sources of strain need not lead to serious disruption of U.S.–allied relationships. There have been several signs of strength and continuity in these relationships in recent years. The basic facts that led to the formation of the Atlantic alliance have not changed—notably the division of Europe and the dependence on the U.S. security guarantee. The divisive issue of strengthening the theater nuclear force balance in Europe by the deployment of new U.S. nuclear weapons has for the most part been successfully managed. The harmony of views on the need for a strong defense policy in the face of the modernization of Warsaw Pact forces has grown. The "peace movement" in

Western Europe that came to life in the early 1980s is now less active as a political force, although its ideas have left a mark on all major political parties. Even the concerns expressed about the SDI fit into a familiar pattern of European anxieties which may be reduced by careful alliance management. There is, however, no ground for complacency. The current controversies on the SDI and new concepts of non-nuclear defense, using advanced technology weapons such as highly accurate battlefield missiles, could slow progress toward the needed enhancement of allied military capabilities, and also offer opportunities to the Soviet Union to exploit internal alliance disputes.

In the face of these strains between the United States and its allies, there is a need for all the allies to avoid unilateral actions that weaken the fabric of their relationship and to accept that, as one participant put it, the time to put weight on a bridge is after it has been strengthened, not when it has been weakened. The current challenges require an effort to strengthen agreement among the allies on objectives and on the strategy for achieving them, as a basis for decisions about new weapons systems and tactical doctrines. In particular, a higher level of allied agreement is needed on whether to reduce reliance on nuclear weapons in the coming years and what are the requirements for achieving this end. Without such agreement on these questions, which the United States, as the acknowledged leader of its alliances, must take the primary responsibility for promoting, there is a danger that one of the key elements of order in the international security system could be needlessly weakened. With such agreements, the allies of the United States would more easily be able to play a larger role in the management of East–West relations and of broader international problems. The United States, accustomed as it has become to a dominant position of leadership, may not always find it easy to accept a more equal sharing of the burden. But this will ultimately be in the interests of all the allies.

The Rio Pact among Western Hemisphere nations is also facing strains in trying to adjust to the changes that have occurred in the region and in the world. The major reasons for the decline of the Organization of American States (OAS) have little to do with the competition between the United States and the Soviet Union. However, the weakening of inter-American institutions has made regional solutions to regional crises more difficult, thereby increasing the possibility of the insertion of the East–West competition into these crises.

THE PROBLEMS OF REGIONAL CONFLICT

The most important regional conflicts, notably those in the Middle East, Central America, the Indian subcontinent, and Southeast Asia, are generally agreed to derive from persistent, long-lived causes within the social, economic and political structures of the regions. Some, notably in the People's Republic of China, see the superpowers' rivalries and their practice of, and pretensions to, hegemony as the root cause of regional instability. But a more general view, with which China agrees, is that the superpowers have merely sought to advance their interests by their involvement in regional conflicts that already existed in other countries and regions, and have often succeeded in aggravating them. They have done so at the risk, which will grow greater as regional instabilities multiply, of being drawn into a process of escalation.

Such conflicts are likely to persist and, in view of the explosive potential of the combination of social tensions, ethnic differences, and economic strains, to grow in number and intensity. The growth of terrorism as a normal tool of both governments and subnational groups, for example in Lebanon and Central America, and the increasing use of force in violation of the U.N. Charter, as in Afghanistan, with no penalty on the violators, are symptoms of this increasing disorder. The challenge to the international community is to find ways either of resolving these conflicts and problems or of living with them without their causing a further breakdown of international order and wider and more dangerous confrontations.

There is general agreement that the ability of the major powers to intervene effectively in regional conflicts has diminished. But their interest in maintaining their influence and control in the world has not declined correspondingly. As the conflicts in Vietnam in the 1960s and 1970s and in Afghanistan in the 1980s have shown, the military power of countries both outside and inside the region can only with the greatest difficulty and at high costs, if at all, contribute to overcoming domestic divisions in other countries. In addition, domestic politics in the United States in the aftermath of Vietnam make it hard for U.S. governments to use military force except where quick and easy success is likely.

Some people draw the conclusion from this situation that the superpowers should define the range of their security interests more narrowly and reduce their involvement in regional conflicts. In this view, the prospect is for a multiplication of incidents that could, if mishandled, lead to a superpower confrontation. Since, in the nuclear age, any one such incident could be fatal, there is a need to establish more firebreaks to inhibit the spread of local conflagrations. It is unwise to rely too heavily on the caution and prudence of the superpowers, given possible fallibility in political and military institutions. This is especially important in view of the prospect of the spread of nuclear weapons to countries that feel their security threatened by internal social and economic pressures, as well as externally. In this view, an important role for outside countries is to help ensure that resources are made available to compensate the losers in regional conflicts. This will help ensure that whatever solutions may be found, whether involving political settlements, territorial adjustments, or movements of population, do not lead, as has happened in the Middle East, to embittered and desperate populations whose primary goal is to restore their losses.

Other people are skeptical whether such superpower restraint is achievable in the foreseeable future, given the expectation of continuing U.S.–Soviet competition. Such people believe that the superpowers have more influence over the course of regional conflicts than this first view admits. Even if the direct control of the major powers has diminished, they still have considerable indirect control. One important means of control is through the supply of armaments, although this is an area in which only the most tacit cooperation between them has been possible up to now. Another is the kind of de facto cooperation, based on their mutual interest, that was seen at the time of the Arab/Israel war of 1973. Moreover, exponents of this view see no reason to believe that restraint by one superpower in a regional conflict will lead to restraint by the other—if anything, the reverse is true. The maintenance of a balance of power remains a vital means of limiting the spread of regional instability.

In this view, the superpowers are unlikely to allow a minor incident to trigger a major conflict, as happened in 1914. Nor is the risk of nuclear proliferation as great as some paint it. Hence, one difficult problem for the United States in the coming years may be to decide how to deal with a growing number of cases where the wind of revolutionary change may blow toward free democratic regimes.

One generally accepted conclusion about regional conflict is the need for Western countries to think in terms of a broad definition of security—"comprehensive national security" as the Japanese call it—which includes economic and political as well as military policies. In this connection, the promising signs of regional cooperation in solving regional problems that have emerged in recent years should be strongly encouraged. The Association of South East Asian Nations (ASEAN), the Gulf Cooperation Council (GCC) and recent diplomatic moves between Brazil and Argentina are all examples of this trend. The Organization of African Unity (OAU), although hitherto less successful, should also be encouraged to take greater responsibility for resolving regional disputes in Africa. The Contadora process in Central America is another form of regional initiative that deserves encouragement.

For these purposes, and also as the basis for some of the more radical solutions that may be appropriate to some regional conflicts, such as resettlement of populations, Western countries will need to devote greater attention and resources than in recent years to economic assistance through both bilateral and multilateral arrangements. This policy will not be popular in countries whose national budgets are already strained. But the short-term domestic advantage of failing to support such policies will be dwarfed by the long-term dangers that will result from this.

THE SPREAD OF NUCLEAR WEAPONS

The spread of nuclear arms to additional nations—nuclear proliferation—continues to pose a grave risk to world peace. None of the panel accepted the view sometimes expressed that further proliferation could be seen as contributing to regional or global stability. All agreed that the effort to halt and reverse proliferation should receive higher priority from all governments.

There is an important connection between nonproliferation and the questions of regional conflict and of alliance responsibilities. Regional tensions are the principal near-term factor motivating the nuclear threshold states to develop or expand nuclear weapons capabilities. Some members of the panel believe that if, in the longer term, the major powers continue to rely on nuclear arms to protect their security they will encourage other countries with acute security problems to reach for nuclear weapons to increase their security. There is, however, no disagreement that this factor has been exploited by proliferating powers to rationalize actions taken for other reasons. Regarding the Western alliance, the successful coordination of U.S. and allied nonproliferation efforts has been important in increasing the effectiveness of the international nonproliferation regime. This coordination should be continued and, if possible, extended.

The international nonproliferation regime, which includes the International Atomic Energy Agency (IAEA), bilateral and multilateral nuclear trade agreements, the Non-Proliferation Treaty, and other elements, has done much to retard the spread of nuclear weapons and deserves continued active support. The recent action of the People's Republic of China in joining the IAEA and its statements opposing further proliferation are welcome in this regard, though China remains critical of the Non-Proliferation Treaty itself. The close cooperation between the Soviet Union and the United States in this area is also a valuable contribution to curbing the spread of nuclear arms. However, U.S.-Soviet tensions in some regions have prevented both powers from taking stronger steps to curb acts by their respective regional friends or partners that lead to proliferation.

There are a number of states whose nuclear activities have raised proliferation concerns over the past decade, including Argentina, Brazil, India, Iraq, Israel, Libya, Pakistan, and South Africa. Ongoing attempts by some of these nations to build or expand nuclear weapons capabilities are evolving in new patterns that pose increasing dangers and necessitate intensified nonproliferation efforts by the international community.

During the 1970s, a number of these nations appeared to be pursuing nuclear weapons through commercial purchases of sensitive nuclear plants as part of their nuclear energy programs. The nuclear supplier countries successfully curtailed sales of these installations, especially enrichment and reprocessing plants that can give access to nuclear weapons material. However, the emerging nuclear weapons states have turned increasingly to developing such installations—in effect, dedicated military installations—themselves, principally by using indigenous resources or through illegal acquisition of nuclear technology from more highly industrialized states.

Nuclear technology controls remain important to counteract these new trends, and efforts should be made to bring new nuclear suppliers to cooperate with supplier restraints. But emphasis must be placed on a broader array of tools for stemming proliferation, including diplomatic pressure, sanctions, and incentives to increase the costs to would-be proliferators of developing nuclear arms. In this respect, and since the technical capability for acquiring nuclear weapons will over time come within reach of a growing number of countries, halting proliferation cannot be viewed simply as a technical problem, but must increasingly be considered a political one. The Israeli bombing of Iraq's Osirak reactor was one manifestation of a more aggressive approach to the problem, but if replicated elsewhere it could lead to escalation of conflict.

Similarly, state-directed violations of supplier-country nuclear export control laws by would-be proliferators constitute a serious assault on the nonproliferation regime. These laws have been implemented by most supplier states as part of their obligations under the Non-Proliferation Treaty. Such violations should be addressed not only by intensified enforcement efforts and prosecutions under domestic criminal laws, but also by appropriate steps aimed at the state encouraging such illicit activities. Increased coordination of intelligence activities by supplier countries is also essential.

Regional measures for addressing specific nonproliferation challenges deserve further support. If, as recent reports suggest, Argentina and Brazil have agreed to open their nuclear installations to mutual inspection, this would represent a confidence-building measure of considerable importance. A "no-nuclear-explosions" pledge by India and Pakistan might similarly serve to reduce nuclear tensions in this region.

Finally, the proliferation of chemical weapons—another weapon of mass destruction—may pose even greater near-term dangers than the spread of nuclear arms, and may be even more difficult to control. Moreover, the acquisition of chemical weapons by one regional power may encourage the acquisition of nuclear weapons by a regional rival. Iraq's recent use of chemical weapons in violation of the Geneva Protocol suggests the need for greater international attention to this difficult problem.

RECOMMENDATIONS

The most important consideration arising from the panel's discussion is that we must pay greater attention to the speed with which the world is changing and the directions that these changes are taking. The affairs of the world are becoming more complex to manage, and this complexity challenges us to find better ways of preserving security. Information technology can help, but can only supplement what we ourselves, both in government and as private citizens, know and understand about our security problems and interests. We draw attention to the following conclusions:

1. The United States, as the leader of the West, will have to pay greater attention to the views and interests of its allies in order to maintain the cohesion and effectiveness of both the Atlantic and the Pacific alliances. Continuing divergences in the way in which the United States and its allies perceive threats and responses raise new challenges for alliance management. The debate on the utility of strategic defenses can be expected to intensify in the coming years.

2. The Western alliances have a strong record of achievement in terms of maintaining peace and security. But all the allies face greater responsibilities for improving the management of global affairs. Their active involvement will continue to be needed in all major dimensions of the East–West relationship—political, military, economic, and social. Allied participation in these areas has often been important in the past. But even greater efforts will be called for in the future if East–West relations are not to be permitted to drift into areas of greater danger.

3. The military capabilities of the Soviet Union and the Warsaw Pact can be expected to continue to develop and pose an increasingly serious challenge to Western security. This challenge is presented not only in the form of military confrontation, but also in terms of attempts to divide the alliance and neutralize it politically. Hence special attention must continue to be devoted to meeting both sides of this politico-military threat.

4. The West should develop, and allocate the resources necessary to implement, longer-term strategies for preventing or limiting regional conflicts. Leadership must in most cases come from the United States, but in some situations, as in the past, individual allies must be prepared to play a leading role. Most urgent action is required with respect to the Middle East, but problems elsewhere, such as in Central America, South Africa, Afghanistan, Kampuchea, and the Korean peninsula, have potential for escalation and must be addressed. Failure to act and accept greater responsibility for initiatives is likely to lead to increased risks both for Western security interests and for global stability.

5. The development of regional initiatives to enhance security, both nationally and collectively, should be encouraged. Organizations such as ASEAN and the Gulf Cooperation Council have shown what can be done. They are worthy of continuing Western support and cooperation, and have lessons for nations in other troubled regions, especially Africa, Latin America, and the Caribbean.

6. The threat of terrorism is becoming more serious as more potent means of violence are acquired by people in desperation in both developed and developing societies. Terrorism is being used as a tool by both governments and subnational groups. Short- and long-term remedies must be sought. Barricades around the White House and the State Department are merely the last line of defense. Forward defense still rests with policies to assist economic and social development, promote political effectiveness, and win observance of human rights in troubled areas. But other approaches, including the use of force to resist and counter terrorists, the establishment of more stringent security systems, and closer intelligence cooperation between friendly governments, are also indispensable.

7. Nuclear proliferation remains a potent threat to world order. New technology and increased concern by potential nuclear powers about regional threats require renewed vigor in dealing with this problem. Firm controls on the transfer of nu-

clear technology must be maintained, and new ways for thwarting the clandestine diffusion of this technology must be devised. The cause of nonproliferation must be kept high on the international agenda. Incentives for proliferation must be dealt with as part of a wider policy for strengthening security, both regionally and globally. None of these problems can be solved in a context dominated by unremitting East–West hostility or the perspectives of any single nation-state. The recommendations of this panel must stand together with those of the two panels on Soviet–American relations.

Study Panel 2
Weapons, Strategy, and Doctrine

INTRODUCTION

This report will summarize a number of themes or issues that emerged in the panel discussions. These include the evolution of U.S. attitudes toward deterrence; factors that have tended to influence weapons developments on both sides; the realities that confront the United States and the Soviet Union and that, in spite of the asymmetries between the two, create areas of common interest; the criteria or critical elements of strategic stability and the things that might be done to foster greater stability; the big issues that need to be faced in the future; and recommendations or specific proposals.

EVOLUTION OF ATTITUDES TOWARD DETERRENCE

There seemed to be a consensus among the American participants that the attitudes on views of deterrence—at least as embodied in U.S. governmental policies—have evolved over time. Early in the nuclear age, the United States turned to nuclear weapons as a substitute for conventional strength in defending Europe (called extended deterrence). From that point U.S. government attitudes evolved toward what came to be called assured destruction. Rational leaders could not use these weapons for rational policy ends against nations similarly armed, but the assured ability to threaten massive destruction would guarantee the deterrence of attacks on the United States and its allies.

By the 1970s some raised questions about the reliability of such an approach to deterrence. Some questioned the logic of an approach that had no political or military rationale and that they claimed had a strategic policy based on revenge; others suggested that for deterrence to be credible the United States needed usable military options that would permit more limited and flexible responses and that would convince its adversary that it could and would actually carry out the threats made.

In the 1970s, U.S. policy gradually began to gravitate in the direction of those who raised these concerns. In policy terms this meant that U.S. deterrent posture became one that employed not simply the threat of assured destruction of a certain percentage of Soviet population and industry but also one that provided for more discrete and limited options for the employment of U.S. weapons. The key factors that produced the change in the 1970s include among other things:

- technological developments that made refinements possible;
- the end of U.S. superiority and the emergence of strategic parity, something many believed would undermine extended deterrence or the ability to deter threats against allies, particularly because of U.S. conventional inferiority;
- the development of Soviet weapons that seemed to put U.S. ICBMs at risk;
- the U.S. perception that the Soviet force posture, exercises, and doctrinal pronouncements indicated that the Soviets did not share U.S. views of deterrence and of war in the nuclear era, and thus, in effect, the Soviets believed that nuclear weapons were not revolutionary, although decisive in wartime.

The shift in the U.S. approach to deterrence has continued into the 1980s with President Reagan stating that the world would be safer, not in an environment of assured destruction or mutual vulnerability, but rather in one of assured survival—where the ability to defend would remove any military incentive in striking first. The feasibility of such an approach remains open to question.

The Soviet participants noted their perception that the development of U.S. doctrines and weapons systems was designed to assure superiority and first-strike capability, and that this remains the direction of the current U.S. strategic policy, including the Strategic Defense Initiative.

FACTORS THAT INFLUENCE MILITARY DEVELOPMENT ON EACH SIDE

For a long time it has been assumed that threat perceptions and a kind of action-reaction cycle have triggered military developments on each side. One of the factors that helped to bring about the evolution of U.S. government attitudes toward deterrence—and the military hardware needed to achieve it—was the development of Soviet military capabilities.

The Soviet participants made it clear that they believed in at least one aspect of the action-reaction model for weapons development: namely, that U.S.

military developments have triggered the arms race and require Soviet counter-measures. The Soviets on the panel emphasized that the United States had initiated all new weapons-technological developments, starting with atom bombs and going through MIRVs, cruise missiles, and so forth; that each such development evoked anxiety on the Soviet side and that the Soviets necessarily had to respond; and that the arms race would end if the two sides would renounce new weapon developments. U.S. participants cited what seemed to them specific counter-examples. However, the action-reaction model is only one factor influencing the weapons developed on each side. Each has very different force postures at the strategic, theater, and general purpose force levels that reflect a series of different inputs.

These inputs on one or both sides include:

- the traditions of the respective military services and their preferred military missions;
- the momentum of technology and the new military means that are created by it (new means that frequently expand the scope of what is possible militarily and thus often drive doctrine rather than the reverse);
- domestic or legislative politics and the political weight of weapon development organization;
- geopolitical needs and different military problems (for example, the United States has been a sea power with a need to keep the sea-lanes open; the Soviets more of a continental power).

Along with threat perceptions, all of these factors seem to have combined in one way or another to shape the force postures on both sides. One U.S. participant on the panel suggested that neither the United States nor the Soviet Union had any kind of long-term strategic plan, and had instead reversed or reshaped their postures periodically.

A U.S. participant noted that there was a pattern of being "out of cycle" in terms of major weapon systems and forces. This pattern has continued through the 1960s and 1970s and up to today. The United States has made investments in spurts of military activity, while the Soviets have had a more steady approach to military force development. This pattern of being "out of cycle" contributed to difficulties in the arms control process.

FACTORS THAT CREATE CONVERGENCE

Though there are many asymmetries and different interests that separate the two sides, it is important not to lose sight of the factors that create a degree of convergence. As one of the Soviet participants put it, "this planet is our common house," and we should proceed from our common interest in preserving it. An important example is the shared interest in nonproliferation, that is, the prevention of the spread of nuclear weapons to additional states.

Nuclear weapons create a threat to that common house, and both sides recognize this. One U.S. participant said that both the United States and the Soviet Union understand that nuclear war would be a disaster; both are aware of the situations that could lead to nuclear conflict (such as escalating crisis or a conventional war) and the need to avoid such situations, and both recognize that they need to maintain survivable forces. Even if neither forswears capabilities that threaten the forces of the other, their determination to maintain survivable forces and to avoid the situations that could lead to conflict are important conditions of stability.

Though another U.S. participant observed that neither side has been reluctant to intervene with military forces in situations where it had a preponderance of force or vital interests, he agreed with the general proposition that both the United States and the Soviet Union have been mindful of the need to avoid situations that could escalate. (One could argue that situations in which one side has vital interests or a preponderance of force are, by definition, not likely to escalate.) In any case, there are certain factors that create a degree of stability in the U.S.–Soviet relationship.

PROBLEMS OF ENHANCING STRATEGIC STABILITY

The stability of the overall U.S.–Soviet relationship is clearly influenced by the stability of the strategic forces themselves, that is, the degree to which these forces encourage or are immune to attack by the other side. The principles that tend to reinforce balance or stability in the relationship of strategic nuclear forces were reviewed next, and here the U.S. and Soviet participants exhibited different mindsets in their respective approaches.

On the American side, there was a consensus that several elements would promote stability in strategic nuclear forces: first, more survivable forces are seen as being essential. Whether or not one believes that a degree of vulnerability creates an incentive for a first strike, it clearly does add to tension in a crisis, and could lower the threshold to preemption. Second, reducing the value of individual military targets on each side would reduce the military incentive for an attack. Third, command and control must be adequate and invulnerable, both before and after any possible attack, to ensure that neither side believes it can destroy the opposing leadership and deny it the ability to use its forces. Fourth, reducing the possibility of surprise will raise confidence in a crisis and further erode the temptation to preempt. (New all-weather, 24-hour-per-day surveillance technologies are emerging and will be helpful in this regard.)

The Soviet participants' response to this was to say that they have a broader approach to strategic stability. For the Soviets, such stability depends on:

renouncing the arms race; renouncing the development and deployment of new weapons systems and all space weapons; renouncing attempts to upset parity and the balance of forces; renouncing attempts to destroy what had been achieved in arms control; and renouncing the first use of nuclear weapons and forces in general.

The Soviet participants made a special point of saying that stability cannot be achieved with new weapons; quite the opposite.

U.S. participants responded to this by saying that there are examples of new weapons that could be far more stabilizing than the weapons they replace, such as small, single-warhead ICBMs, small SSBNs, etc.

One of the Soviet participants responded by saying it was hard to define which weapons are stabilizing and which are not. He observed that any new weapon changes the environment, and certain theories might not hold up in those new environments.

While there was no meeting of the minds on this issue, there was agreement that technical means alone cannot resolve the issue of stability. Confidence-building measures and improvement in signalling and ensuring that each side will be understood in a crisis were also identified as important criteria for enhancing strategic stability.

PRINCIPLES TO ACHIEVE GREATER STRATEGIC STABILITY

In discussing what we should act on now to achieve greater stability, the issue of reducing the vulnerability of forces was raised.

One U.S. participant said that if the U.S. wants to reduce the vulnerability of forces, it has basically three alternatives: (1) It can take unilateral steps with respect to offensive forces—concealment, mobility, etc. (2) It can try to develop an arms control regime. (3) It can defend the forces.

The group recognized that there could be tensions between any of these alternatives; for example, that weapons development or practices such as concealment and mobility could complicate arms control efforts because of the verification problems. The consensus on the American side was that it is more important to enhance strategic stability, and that this should not be subordinated to absolute arms control verification. It was also noted that if small mobile ICBMs like the Midgetman replaced the current ICBM forces, verification and numbers would be less significant, since preemption and ''break-out'' would pose less of a risk.

On the question of strategic defense, there also seemed to be a general consensus on the American side—that strategic defense ought to be evaluated as one of the ways to reduce the vulnerability of forces. It was suggested that its costs, feasibility, and political implications must be weighed against the various alternatives.

Concerns about the potential problems with strategic defense were raised by both American and Soviet participants. A U.S. participant raised the concern that the objectives of strategic defenses—such as, protecting missiles or protecting population—are not so easy to distinguish. Such ambiguity and doubt may trigger offensive countermeasures or responses.

Soviet participants said that a large-scale ABM defense—exceeding levels permitted by the ABM treaty—such as envisioned in the administration's Strategic Defense Initiative would not enhance stability or invulnerability of forces; that offensive forces would be perfected in response; that, as a result, there could be no agreement on reducing offensive forces if the development of strategic defenses went forward; and that the ABM treaty and all other arms control agreements would inevitably be destroyed by any such development.

ISSUES FOR THE FUTURE

American participants raised two issues that they felt needed to be thought through as we begin to deal with the problems of the future. One is the issue of strategic defense and the other is that of space.

With regard to strategic defense, one participant noted that technologies are emerging that may enable the rapid detection, correlation, discrimination, and targeting of large numbers of attacking warheads. New decisions may need to be made. Relevant questions that arise include: Can such capabilities work effectively in nuclear war when advanced technology is available for countering such systems? Should the focus be only on ground-based strategic defense or include space-based weapons? Should or could the technology be banned altogether, or should there be some collaborative U.S.–Soviet approach? Soviet participants on the panel were very skeptical about the prospects for such collaboration, and favored an outright ban.

Another U.S. participant said there were also a number of questions regarding the uses of space. Should there be a treaty on ASAT? Should there be an extension of the ban on weapons of mass destruction in space to include all weapons? Is there a basis on which to develop even a tacit understanding with the Soviets on the uses of space? Another U.S. participant said that the guiding principle ought to be that both sides have important assets in space that should not be threatened.

The Soviet participants reiterated the critical importance of banning all space weapons.

SOME SUGGESTIONS

A number of specific recommendations or proposals for stabilization were made and are summarized below:

1. A U.S. participant proposed a sharp reduction of offensive forces, to a total of 1,000 warheads on each side. Another U.S. participant proposed de-MIRVing all systems, and going to only single warhead systems. This was proposed as an alternative to deploying a strategic defense with the object of enhancing the survivability of offensive forces. The Soviet participants supported sharp reductions.
2. Another U.S. participant proposed modifying the current situation by eliminating very short-range nuclear systems in Europe. This would reduce the prospect of their being overrun in wartime and pressure for early use of them. (Another participant feared this could actually lead to some "decoupling," and an erosion of the edifice that has worked so well in Europe.)
3. One U.S. participant suggested that the importance of our satellites in space made it essential for us to ban ASAT tests and all space weapons. The Soviet side was in favor of this suggestion as well.
4. In light of the suspicion and fears on each side, a U.S. participant proposed that we should discuss in advance with the Soviets weapons we each might deploy and the reason for such development/deployment. This might reduce fears and perhaps even preempt certain deployments.

Study Panel 3

Negotiation and Diplomatic/ Political Aspects

In the context of international security and arms control, the panel proceeds from the premise that the single most important goal that negotiations and diplomacy can help to achieve is the avoidance of war, both conventional and nuclear.

In connection with this goal, the United States and the Soviet Union have a number of parallel objectives, including survival, security, equality, and curtailing military expenditures. At the same time, it should be borne in mind that the two nations differ in a number of respects, both regarding the means by which their objectives can or should be achieved and, indeed, regarding their meaning (even when the same words are used). For instance, equality, seen from each of two different perspectives, is defined differently.

Moreover, the political aims of each side differ widely. Not only do the two superpowers espouse widely different political philosophies, but they also have highly divergent interests throughout the world in practical, nation-state terms. Thus, a state of competition at best or hostility at worst is virtually unavoidable. At the same time, the avoidance of war and of the destruction of the countries is, as stated, the paramount objective.

Arms control negotiations and agreements are an integral part of efforts to avoid war, as are many of the goals previously mentioned. However, arms control by itself cannot prevent war, and must be treated as one element albeit an important one, in an overall strategy for assuring national and international security, strategic stability, and a peaceful world.

In this connection, the panel reviewed ongoing negotiations, both multinational and bilateral:

- the Vienna negotiations on troop reductions in Central Europe;
- the Stockholm Conference on Confidence-Building Measures in Europe;
- the multilateral negotiations at the Geneva Conference on Disarmament on a complete worldwide ban on chemical weapons;

- the negotiations between the United States and the Soviet Union concerning space and nuclear arms of both strategic and intermediate range that opened on March 12, 1985;

and addressed facets of arms control which should be considered in assessing future steps.

The different systems of the two countries mean that arms control policies are not arrived at in the same ways. What matters most, however, is the policy that results.

Both sides' policies are affected by external pressures, but domestic politics play a particularly significant role in Western countries. The United States Congress has become increasingly involved in arms control. In the United States, public opinion over time has often been steadier than government policy, but it has become increasingly difficult in recent decades to keep foreign policy nonpartisan. While media coverage of the issues has not always been perfect, the media have not been primarily responsible for the swings in public mood.

Public opinion has emerged as a major factor, particularly in Western Europe, as reflected in the debates of the past several years over deployment of U.S. intermediate-range missiles. Both American and Soviet negotiating positions and public postures have been substantially affected by the consideration of the reaction of Western audiences, and this has led the superpowers to play to the grandstand.

The Soviet member disagreed with the characterization of the Soviet negotiating position. One Western member disagreed with the characterization of the American negotiating position, and underlined the determination of the American negotiators, supported by the allies, to achieve a balanced outcome at the lowest level of intermediate-range missiles.

In this connection, it was noted that, as the Geneva negotiations have dealt increasingly with weapons systems affecting the military situation in Europe and elsewhere, in addition to the direct confrontation of the superpowers, consultation with allies has increased proportionately. This was seen to be a necessary and helpful development and one that is expected to be continued.

There is difficulty in making arms control policies consistent with military procurement and production decisions. Both sides tend to try to limit the other's modernization while keeping their own options open. The future impact on arms control is not always considered when research and development decisions are made. The problem is further complicated because both sides' military modernization programs are out of phase with each other. Agreements with longer terms might help deal with this problem, since five years—the term of previous strategic offensive arms limitation agreements—is not long enough to affect research and development decisions.

The more complex and wide-ranging arms control negotiations become, the more important will be the issue of treaty compliance. Both sides have committed technical violations in the past (such as "venting" into the atmosphere from underground nuclear tests). There have been problems in interpreting the terms of treaty requirements, as well as in determining the facts of alleged violations. This has not been a major problem until recently, however, because first, it was not clear that such cases were deliberate; second, they were dealt with satisfactorily in discussions in the Standing Consultative Commission, which was established to deal with such questions; and third, none of the issues went to the heart of the purpose of the treaties. However, most members of the panel believe that over the last few years there has been increasing evidence of Soviet violations of existing agreements, both ratified and unratified. Because of the nature of recent questions about compliance as well as other factors, the issue of verification is becoming much more politicized. Maintaining secrecy is also becoming a more difficult obstacle to further progress in negotiation.

There was agreement that the ABM treaty is a requisite for maintaining a stable deterrent for the foreseeable future and should be affirmed. Research on ballistic missile defense is allowed by the treaty, and in any case is not monitorable. It was also noted that it is uncertain how research programs could be controlled by negotiated agreements, and that the issue will be more significant further in the future if U.S. and Soviet research programs begin to identify promising technological possibilities. Most participants agreed that, while strategic defense may occur, both superpowers' strategies will, for the foreseeable future, continue to depend on offensive retaliation.

The panel agreed that the serious negotiation of arms control agreements in itself provides an important channel for dialogue and can thereby contribute to the reduction of misunderstanding and the increase of unilateral confidence. Arms control is not only a matter of immediate practical importance in avoiding war, but can also be a significant part of a long-range process of creating a structure of peace.

Based on its discussions and the comments noted above, the panel recommends:

- that the United States and the Soviet Union continue to adhere to the Antiballistic Missile Treaty and the Outer Space Treaty, and that no steps be taken contrary to the terms of those treaties without negotiation.

- that the United States and the Soviet Union continue their existing policies of not taking steps to undercut the provisions of treaties agreed to but not formally in effect, including the Interim Agreement on Offensive Arms, the Threshold Test Ban Treaty, and SALT II; the definitions and other noncontroversial provisions of the last should be carried forward into any future agreement.

- that the United States and the Soviet Union pursue negotiations to reduce and further limit offensive nuclear arms, both intercontinental and intermediate, taking into account but without letting the possibility of future developments in strategic defensive systems inhibit such reductions and limitations; any such agreement should create a more stable balance at lower levels of weapons and contribute to overall strategic stability.

- that the sides should take more constructive and imaginative steps regarding verification of compliance with future agreements, including cooperative measures as appropriate and necessary to enhance such verification.
- In this connection, issues of compliance should be dealt with by both sides in a manner which is aimed at their resolution, not their exploitation for political or propaganda purposes, and that the same criterion be applied to negotiations themselves.
- that the United States and the Soviet Union address with the utmost priority the question of establishing mechanisms aimed at crisis prevention and crisis management in order to avoid misunderstandings and/or miscalculations which could lead to conflict.
- that current and future negotiations continue to take into account the interests of allies and other countries in the avoidance of war and enhancement of stability.
- that current and future negotiations, while not conducted in a vacuum, should at the same time not be held hostage to linkage with other, unrelated issues between the sides.
- that neither side seek to achieve superiority through negotiations.
- that in the future both sides move more ambitiously in limiting and reducing offensive arms without excluding limited steps in the short term.
- that the public in both countries be educated to the fact that the issues are complex and that both sides enter the negotiations with major asymmetries, many of them immutable.
- that the sides should take more constructive and imaginative steps regarding verification of compliance with future agreements, including cooperative measures as appropriate and necessary to enhance such verification.

Finally, the panel is greatly concerned about the danger that the new negotiations in Geneva are heading for an early stalemate. The Soviet side appears to be unwilling to consider deep reductions in strategic offensive weapons so long as the possibility of new strategic defensive deployments is not definitively foreclosed; the American side wishes to negotiate precisely such deep reductions while holding open the strategic defense option, pending completion of research to establish its feasibility. The panel believes that negotiation must proceed with full account of the strategic offensive-defensive interrelationship, exploring offensive *and* defensive arms limitations.

The panel believes further that an unregulated competition in both offensive nuclear weapons and strategic defenses would be disastrous, and that a cooperative transition toward deployment of extensive strategic defenses may not be feasible on either technical or political grounds, even if desirable in principle. Therefore they recommend that the two sides now begin to examine what kinds of more far-reaching arms control agreements limiting offensive forces might be sufficient to stabilize the competition in a manner that would minimize the incentives of either side to deploy extensive strategic defenses.

Index

About the Editors

Ellen Propper Mickiewicz is Professor of Political Science at Emory University, where she also served as Dean of the Graduate School of Arts and Sciences. She was co-director of the Consultation on International Security and Arms Control, chaired by Presidents Carter and Ford and held at the Carter Center of Emory University. She is editor of the scholarly journal, *Soviet Union*, and author of *Media and the Russian Public, Handbook of Soviet Social Science Data*, and *Soviet Political Schools*. Her articles have appeared in the *Journal of Communication, Public Opinion Quarterly, Slavic Review, Nieman Reports, The New York Times, Corriere della Sera*, and other journals. Her current research on Soviet and American media is supported by grants from the Markle and Rockefeller foundations.

Roman Kolkowicz is Professor of Political Science at the University of California, Los Angeles, where he was the founding director of the Center for International and Strategic Affairs. He served as co-director of the Consultation on International Security and Arms Control, chaired by Presidents Carter and Ford. He is the author of *The Soviet Military and the Communist Party*. His work in the fields of Soviet foreign and military policy has appeared in *ORBIS, Journal of Strategic Studies, World Politics*, and other scholarly journals. His most recent works include *Soldiers, Peasants, and Bureaucrats* and *National Security and International Stability*.